To

MW01145810

Welcome to the

rolling revolution!

Teresa
Richards

♡

TERESA RICHARDS

Evernight Teen ®

www.evernightteen.com

Copyright© 2023

Teresa Richards

ISBN: 978-0-3695-0792-1

Cover Artist: Jay Aheer

Editor: Melissa Hosack

TERESA RICHARDS

DEDICATION

To my teenage self and everyone else still learning to love themselves. Keep working at it for as long as it takes. You're worth the effort!

ACKNOWLEDGEMENTS

This is the book of my heart. It's taken me a couple of decades to really learn to love myself, and this story reflects the way I wished I could have come to view myself in high school. But you can't tell a story like this without going through it and coming out on the other side, so I'm grateful for the life experiences I've had, and the people who supported me through them, that have gotten me to where I am today.

Thank you to my first and wonderful-est writing group, the Fairfield Scribes. Though we've been apart in distance for a lot of years now, you will always be so close to my heart. Thank you always for the laughs, the support, and of course the honest and heartfelt critiques of my words. Spending time with you has shaped me into the writer I am. Thank you to my early readers and critique-ers of this book, especially Mallory Brown, Rie Neal, Dawn Frederick, Sabine Berlin, and Ashly Clark. And for the writing support and many beta reads over the years, thanks to Cindy Jewkes, Nikki Trionfo, Sarah

Beard, Heather Clark, Amy Wilson, TJ Amberson, Madeline Malmstrom, my mid-south SCBWI pals, and my Storymakers family.

I have to thank the 80's for gifting me with a love of roller skates, roller rinks, and bright colors. Thank you to Indy Jamma Jones, Estro Jen, Pigeon, and the Moxi Skate team for your incredibly fun and jaw-dropping videos that were the inspiration for this book. Thank you to Ellie Slay and the Derby City Roller Girls for letting me sit in on your practices and bouts and answering roller derby questions for me. Thanks also to Dawn Frederick for seeing something in this book and helping me take it to the next level with your joint publishing and roller derby expertise.

Thank you to my wonderful agent, Kelly Van Sant for your wisdom, encouragement, insightful feedback, gentle guidance, and just all-around awesomeness. This book has been on a long and twisty journey since it found its way to you, and you have helped me shape it into something truly incredible. Thank you to KT Literary for the wonderfully supportive author home you are. I am so grateful to be part of such a talented and knowledgeable bunch.

I could not do this without the support of my amazing husband and awesome kids. Frank, you are the rock I know I can count on day in and day out, and your belief in me over the years has truly made all the difference.

Thanks to my teens and their friends for helping me refine the pitch for this book and for being some of my biggest online cheerleaders. Also, for providing highly entertaining conversations as I drive you all over creation—these are some of the best moments of my days. You are strong and beautiful and kind, every one of you, and I feel incredibly privileged to be a part of your lives.

And to my readers, thank you! I hope you will love these characters as much as I do and that you will see a reflection of their strength and courage and light in yourself. Because, in the end, my characters are only a reflection of you.

TERESA RICHARDS

FLIPPIN' SKATERS

Teresa Richards

Chapter One: Derby Girls

The day my sister, Jojo, skated in her first roller derby bout was the day I quit skating forever. I had to. It was self-defense. She was eleven and I was ten.

It was just a few weeks before our brother, Nate, was born. Sitting there with my family, watching Jojo skate, I remembered thinking Mom was going to go into early labor with how many times she jumped out of her seat, cheering and screaming her head off as my sister hip-checked and dodged the other skaters. It was like watching an episode of Dance Moms, only with mouth guards and bruises instead of tights and tiaras.

Now, seven years later, Mom was just as vocal, and completely unaware of the public spectacle she made of herself every time Jojo played. Sometimes I thought my mom should join roller derby herself with how competitive and crazy she got during my sister's bouts. She never got like that at any of the football games I cheered at, even though I was the best tumbler on the squad.

So, my sister was eleven when she found her calling in life.

At sixteen, I was still searching for mine.

"You're late," Mom said when we joined her in the front row of the roller dome, my dad carrying a tray piled with concession stand food. Greasy food was part of the experience, but usually these things were in the evening. Today was tournament day—day two, actually, since Jojo's team had dominated yesterday—and Sunday before noon didn't seem like the best time for corn dogs and fries.

Especially since I'd spent the morning throwing up.

My mom was fresh off her overnight hospital shift, and if she figured out I wasn't feeling well she'd go all Doctor Mom on me—which would lead to some very specific questions about last night that, in all honesty, I probably couldn't answer.

It was a good thing my dad had been the one in charge last night.

I sat down and tried to ignore the pounding in my head.

"It doesn't start for ten minutes," Dad said, getting Nate settled with a plate of nachos. "Plenty of time."

"You missed warmups."

Eye roll. We'd seen Jojo warm up a thousand times.

"She's looking good," my mom continued, grabbing a fry from my dad's tray and popping it into her mouth. "I think the new skates are making a difference."

Jojo was good with or without new skates. At eighteen, she was already Seattle's favorite derby girl—a legend in the making, the local papers said. Her derby name was Red Thunder, because her curly red hair was the first thing people noticed about her and, supposedly, when she hip-checked you in the rink, it was like being rocked by thunder.

My hair was red and curly too, but mine was not so red as to be the first thing people noticed about me, like hers was. Mine was more auburn, and less curly than it was just big. Jojo always said mine was better, but I disagreed. If you're going to be red, *be red*. Don't skulk around, being *almost* red.

Anyway, the hair gods got it right, because Jojo was the supercharged version of me. Or I was the watered-down version of her, depending on which way you looked at it.

I didn't miss her. I really didn't. College could have her all it wanted.

Except ... there were times I wished I could talk to her like I used to. Today, for example. Absently, I reached over my little brother and stole one of his nachos.

"Hey, that's mine!"

I regretted it the moment I bit down—not because of his whining, but because of my upset stomach and throbbing head.

"Dad, Aspen ate one of my chips."

"Ugh, fine, you want it back?" I opened my mouth, pretending I was going to take the mushy pieces out and put them back on his plate.

"Aspen, don't you dare," my mom said.

Okay, I wasn't actually going to do it. Obviously.

The overhead lights in the roller dome dimmed, and Nate's voice ticked up in pitch. "Aspie, it's starting!"

Multicolored laser lights appeared, roaming the arena as the background music got louder. A man's voice came on over the loudspeaker. "Good morning derby fans, and welcome to the Metro Roller Dome where we are just a few matchups away from crowning our tournament champions!" He paused, drawing out the drama of the moment while the crowd cheered. "This morning, Seattle's own Metro Roller Girls are facing the Eastern Washington Skull Smashers."

The opposing team filed out of the locker room on their skates, wheels gliding smoothly across the hardwood track. They wore tiny shorts and neon knee-high socks, along with helmets, mouth guards, and knee and elbow pads. The audience cheered while the music pulsed in the background.

Once the Skull Smashers were in place, the announcer continued, stretching out the words dramatically. "And now, put your hands together for your very own Metro Roller Girls!"

The room erupted in applause, but you could barely hear it over the music that came on—the kind that made you want to jump out of your seat and start dancing or do a hundred jumping jacks or scream your head off.

Today, it just made me want to pound a nail through my brain to stop the waves of pain.

Jojo's team filed out of the locker room on their skates.

Nate forgot all about his nachos and watched in wonder as the Metro Roller Girls skated past us, even though he'd seen this almost as many times as I had. He'd grown up at these things.

I had to admit, the team looked extra fierce today. Some of the girls wore torn fishnet stockings, some had body paint and hair dye, and others had new tattoos. Beneath their helmets, their eyes were laser focused. It was like watching a pack of lionesses before a hunt.

I found Jojo among them, her hair wild and loose where it extended below her helmet. With her mouth guard in, she looked like she could rip your throat out in a single move.

The roller girls were all different shapes and sizes, but they shared the same ferocious dedication to their alter egos. It didn't matter who these women were in real life—lawyers or dental hygienists, college students or stay-home moms—once they put on their skates, they were derby girls and that's all that mattered.

I felt a twinge of envy. As much as I enjoyed the tumbling I did in cheerleading, it in no way compared to the very real grit these girls had. Sure, what I did was hard, and required a ton of technical skill. No arguments there. But I'd never experienced the passion that was so evident in their faces. Next to them, I kinda felt like a kid doing somersaults in the backyard—still trying to find my place long after I already should have.

I wondered if Jojo ever thought about me now that she was an official grown up.

The bout started. Wheels clonked against the hardwood as blockers set their feet down and fought to keep the jammers from getting by. Skates squeaked as the players turned, started, and stopped on a dime. Roller derby was unique because both teams were running offense and defense all at the same time, which made it exciting to watch. But I'd seen Jojo skate a thousand times, and I didn't need to watch to know she would dominate.

I pulled out my phone and the lock screen appeared, with a picture of me and my two best friends, Rhea and Chase. They were dating each other now, but this picture had been taken years ago, before all that. It showed us at the state fair, our smiles sticky with fried dough and powdered sugar.

Now, after last night, I knew things would never be the same again.

My mom jumped up, yelling at the ref for something happening on the track, and my dad scrambled to catch the plate of fries she'd knocked off his lap. One of the girls on Jojo's team—Peanut Butter Jamma, it looked like—headed for the penalty box, to a chorus of boos.

I started scrolling through my social feed as the skaters reset for the next jam. There were a bunch of pictures from last night, at the music club where the band Appellooza had played. Everyone had been there. When a band made up of kids you've known since kindergarten reaches even the fringes of making it big, you go.

A whistle blew and the action on the track started up again.

I commented on a picture. Laughed at another. Liked a third. I scrolled through my feed, catching up on the morning's gossip.

And then something caught my eye. The kind of something you never want to see.

It was a picture of me.

On a stage.

Wearing nothing but a lacy red bra and panty set I had never before seen in my life.

Chapter Two: Viral

I stared at the image—me practically naked onstage—while my world rocked. As if on cue, the action on the track kicked into high gear, the crowd roaring at something I hadn't seen. I jumped, flipping my phone over to hide the screen.

That picture had to be fake.

I didn't own underwear like that—I would never in a million years buy underwear like that, let alone put it on display for everyone to see. And, anyway, that hadn't looked like my body.

Easing my phone over but holding it close so only I could see, I examined the image again.

Yep, the legs were too long and the stomach too toned. It wasn't me.

But that was my face, and that was definitely my hair—one-hundred-percent, that was my hair. So, what, had someone Photoshopped an image of me and put it online? It was good editing work, too—not some crude cut-and-paste job.

But *why* would anyone do that?

Mom jumped out of her seat again, and I glanced up just as Jojo dodged past the pack of blockers for another four points. A chant started up in the crowd— *Thun-der, Thun-der, Thun-der.* My parents and brother joined in, urging Red Thunder on. No one was paying any attention to me.

I went back to my phone and sucked in a breath when I saw the comment count. There were ninety-two comments.

Ninety-two!

And then there were ninety-three.

No, wait, ninety-four.

The chanting around me continued in perfect

time—*thun-der, thun-der, thun-der*. It was like clockwork, marking each new comment as it appeared.

Thun-der. Ninety-eight.

Thun-der. Ninety-nine.

I pressed a hand to my head, trying to squash my headache, as the comment count skipped right over one hundred and went straight to one-oh-four. My stomach lurched with a fresh wave of nausea.

One-hundred-and-ten.

Then one-thirteen.

What in the world were people saying about me? I clicked on the thread.

jazzyjay: **hey Aspen, backstab much?**

$ydneeee: **Poor Rhea**

Seahawksfan99: **how does she hide her giant butt under that tiny cheerleading skirt?**

alex451: **dude, no. just … no.**

flippinrick: **No way Chase would ever leave Rhea for Aspen. Just sayin**

Bile rose in my throat. Who had even posted this? Maybe I could convince them to take it down.

I scrolled back to the top—and nearly fell off my seat. This was *Chase's* post. Chase with the powdered-sugar smile. Who I'd been friends with since the day I was born because our mothers were best friends and we'd grown up together. Chase, who'd had my back ever since elementary school when the other boys started making fun of my giant hair.

He posted maybe twice a year because he'd—quote—*rather be throwing a football than gossiping online*. Along with the picture, he'd included a caption I hadn't noticed until now: "*Sorry Aspen—I'm with Rhea. I thought we were friends.*"

My face burned like I'd been slapped. Why was he doing this to me?

Then I remembered what I'd witnessed in the bathroom last night and, suddenly, I knew. This was because of Rhea. Because of what I'd seen.

I closed my social feed and stood up.

"Is everything okay?" my dad asked.

"I need to make a call." I tapped on Rhea's name in my favorites list and made my way to the exit. It took her four rings to answer.

"Hey, meanie," she said. The sound of a blow-dryer whirred on her end of the line.

My head pounded.

The response she expected sat on the tip of my tongue: *Hey, meanie.* We always started our conversations this way, thanks to the lyrical genius of Taylor Swift and her song Mean. Sometimes we quoted the lyrics, too.

But I couldn't say them. Not today. Quoting Taylor would mean everything was okay.

"Aspen?" Rhea said. "What's wrong?"

I took a shaky breath. "What did you say to Chase after I left?"

"Huh?" The blow dryer stopped.

"Last night after I caught you with Drake. I left the club, but you were still there, and now there's this awful picture of me online—that *Chase* posted—and I know he wouldn't have done that unless he was either super mad at me or super hurt. So, again, *what* did you say to him?"

"Nothing. Drake and I left after you found us."

My grip on the phone tightened. "That's not possible. You had to have said something. Did you tell Chase I was into him?"

"*Ew.* You two are like siblings."

"I know! That's why I know you said something. Were you trying to distract him so he wouldn't figure out what you'd done or discredit me so he wouldn't believe it when I told him?"

Rhea's voice took on a sharp edge. "You said you weren't going to tell him."

"Well, I will if you don't," I snapped. "He deserves to know."

"Look, Aspen, I didn't say anything to him last night, but maybe I should have if you were planning to rat me out. Maybe you don't deserve a friend like Chase. Maybe you don't deserve any friends at all."

The line clicked and went dead.

I huffed, stuffing my phone in my pocket. I was a great friend. If anyone deserved to be friendless, it was Rhea, not me. *I* was the one doing the right thing.

Suddenly, saliva flooded my mouth and my stomach clenched. I scrambled to the nearest bathroom, even though there couldn't possibly be anything left after how much I'd thrown up this morning.

I was wrong.

Time slipped by as I knelt beside the toilet. The concrete floor pressed against my knees. Dry-heaving set in. And my thoughts drifted back to last night.

The music, so loud I could barely hear myself think.

My naturally un-tamable hair reaching epic-level proportions of wild as I danced with my friends.

A glassy-eyed Chase, begging me to help him find Rhea, who he'd lost track of in the crowd.

I'd found her making out with Drake in the girls' bathroom. Pothead Drake, of all people. If you were going to cheat, there were infinite choices better than Pothead Drake. I'd never even spoken to him and, as far as I knew, Rhea hadn't either. But when I walked in on them, he'd said, "Hey." Like me catching them was just any old thing.

Rhea's gaze ping-ponged between me and Drake. "Aspen, please don't tell Chase."

"So you want me to lie?" I'd said. "How long have you been cheating on him?"

She'd looked away, like my gaze was physically painful.

"Rhea, how long?"

She fidgeted. "I just met Drake tonight."

"That does not answer my question."

"Fine, there were others before Drake," she finally said, her voice going quiet. "I don't love Chase anymore."

My hands tightened into fists. "If you don't even have the decency to break up with him before moving on to someone else, then you never loved him at all. I'm going home. I can't do this right now."

Rhea's voice went shrill. "But you're not going to tell him, right? There's a big game this weekend. It'll totally throw him off."

"Actually, it will ruin him. But no, I'm not going to tell him. That's your job. You don't get to look away when you're breaking someone's heart." I whirled around and, for once, my hair did me the favor of matching my mood—wild and fierce and one strike away from going up in flames.

After that, I'd left the club. That had been my only choice. I couldn't stay and face Chase, knowing his girlfriend was cheating on him, and not say anything. But telling him was Rhea's job, not mine. I'd done the right thing.

So why was there now a Photoshopped image of me online—my head on some random girl's body—dancing on a stage in nothing but her underwear?

As soon as my stomach calmed down, I left the bathroom stall. But I didn't want to go back to my family.

I took my time washing my hands, letting the water run until it was almost scalding and watching it cascade over my fingers. But the burn on my skin did not thaw the ice growing inside me.

I couldn't unsee that image of me. Whenever I closed my eyes, it was there—the flesh, the red lace, my wild hair—seared into my brain. Sure, *I* knew the picture wasn't real, but nobody else did. They all thought that was really me, making some slutty power play to steal my best friend's man.

Steam was now rising from the faucet. I shut it off and stuck my hands under the air dryer, letting my gaze catch on the words *Zeke-n-Loni 4 Eva* written in ballpoint pen on the painted cinderblock wall.

Rhea had to have said something to Chase—had to have made him believe I was the bad guy. Why else would he go to all that trouble?

And, come to think of it, Rhea had never spoken to me like she had this morning. We'd been friends all the way through middle school, and everyone knows middle school is the worst. If she was going to turn on me, she'd had plenty of chances before now. Like the time I accidentally left her phone in the shoebox of a pair of shoes she'd tried on. Or when we were both crushing on Grant Koh in the sixth grade and his friend told our friend that he liked me better than her.

Why couldn't she understand that if she wasn't going to tell Chase she was cheating on him, I would have to? She knew how close we were. She'd known when she begged me to set them up freshman year.

Suddenly the air coming out of the dryer felt too hot, and I realized my hands were an angry red. I scrambled back to the faucet to douse them with cool water. As the water dribbled off my fingertips, I took in a long, slow breath and released it just as slowly.

Outside the bathroom, the crowd started up again with their chanting.

Thun-der, thun-der, thun-der.

And my head throbbed harder than ever.

****

The bout turned into a double header because Jojo's team won, and then an awards ceremony because they won again. My butt felt numb—I hadn't moved in hours.

"Aspen, are you sure you don't want the rest of your hot dog? You've barely eaten anything today." My mom held out a sagging paper plate with an hours-old hot dog on it while my dad folded up our bleacher seats.

Ugh, I couldn't look at the hot dog. "No, I'm done."

She tossed it out with the rest of our concession stand dinner.

I *was* getting hungry, but I wasn't about to take any chances until we were safely back home. My body felt like it was made of wet sand, and my head felt full of cotton balls. I really just wanted a bed and a fluffy pillow.

The notifications had started shortly after I'd left the bathroom—people texting and messaging with varying levels of concern.

Zuri: **hey, I saw Chase's post. r u ok?**

Sara: **how r u feeling? better not get online rn, btw**

Paloma: **ur sick. trying to steal your bff's bf is so messed up**

Jace: **finally showing your true colors and they're ugly af**

But there was nothing from Chase. Part of me wanted to confront him—march over to his house and figure out what the heck his deal was. But the other part of me—the bigger part—was too hurt. Chase should be the one coming to me.

I'd finally turned my phone off halfway through Jojo's second match, drained of the energy required to process the messages.

Now that everything was over, we made our way to the track, where my mom and Jojo would rehash the highlights of each jam, and Nate would tug on my dad's arm, begging to stop for ice cream on the way home, and I would stand by like a mute zombie. Today I actually felt like one.

Jojo's smile was electric as she skated over to meet us, her hair sweaty and matted around her forehead where her helmet had been. "Can you believe it? I got the Energizer, Deadliest Bootie, *and* Bloodsucker awards." She still had her skates on—they were basically extensions of her legs these days—and I could almost see the adrenaline rolling off her as she moved in fluid circles around us.

"The Bloodsucker award?" my dad said. "What's that one for?"

Jojo grinned. "The skater who drew the most blood this weekend."

"*And* you're tournament champions," my mom added, her voice going up in pitch like a tween at a boy band concert.

Jojo laughed, a musical, carefree thing. "Yeah. And there's that."

"Well, we're so proud of you." Dad shifted his weight as Nate tugged on his arm and said, "Can we get ice cream now?"

Called it.

My mom said, "My favorite part was in the fourth jam against the Crashionistas when you jumped over that girl. You got so much air!"

"I had to—it was either jump or get my teeth

knocked out."

"Isn't that what your mouth guard is for?" I said, feeling like I was pointing out the obvious.

Jojo stilled, staring at me. "Well … okay, yeah. My teeth probably would have been fine. But still—you didn't want me to start a pile-up, did you? I had to do something—why not try a jump? And, anyway, I made it past all the blockers with that move so it paid off."

"Well, it was amazing," my mom gushed. "Hopefully the photographer got that on camera—you'll make the newspaper again for sure."

One of Jojo's teammates, Penny Pulp-inator, skated over. "Hey, Thunder, we're giving Coach her award now." The girl winked.

"Ooh, I gotta go. But I'm so glad you all got to see this. Best derby weekend ever!" She pumped her fist in the air a few times, circled and gave us all high fives, then headed for the locker room.

My hand stung from how hard she'd slapped me five.

We wouldn't see Jojo again until her next bout, since she lived on campus at the University of Washington—U-dub—now.

My family turned to go, but I found myself rooted in place, staring after Jojo's retreating figure and fingering the corded leather bracelet I always wore. Jojo had its twin—our parents had brought the bracelets home for us from Mexico last summer right before Jojo left me behind. Hers was probably sitting at the bottom of some junk drawer labeled 'Not important enough to take to college'.

I rubbed my palm absently, watching my sister go. And then, suddenly, my zombie legs flooded with life and I was following her.

"Aspen, where are you going?" my mom said.

"Just a sec—I need to talk to Jojo."

"That's what we were just doing," Mom called after me.

But I was now running, a panic creeping up my throat. I was in over my head, and suddenly, desperately, I needed to talk to my sister.

Chapter Three: Locker Room

I headed for the door that Jojo and Penny Pulp-inator had just gone through, a knot forming in my stomach. What would I even say? How do you make someone understand your insides are a trash fire without being able to open yourself up and let them experience the horror for themselves?

A girl skated past, bumping my elbow and knocking me off-balance. Her jersey said *Skull Smashers.* "Junior league meets at the playground," the girl said, without even a backward glance.

I made my way into the locker room and heard a different girl's voice, coming from somewhere ahead. "... best coach, friend, mentor, all of it," she was saying.

I continued, rounding a few bends, until the speaker came into view. It looked like Rocka-fell-her, from Jojo's team, but it was hard to be sure since I'd only seen these girls from far away on the track or as glossy head shots in the program.

The girls, most of them still in their skates, were clustered around their coach. I spotted Jojo among them—huddled at the rear of the group with Penny Pulp-inator. The two of them were bent over a cooler.

"Jojo," I hissed, coming up behind her.

My sister jumped, nearly dropping something she'd just pulled out of the cooler. It was ... a pie. Well, a mini pie. Banana cream, from the looks of it.

I pointed to it. "What's that for?"

"Geez, Aspen, you scared me," she whisper-hissed. "What are you doing here?"

"I need to talk to you."

Penny Pulp-inator snapped her fingers in Jojo's face. "Come on, Rock-a's almost done. Hand me another

25

one."

"Aspen, I can't talk right now." Jojo handed another pie to Penny, who passed it to the girl beside her. Actually, there was a whole assembly-line-type thing going on, pies making their way through the entire group.

But Jojo would help me if she understood how important this was. I had to make her understand. "There's this awful picture of me that went viral this morning," I said, kneeling beside her, "and I don't know what to do about it. I need your help."

Jojo finished up with the pies and passed out a few cans of whipped cream. "Awful pictures go viral all the time, Aspen. Suck it up."

At the front of the group, Rocka-fell-her was finishing her speech. "And that's why we want to give you the Pie Face award. For being so sweet you make us sick and yet, somehow, we just can't get enough."

Someone handed Rocka-fell-her a pie, and in one smooth motion, she smashed it into the coach's face.

As if on cue, the room suddenly exploded into a flurry of activity. Pies flew through the air. Streams of whipped cream went off like fireworks. Jojo flung a pie across the room only to be hit by some flying crust a moment later.

Shrieks, cursing, and laughter filled the air, punctuated by the sound of roller skates clonking and sliding around on the cement floor, which was quickly becoming a sticky, slippery mess.

"Jojo," I called. She didn't look at me. "Jojo!" I tried again, louder.

My sister was ducking and skating around the room, laughing and shrieking with the others. Her laughter was infectious. There was a time when that laughter made me feel important. Like I mattered to her and that she liked being with me.

But today, right now, it seemed she was laughing *at* me. Just like everybody else.

My arms crossed over my stomach and I turned to go, casting a final glance at my sister. There was no way I was getting her attention anytime soon. As I retreated, something hit the back of my head.

I reached up and got a fistful of banana cream.

****

In the car, after insisting to my parents that I hadn't been crying and had just walked into the middle of a food fight and must be allergic to bananas or something, I leaned my head against the cool glass of the window.

My dad turned on some jazz. Nate was playing a game on my dad's phone. Mom was in her own car, since she'd come straight from work.

"You feeling okay, Peanut?" my dad asked.

"Yeah. Just tired."

When we got home, I showered, slipped into my PJs, and climbed into bed even though it was well before bed time. Miraculously, I slept all night. But the next morning, surrounded by the chaos that was my room, I realized it was time to face facts. And the facts were these: All the weekend's gossip had been about me.

I couldn't turn to my sister, or either of my best friends.

And now I had to go to school and face everyone.

Chase's post now had two-hundred-and-eighty-seven comments. I'd missed a call from him last night, but he hadn't left a message.

My finger hovered over the comment thread and, for the teeniest, tiniest moment, I actually considered clicking on it and reading them. But I knew better.

My gaze caught on the pile of clothes I'd peeled off and tossed aside yesterday morning. After coming home from the music club, I'd apparently fallen asleep in the dress I'd gone out in, and one of my sister's U-dub hoodies, which I didn't even remember taking with me.

By the time I made it down to breakfast, with my phone silenced at the bottom of my backpack, my family was already at the kitchen table. Dad held the morning paper, studying the daily Sudoku puzzle, while Nate dug into his overfull bowl of cereal. Mom was already in her scrubs for her hospital shift and popping the last bite of a breakfast muffin into her mouth.

"She's alive!" my dad said as I walked in.

Mom came over and pressed a hand to my forehead. "Are you feeling okay? You've been asleep forever."

"I'm fine." I ducked away from her to get a bowl.

"You'd better eat fast," Mom said. "Chase will be here soon."

Umm, no. I definitely would *not* be riding to school with Chase today. "Actually, I'm taking my bike."

Dad looked up from his Sudoku. "You can't take your bike. It's going to rain later."

"Dad, we live in Seattle. It's always going to rain later."

"Exactly. That's why you should let Chase drive you."

"Don't you have cheer after school and a football game tonight?" Mom added. "I don't want you riding your bike home in the dark."

Ugh. I'd forgotten about the Monday night game, rescheduled from last weekend due to a thunderstorm. Rhea was cheer captain and Chase football captain—a match made in heaven, everyone said—so I'd be spending the evening with both of them. Super.

"I just want to ride my bike today, okay?" I shoveled a bite of cereal into my mouth. The food tasted like sand, but I chewed anyway. "I'll get a ride home with Sara—she can throw my bike in the back of her truck."

Mom frowned. "Sara?"

"She's the new one—the senior who transferred in this year."

"Oh. Well, I guess that's okay." Then, to my dad she said, "I forgot to tell you—Joelle said they added some more bouts to the schedule. I'll send you the dates."

With that, they were done worrying about me. I got up and dumped my cereal down the drain. Jojo—or Joelle, as my mom insisted on calling her even though nobody else did anymore—was still the center of attention. Nothing new there.

What would Jojo do in my place?

She'd probably shake it off. Then she'd punch everyone in the throat. So I guess that's what I'd have to do.

Too bad I'd never learned how to throw a punch.

Chapter Four: Social Tsunami

The day was gloomy and cold. I pedaled to school slowly, hoping my racing heart would take a hint and slow down already. It didn't.

I'd never worried about what people were saying behind my back, or if I'd have anyone to sit with at lunch, or even whether I'd have plans over the weekend. Sure, Jojo was the superstar of the family, but I'd always had lots of friends. I'd done gymnastics through middle school, and when I'd decided to quit because I wanted to have a life outside of leotards and floor routines, it had been an easy jump to cheerleading.

But now there was a massive pit in my stomach, growing larger by the second. The sun emerged for the tiniest moment, but the cloud curtain came back almost as fast, once again casting the world in gray. I pedaled and pedaled, the wheels of my bike whirring faster and faster as the pit in my stomach grew.

Breathe, Aspen.

Breathe.

It's just a storm—a big, old suckstorm, sure—but still a storm. And storms always pass.

****

Chase found me while I was locking up my bike. "I came by to get you—why didn't you wait for me?"

I snapped my bike lock shut. "Seriously? That's all you have to say to me right now?"

He gripped one my bike handles, his shaggy brown hair falling into his eyes like it had done every day since kindergarten. "Actually, no. I was going to ask what got into you at the club, since you didn't answer my call yesterday. I was trying to ease into it."

I gawked at him. "What got into *me?*"

"Yeah. You've never acted like that before."

"Well, excuse me for leaving without saying goodbye. I was trying to *protect* you, because that's what friends do."

He frowned. "Protect me from what?"

I opened my mouth to tell him about Rhea and Drake—I could really dig the knife in—make him hurt as much as I did. After what he'd done to me, he deserved it.

The words that would break him teetered on a razor-thin edge, at the tip of my tongue.

I swallowed them whole. I couldn't hurt him that way. "Why'd you do it, Chase? That's all I want to know."

The picture he'd posted flashed through my memory, along with his words: *Sorry, Aspen—I'm with Rhea. I thought we were friends.*

Suddenly, I couldn't even look at him. "You know what, never mind. I thought we were friends, too."

"Aspen, wait. You're not making any sense."

I turned and walked away from my best friend in the world, heading into a storm I was so not ready for.

The crowd of students didn't actually part, like I'd been afraid it might, as I entered the school. But I felt the weight of too many gazes on me as I walked to my locker.

"Hey, Aspen, nice show," a guy said. I didn't even know who he was.

"Yeah," another one added. "Why don't you show us some more?" The two guys laughed and fist-bumped each other.

I swallowed, swiping a section of my hair away from my eyes. It bounced back immediately. *Punch everyone in the throat,* I reminded myself.

Some people ignored me. Actually, a lot of people

ignored me.

But too many didn't. There were those who stared. Those who spoke in rushed conversations that died off as I drew near. Those who looked away quickly as I approached.

Then a guy named Tim that I'd known since freshman year sidled up to me. Right up in my personal space. I could smell the bacon he must have had for breakfast.

"Aspen, baby, you're a star." He grabbed my butt and gave it a good squeeze.

I jerked away, smacking him on the shoulder. "Don't touch me!"

A girl in my science class, Marissa, came over and shoved Tim away. "Get lost, loser." She fell into step beside me. "Ignore him, Aspen. Do you want to talk about it?"

My brain was struggling to form any thought other than *punch everyone in the throat*, and I was pretty sure any attempt to talk would end badly. I shook my head.

Marissa stayed by my side but didn't make me talk.

My locker came into view and I stopped short. Crude letters in black Sharpie stretched across the green metal surface of the locker—*Slut*—like a slap in the face. The artist, whoever it was, had kept their work neatly inside the lines—for my space only.

I glanced around and was met with averted eyes and turned heads. Oh, so now no one could even *look* at me?

Marissa was the only person not acting like a witness at a crime scene.

Then, someone else spoke. "Nice job, Aspen."

I whirled around.

Paloma stalked toward me, along with Jasmine and Bianca, all members of the cheer squad. My so-called friends.

"How could you do this to us? Didn't you think about the squad?" Bianca said.

Marissa edged away, her gaze darting between me and my friends. She wasn't part of our group.

"Yeah, we needed you," added Jasmine. "Regionals are only two weeks away."

Paloma turned up her nose.

My brain struggled to keep up. "I didn't do anything to hurt the squad."

Marissa had retreated to her phone, becoming just another face in the crowd.

Jasmine lowered her voice. "Don't lie to us, too. How dumb do you think we are? We know you're going to have to quit cheer now."

"Seriously? *I'm* the victim here. You were at the club, that picture of me is totally fake. I didn't do anything to Rhea. Can't you talk to her?"

Paloma took over. "Talking won't undo the fact that you're pregnant with Drake's baby."

My mouth dropped open. Maybe I should have read through all those comments.

"Pothead Drake?" As in, the Drake Rhea was making out with last night. I stared at the three of them, waiting for the punchline. "Am I being punked right now?"

My friends just stared back.

"You can't possibly believe that's true. Trust me, there's no *way* I could be pregnant, especially with Drake's baby. Ew."

The girls finally broke their silence and spoke in rapid-fire succession.

"We know you've been hooking up with him

since homecoming."

"I heard there's all kinds of proof."

"It's just sad, Aspen, really—that you value yourself so little."

My gaze wandered to the word on my locker as my friends catalogued all the supposed proof against me. The black letters cut through the green painted background, just as sharply as the words coming from their mouths.

The girls finished talking and stood there, watching, waiting for me to say something.

But what do you say when you realize your friends didn't know you at all? So I turned and walked away. The warning bell rang, and lockers slammed shut around me.

I walked faster.

As I fled, Marissa called, "Aspen, are you all right?"

As if the answer wasn't obvious.

My legs carried me past rooms, around bends, and down hallways I'd never had reason to go down. And then I reached a dead end, with only one door left. A placard said it was a darkroom—like for developing photos, I guessed. Perfect. Nobody actually did that anymore, right?

There were two sets of doors to push through before I entered a deserted, mostly darkened room, lit only by a dim reddish light. It smelled funny, but it was empty. I sank to the floor, my back up against a wall, and pressed my head into my hands. How had it gone from one doctored pic to *'Did you hear? Aspen is carrying Drake's baby?'* in a matter of hours?

How could I fight this without knowing what was going on? I had to read the comments.

I yanked out my phone and found Chase's post. In

the picture, too much flesh was showing, and the girl with my head was posing like some sort of supermodel-wannabe, her giant hair cascading over mostly-bare shoulders.

Oh, come on. I was the queen of awkward and I didn't have a sexy bone in my body. Why did people believe this was real?

The latest comments were:

Addikay: **I can't believe I thought she was cool**

EricandSasha4ever: **Save football season—ditch the ho!**

PotBot: **Drake is too good for her**

I scrolled up, searching for the first mention of Drake. How and when had he come into the picture?

The closer I got to the beginning of the comment thread, the tighter my insides knotted up. Then, suddenly, there were no more comments on Chase's post. And there'd been no mention of Drake, or of me being pregnant.

I went back to the newsfeed from that morning, frowning.

And that's when I saw it: another picture of me.

And another.

And.

Another.

They were all similar. They'd been posted by people I knew and people I didn't know. Seriously … *what?* Had Chase been handing out altered pictures like some sort of sick party favor last night?

The comments on the other posts only made things worse. I couldn't stop reading them, though, even though each one was a fresh cut on a still-open wound.

And then … there …

A post about Drake, from a profile I didn't recognize.

APGrl: **Aspen Heathrow is a backstabbing fake. She's been hooking up with Drake since homecoming, and now she's pregnant with his baby. She probably has an STD and was trying to give it to Chase. Some friend.**

My throat closed up and my vision blurred with unshed tears as this lie combined with all the others. The hateful words seeped into my fog-filled brain. But I kept scrolling. Kept reading. There had to be something good—just one person telling everyone to stop being stupid and give me a break. Just one person pointing out that maybe the pictures were fake. Obviously, the pictures were fake.

But nobody had anything nice to say.

At all.

A text from Zuri popped up on my screen. Oh good, I still had one friend.

Zuri: **Are you ok?**

Zuri had been at the club, too, but she hadn't been part of the group at my locker.

My eyes flooded and I gripped my phone harder, blinking. I started typing a response, but didn't know what to say. I was not okay. Obviously. But what was Zuri supposed to do about it? I deleted what I'd written and fired off a quick response.

Aspen: **yeah. thx for asking**

Zuri: **Mr. Mead is looking for you**

The guidance counsellor. Super.

"Don't read the comments," said a voice.

I jumped, swiping at my face. My phone slid off my lap and clunked to the floor.

A figure loomed before me, then crouched by my side.

It was a girl I didn't recognize.

"Too late." My voice wobbled. I cleared my

throat and tried again. "I thought this room was empty."

"I know," the girl said. "I was going to try sneaking out, but there was no way you wouldn't have noticed me. I'm Summer." Her dark hair was twisted into a messy bun on top of her head, held in place with a pencil shoved through the center.

I stumbled to my feet. "Sorry for barging in on you." I turned to go.

"Wait," Summer said, standing. She was shorter than me—although her hair added several inches to her tiny frame—and had delicate, pixie-like features. "Do you wanna talk about it?"

I hesitated. The cold metal of the doorknob pressed against my palm. "You don't even know me."

"Maybe that makes me a good person to talk to."

I considered her words, but I knew the truth. "Or it makes you lucky." I turned the knob and left.

Last year, Jojo would have been here to walk through the halls with me. She would have been here to tell me everything was going to be all right and, if needed, punch everyone in the throat, since I didn't seem capable of doing it myself.

But she was gone and I was alone.

I fingered my leather bracelet. Why couldn't life be as simple as when my sister and I spent our days hanging from trees and fighting over dolls?

A bell rang and students filled the hallways. First period was over. I was standing right by a side exit. Before round two of the Aspen Humiliation Show could start, I left the building.

No way was I going to class today.

Chapter Five: Alter Ego

It started raining (of *course*) as I rode my bike home considering my options. I could move to Alaska. Or drop out of school and become a professional hermit. Or join a nunnery.

Actually, the nunnery probably wouldn't take me because my hair would never fit under one of those little things they wore on their heads.

My phone sounded with Chase's ringtone, but I'd probably fall head first into a puddle if I tried answering it. Anyway, I didn't want to talk to him.

I focused instead on what I *did* want, which was to be someone else right now.

When Jojo wanted to be someone else, all she had to do was put on her skates and head to the rink. It was that simple. So, yeah. All I needed was a secret alter ego.

So … maybe I should go join a Renaissance fair. Or find one of those role-playing group games. Or attend Comic Cons.

But then I'd have to start reading comics and watching superhero movies and, like, learn how to swordfight. Not really my thing.

What was my thing?

It wasn't really cheerleading, even though that's where I'd spent most of my time the past several years. And gymnastics was too serious. Even though I loved the feeling of flying through the air on a tumble track, there was so much emphasis on perfection that it was hard to have fun doing it.

I pulled the bike into my driveway and punched in a key code to open the garage. Both of my parents were at work, so the garage was empty. As I parked my bike, my gaze caught on a pair of Jojo's old skates hanging from a hook on the wall, along with some of her gear.

I fingered the skates. I'd been happy skating once, a long time ago. Before all the drama.

In an instant, I was running inside and dumping out the contents of my cheerleading bag. I refilled it with some of Jojo's old clothes, her skates, and some makeup. I also grabbed a fabric eye mask from Nate's costume box, because I really wanted a secret identity right now and a mask was kind of an alter ego essential.

As I headed on foot to the bus stop, I pulled out my phone to check the bus schedule and figure out which stop was closest to the skating rink. Then I saw the voicemail notification. Right. Chase had called.

My finger hovered over *delete*.

I hesitated.

And then I pressed play.

"Aspen," Chase's voice started.

There was a long pause. When he continued, his voice sounded stripped bare.

"I don't want to leave a message, but you're probably not going to answer a call from me anytime soon, and I really need to say this. I want you to know that I *just* found out about everything happening online. When I saw you this morning, I had no idea what was going on—you know I'm never on social media. Aspen, I *swear* I don't know what happened. I would never hurt you, ever. Posting that picture of you was sick—I don't remember doing it. But ... I guess I did? I mean, obviously, I did. All I can say is, I must have been really, *really* drunk and I am so, *so* sorry. Please forgive me. I'll do whatever it takes."

There was another long pause. Finally, he said, "Goodbye."

He was *drunk?* That was his big excuse?

People got flirty or mean or paranoid when they

were drunk. But Chase had altered pictures of one of his best friends and posted them online. What even was that? And he was just going to leave a message saying he was sorry? I mean, come on. If he was really sorry, then he needed to fix it. He needed to put all the rumors back in the box and repair my reputation. Scrub the Sharpie off my locker. Scrub those pictures from my brain.

****

The roller rink was closed when I got there.

I mean, of course it was—everyone was in school right now, plus the universe was so obviously against me this morning. A quick phone call and pre-recorded message told me they offered afternoon skate sessions daily, and evening sessions on select nights and weekends.

But I was itching to skate, so I sat down on a nearby bench. Jojo's feet were smaller than mine and my toes scrunched together inside the skates when I pulled them on, but I laced them up anyway.

Only, I hadn't been on skates in years. As soon as I stood up, I realized that the sidewalk was sloped and I had no idea how to safely stop myself if I got going too fast down a hill. I sidestepped to a flatter, plaza-like area in front of the roller rink entrance. The surface there was awful for skating—bumpy concrete, with sticks and rocks and stuff from the trees littering the ground, but I took a few strides anyway.

Then one of my skates hit a rock and I went down, hard. Palms stinging from breaking my fall against the pavement, I decided to just wait. It was only a few hours—I'd go find a place for lunch.

Once I was settled at a table, my feet safely back in my shoes and a large plate of loaded nachos in front of me, I typed *sports played on roller skates* into my phone. If skating was a thing I wanted to do for more than just an afternoon, I needed a solid plan. Because becoming a derby girl was out of the question. I was already known as Joelle Heathrow's little sister, and I didn't need another place where I had to walk in her shadow.

I popped a chip smothered in cheese and sour cream into my mouth and scrolled through the results.

There was something called artistic roller skating. Which sounded stupid.

There was speed skating, where you skated around and around in circles. Boring.

There was roller hockey. Eh, I didn't love the idea of having to carry a stick around while I skated.

There was jamskating, which was like breakdancing on roller skates. But I was a tumbler, not a dancer.

Then I saw a video labeled *Jetsi Girls skate.* I clicked on it and waited for the content to load as a server walked past with a sizzling skillet that smelled divine. I bit into another chip, savoring the melty cheese on my tongue.

The video finally opened, showing some girls roller skating down a wide street. Dance music played in the background. The beach was visible behind them, with the ocean in the distance. The girls wore helmets, short shorts, and retro knee-high socks. Their skates were from a color palette that was like a bag of saltwater taffies.

And then they started doing tricks.

Spins. Jumps. Cartwheels, even.

The video cut to a shot of them at a skate park, where they skated the ramps just like skateboarders, only on roller skates. They did handstands, tucks, and jumps—all on the ramps. Then one of them skated up a ramp, did a backflip at the top, and landed backward on her skates. She skated backward until she reached the bottom of the ramp, then spun around and kept skating.

"No way," I breathed.

Then I noticed that the video was tagged *roller skating gymnastics.*

My world rocked. I actually felt it, like I'd just stepped onto one of those wobbly sidewalks at the fair. Or maybe like I'd just stepped off of one. I wasn't sure which world was the right one anymore.

I backed the video up to watch it again. Then I clicked on an attached link, which led me to the Jetsi Skate Shop. It was a store in Long Beach, California, that sold skates—the saltwater-taffy-colored ones the girls in the video had been wearing. They were both retro and cool at the same time—with tons of ankle support for landing tricks.

Right.

Roller derby skates were just designed for speed. None of the derby girls did actual flips and tricks, for which you'd need massive ankle support. I couldn't believe these girls were doing gymnastics on freaking roller skates. It was insane! It was unthinkable.

But they were doing it. They were *killing* it!

These Jetsi Girls had invented a whole new sport!

I played video after video of the Jetsi Girls. They skated along paths by the beach, in empty pools, on half-pipes, and at skate parks built for skateboarders. They did handstands and cartwheels and aerials. They even used trampolines and ran up stairs, using the toe-stops on the fronts of their skates.

And they had skater names just like the derby girls.

Watching them felt like some sort of rebirth, like learning magic was real or money really did grow on trees.

My plate of nachos was growing cold, but it was hard to care about that in the face of this new information. Skater girls could fly. And I wanted to learn how.

****

A skating rink employee finally came and unlocked the doors at 2:58 PM, twenty minutes after they'd noticed me standing at the front door watching them, and forty minutes after I'd started mind-begging them to open early. I was the first one in, but others trickled in behind me. I paid my admission and headed straight for the bathroom to complete my transformation into a skater girl.

I painted my lips cherry-bomb red, then used black eyeliner to draw a tattoo just below my collar bone—sk8 with a tiny heart below it—because, why not? I put my hair in two bunches at the nape of my neck because the goal here was to look like someone else, and my giant hair was my most distinguishable feature.

Now for the eye mask. The one I'd borrowed from Nate's costume box was a simple black fabric one. I tied the straps behind my head and pinned them in place with bobby pins so they wouldn't slip while I was skating. Then I stepped back to survey myself in the mirror.

The girl looking back was not me. *This* girl had attitude and fire and totally normal-sized hair. Suddenly, the person who'd taken that humiliating walk down the school hallway this morning was somewhere far away, and I knew that coming here had been the right thing to do.

I stuffed my feet into Jojo's too-small skates for the second time that day and stashed my cheer bag in a locker. I wobbled as I stepped out onto the rink, joining a dozen or so other skaters. But I found my balance quickly, my skates gliding along the smooth surface as I built up speed. I felt myself relax into the familiar movements.

Jojo and I used to skate a lot together, back before we stopped playing with dolls. I'd been good at it. But, as with everything else we'd done together, Jojo had been better.

Once I felt comfortable, I started practicing my stops and spins. I let my body move naturally, pumping and skating by feel. I skated until my toes were numb, and then skated some more. Just moving. Gliding. Free.

When I stopped, I knew I wanted to make skating a bigger part of my life—a new part of my life. *This* was the alter ego I needed right now.

So. My new plan.

I was not going to move to Alaska, or become a nun, or even a derby girl. I was going to be a Jetsi Girl. The team was located in Long Beach, California, but there was an easy solution to that.

I'd just start my own team.

Chapter Six: Botched

The skating rink slowly filled up as the clock crawled past four. My feet were going numb because Jojo's skates were too small, but I didn't care.

I hadn't heard from my parents yet, but that didn't mean the school hadn't called them. My mom worked at a busy hospital, and my dad operated a crane at the docks—both were only able to check messages on their breaks. I'd be in trouble for ditching today for sure, but I was going to milk my delinquency for as long as I could.

I took a break from skating and watched another Jetsi Girl video, trying to soak up everything I could. If I was going to be one of them, I needed to watch every single one of these videos.

Also, I'd need a skater name.

The Skate Smacker?

Skater Rager?

Lady Ragemaster?

Okay, no. I'd work on the name later.

A text popped up on my screen, interrupting the video I was currently watching.

Zuri: **rhea is pissed**

Another message came in right after the first.

Zuri: **where r u?**

Aspen: **left school early. sure you can guess why.**

Zuri: **we're supposed to debut the new cheer move, remember?**

For one delicious moment, I had no idea what she was talking about.

Then my stomach lurched. The football game— I'd totally forgotten! There was a pep rally right after school, and Rhea had called a practice between that and the pre-game stuff.

But would my squad even want me there? After the way they'd treated me this morning, it seemed like everyone needed some time to cool off. *I* needed some time to cool off. Anyway, didn't they all think I was pregnant?

Zuri: **rhea freaked when u didn't show up for the pep rally. ur the only one who can land that move**

Right. I was the star of the routine Rhea had choreographed—the one that was supposed to take us through regionals and right into states.

The freedom I'd felt the past few hours flitted away like a dream. I sat still for a moment, mourning it. Then I texted Zuri.

Aspen: **be right there**

I hurried through the carpeted lobby, almost running into a little kid as another text came in. I glanced at it and froze.

Zuri: **aspie...**

Something about that one little word. My nickname. It felt like a bomb was about to drop.

Zuri was typing.

People made their way around me as I stood shock-still in the middle of everything. Jojo's too-small skates pinched my feet and my toes throbbed, screaming to be set free.

Zuri's text appeared.

Zuri: **when u didn't show for the pep rally, rhea kicked u off the squad**

All the breath went out of me in a whoosh. I actually heard it leave my body, and then I couldn't breathe back in.

Zuri: **she said our squad was no place for slackers and sluts**

I forced my lungs to expand, drawing in a breath

that scraped at the sides of my throat like nails on glass. I fired off a response.

Aspen: **she should tell that to herself**

My words sounded snappy, but my brain felt more like the nacho cheese now congealing in my stomach. How could Rhea kick me off squad for missing one measly pep-rally? Bianca had missed a whole week when she got her wisdom teeth out. And Paloma had gone to France the month before school started, missing almost the entire pre-season, and she'd been treated like a celebrity when she got back.

Rhea was doing this because I'd caught her with Drake.

Wait … my mind snagged.

Did Rhea actually *like* Drake? Did she believe I'd hooked up with him and was now carrying his baby? Was *that* why she was so mad?

Zuri: **im sooooo sorry**

I stared at my phone, my body deflating. All my friends were on the squad. It was the only placed I mattered, since my grades sucked and my sister was the superstar of life. As sick as I felt about the way everyone had treated me, if I lost my squad, I had nothing.

Zuri: **ill really miss u. cheer wont be the same**

Aspen: **what did coach say?**

Zuri: **she looked surprised, but didn't interfere**

No, she wouldn't. Coach was big into letting the squad-elected captain lead.

Zuri: **she wants to talk to u tho**

My body felt so heavy. Too heavy. Like I was going to sink right through the floor. I stood there in the middle of the lobby, staring at my phone, my fingers going white at the knuckles as I squeezed it.

Then my hand was shaking and, suddenly, I let out a primal yell and threw my phone across the room with all the force I could muster. It slammed into a case of trophies, narrowly missing a guy who was walking by, and clattered to the floor.

The guy, who was about my age, gaped at me. "Did you seriously just throw your phone across the room?"

I stared at him, my chest heaving.

The vending area behind me had gone silent, people frozen mid-slurp, mid-bite, mid-whatever. The lobby went similarly still.

"Yep." I left my phone right where it was and half-skated, half-stomped across the carpeted floor to the lockers. Jojo's stupid skates were squeezing my feet to death. I tore Nate's face mask off, bobby pins flicking away.

The guy picked up my phone and followed me, tapping at the screen. "Oh, good, it still works. Screen's cracked, though." He held my phone out.

"I don't want it." I sat down and yanked at the laces. Seriously, my feet were in danger of falling off.

"Come on, you don't mean that," the guy said, sitting down beside me. He wore a gray beanie, and a few locks of dark hair curled up around the bottom edge.

I looked at the curls, and then at the stubble on his jaw. He was very close. I wondered what it would be like to kiss him.

Then I wondered what was wrong with me.

I stood, my chest heaving from the crazy mixture of rage and hurt broiling there. And now hormones, too, apparently. I opened the locker where I'd stashed my stuff and pulled out my gym bag.

The guy held my phone out again. The screen was indeed cracked—large spiderweb veins now running across the surface.

I ignored him and sat back down so I could get

my skates off. My fingers felt raw as I tugged at the knots. The laces came loose and, finally, the first skate was off. I wiggled my toes, trying to get some feeling back.

"What made you do it?" he asked.

I tugged off the other skate. "Do what?"

"Throw your phone across the room."

There was a reason, sitting just below the surface of my anger. Something tender and fragile. But I wasn't about to go there right now. "Maybe I was mad and wanted to throw something."

My gaze caught on his lips, and this time I didn't give myself time to reconsider. I just grabbed his face and went in, thinking, *I am a Jetsi Girl and I'm going to kiss this stranger.*

In the second before I did it, I saw it all play out in perfect clarity. I'd grab this guy's face, maybe twine my fingers into his hair, and then kiss him like he was the last Popsicle on the planet. And, suddenly, I'd be fiercely in control of my life and nothing else would matter.

Only…

I must have misjudged the distance between my lips and his. Or maybe he moved or something. Because the next thing I knew, we were lip-to-teeth and it hurt. And I couldn't tell if I'd bitten him or he'd bitten me or if we'd just knocked teeth.

My upper lip throbbed and I tasted blood.

The guy pulled away, his eyes going impossibly wide. "Did you just try to kiss me?"

The key word being *try*.

I didn't have to see myself to know my face was turning red. It was on fire—a giant hot-air balloon, going up in a blaze of flaming glory.

"I'm so sorry!" I said, my hands fluttering in front of my face. To hide myself, or to fan away the red, or maybe just to distract him in the hopes that he wouldn't look at me. Either way, I could now add *Worst Impromptu Kisser Ever* to my growing list of titles.

I bent down to grab my skates, wanting to add something like *'I promise I never do stuff like that'* or *'Surprise, you're on a hidden camera show—I'm not really a psychopath'*.

But I'd apparently lost the ability to speak.

Where was my gym bag? Had I even gotten it out of the locker? You know what, I could just leave it here.

I fled.

But a hand caught my arm. "Hey," the guy said.

Oh, I wanted to die. Just sink through the floor and lay here in the annex of the skating rink for eternity. They could memorialize me as the girl whose final act in life was to ruin a century of swoon-worthy surprise kisses with that epic disaster of one.

I stopped, feeling the weight of his hand on my arm, but I didn't look at him. I couldn't. "I'm sorry," I said again. "I don't know what I was thinking."

He didn't say anything, and he didn't let go. Eventually the silence became too much and I had to look at him. Just a peek.

When I did, he smiled. "I'm Brogan." He tucked my phone into a side pocket of my bag, which I now remembered yanking out of the locker and setting down on the bench. He handed the bag to me, patting the pocket where he'd put my phone. "For later."

Then he winked, stood up, and walked away.

I dropped my head into my hands. My life was over. It was just completely over.

At least I'd never have to see him again.

Chapter Seven: Gymnastics in the Park

I stopped at the drug store for some cans of temporary spray-in hair color for the next time I went skating. If I was going to become a Jetsi Girl, I'd need a new image. Also, I needed a real skater name and some actual game, which that kiss proved I didn't have.

I'd also need some teammates.

My thoughts drifted to my squad. They were probably working out their halftime routine—modifying it since I wasn't going to be there.

Well, I hadn't wanted to go to a football game tonight anyway.

"Aspie, you're here!" a voice said when I let myself into the house.

Crap. Why was Nate home? He usually went to a friend's house until my parents got home from work. Which meant … one of my parents had come home early.

Nate attached himself to my leg with a Godzilla-like grip. "Go!" he said.

I swiped a hand across my cheek. Not that I'd been crying or anything. Just in case there was some smudged eyeliner or something. "Not right now, Nate." I tried shaking him off while I peered around the living room, trying to figure out which parent was home.

"Koala ride!" he demanded. "Go, Aspie, go!"

Ugh. I dragged him into the next room where I saw my dad hurrying down the stairs, a pinched expression on his face. He relaxed when he saw me. "Aspen, where have you been?"

Crap, crap, crap. I'd completely forgotten to prepare for this conversation. But at least it was Dad—he'd be easier on me than Mom would.

"Hey, Dad," I said, drawing it out as much as I

could. What the heck was I going to say?

"*Hey, Dad*?" he said, repeating my words back in response. "I get a message that you weren't in school today, and then I get home and you're not here, and your coach says you're not at cheer and, by the way, she wants us to come in for a chat. And, to top it all off, you're not answering your phone. And '*Hey, Dad*' is really the best you can do?"

I hadn't touched my phone, or heard it ring, since I'd thrown it across the skating rink—maybe the damage was worse than just a cracked screen.

Wait, he'd called my coach?

"My phone is broken."

Dad raised an eyebrow. "That does not explain why you missed school."

A flood of emotion welled up inside me. How could I possibly explain everything that had happened today? "Dad, I'm sorry…"

Suddenly, I was crying. Then sobbing. On top of everything else, I was falling to pieces right here on my living room floor. "I just couldn't … do school … today." It was all I could get out.

Suddenly, my Dad's arms were around me, pulling me into a hug. "Okay, okay. Shh. It's okay."

I let him hold me as I got control of myself.

He pulled away and examined my face. "I'm assuming you're not going to the football game?"

I shook my head.

"Do you want to talk about it?"

"Not really."

He eyed me, frowning. Thinking. Finally, he said, "Why don't we go to The Tin Roof for an early dinner?"

"The Tin Roof?" Nate said, his voice ticking up in pitch. "Can I get ice cream?"

"Only if you eat your dinner."

"They have mac and cheese, right?" Nate's grip tightened around my legs.

"Yes, they have mac and cheese," Dad said.

I really just wanted to spend the night in my room, but I owed him for not making me talk. Also, The Tin Roof was my favorite diner. "Okay."

"Good. You'll feel better after a night of family time."

He headed for the garage, but Nate was still clinging to my leg.

I eyed my little brother. Usually I'd be annoyed, but today, weirdly, it wasn't so bad. My social life might be in the toilet, but this little person wanted to hold onto me.

My dad turned around and saw us still standing there. "Nate, let go of your sister."

Nate didn't budge.

"I bet you can't beat me to the car," Dad said, jangling his car keys.

Nate scrambled up from the floor, frantic now that my dad had thrown down a challenge. "Oh yes I can!"

I dug my phone out of my bag and followed them out the door. My phone appeared to be working, even with the giant crack in the screen, but it was switched over to silent, which I had not done. Maybe hitting the floor had jolted the silent switch.

I texted Coach Irina.

Aspen: **Please don't bring my parents in for a chat. I'll come in tomorrow and explain everything, I promise.**

She didn't respond, but that wasn't a surprise with the football game and all. Hopefully she'd give me a chance to talk things over before contacting my parents again.

****

When we got home, my mom had just gotten off her shift.

Dad gave her a kiss and handed her the to-go container of food we'd brought her.

"Ooh, thanks," she said. Then to me, she added, "Aspen, will you take your brother to the park?"

I hesitated, gauging her mood.

She raised an eyebrow at me. "Your father and I need to talk."

Okay, there it was. They'd talk about what a delinquent I was and come up with a plan.

I sighed. "Nate, wanna go to the park?"

"Can I ride my bike?" He didn't even wait for my response—he was already running out the garage door.

"Make sure he wears his helmet," my mom said, digging into her dinner. "And it'll be getting dark soon, so watch for cars on your way home."

My brother and I biked the few blocks to the park.

Nate ran straight for the tire swing. "Will you push me, Aspen?"

"Push you? Get real, I'm going on with you." What better way to forget about my stupid life than pretend I was a kid again?

Nate eyed me. "Mom usually just pushes me."

"I know, but that's really boring for the pusher. Here, you get on first, then I'll twirl it and jump on. Haven't you ever done this with your friends?"

He shook his head but got on the swing.

I backed up and pushed the tire, sending Nate away from me in a big arc.

There was a girl around my age doing a handstand beside a nearby bench, using the back of the bench like a wall to help hold her up. Her legs were pretty straight, and she actually had her feet together.

The tire swing came back around and I pushed it

again, higher this time.

The girl lowered herself out of the handstand and stood, adjusting a bun on top of her head. She seemed … familiar. Silky black hair, tawny-colored skin, delicate build.

Nate came around again and I gave him another big push even as I eyed the girl, trying to figure out where I'd seen her before.

"Aspie, when are you jumping on?"

Oh, right. The swing was at the perfect height. I tracked its path with my eyes and reached out so I'd be able to grab it when it came around.

Beyond Nate, I saw the girl start a series of cartwheels.

The swing approached.

She ended in a perfect round-off. Ooh, maybe she could be my first Jetsi recruit!

My hands closed around the chains of the tire swing in preparation to pull myself on, but I didn't jump fast enough and the swing yanked me off my feet. The chain was ripped from my grasp, and I landed face-down in the dirt, palms stinging and knees throbbing while the tire spun above me. I shimmied out from underneath.

"What happened? Why didn't you get on?" Nate said, his voice alternating from quiet to loud to quiet again as he spun.

Wow, what *had* happened? I used to be really good at that.

My whole front was covered with dirt. I brushed myself off, glancing back at the girl doing gymnastics before refocusing on Nate. "I guess I got distracted. Maybe I'll just stick to pushing."

As I pushed, I tried to keep my thoughts from circling back through the day's events—tried to think about the Jetsi Girls instead of everything else.

I tried and I failed.

The memories sucked me under, playing on an endless loop until I felt like I was reliving it all over again—the Photoshopped picture, that horrible walk through school, my friends icing me out, Zuri telling me—no, texting me—that I was off the squad, trying and failing to kiss a stranger, and now probably getting grounded for skipping school.

"I'm tired of swinging," Nate said, dragging me out of my mental whirlpool. "I want to ride my bike." He hopped off the still moving swing and ran over to his bike.

Handstand Girl wasn't by the bench anymore. I glanced around, looking for her as I unlocked the bikes, but she was gone.

"Aspen, let's race!" Nate didn't wait for my response before pushing his bike off and, after a wobbly moment, pedaling down the paved path that led around the park.

His little body swayed from side to side as he pedaled madly, and a smile tugged at the corners of my mouth. I hopped on my bike and left the park behind, wishing my worries were as easy to flee.

Nate and I raced all the way home.

Chapter Eight: Guidance

Mom and Dad were still talking when Nate and I got home. "Aspen, why don't you go get some rest?" my mom said.

I frowned. Was she sending me to my room?

She raised an eyebrow at my hesitation. Okay, I was being sent to my room.

While I was getting ready for bed, a text came in.

Coach Irina: **Come see me first thing tomorrow. I'll wait to take any further action until after we speak.**

Well, that sounded serious, but at least she wouldn't be calling my parents tonight.

I typed out an apology text to Rhea, but deleted it before sending. I asked her how the game went, then deleted that, too. I typed out *why do you hate me???* then backspaced it away. Finally, I settled on something simple.

Aspen: **hey meanie**

I waited, hoping for the response that would mean we were still friends. Some lyrics, or at least a quick *hey meanie* back.

It didn't come. Nothing did.

The next morning, I tried to put a positive spin on things. The thought of becoming a Jetsi Girl was exciting. It would give me an alter ego—just like the roller derby girls had—*and* I'd get to do gymnastics.

I went to the bathroom and scrubbed off yesterday's fake tattoo. Then I drew a new one, going with a coiled up viper instead of the sk8-with-heart combo I'd drawn at the skating rink. Vipers were poisonous and fierce—just like I was trying to be.

Maybe my skater name should be the Venomous

Viper.

I examined my handiwork, then wiped it off because it looked too much like a pile of poo. I'd have to practice drawing snakes. Then I got dressed and headed down to the kitchen for breakfast, where Jojo and my dad were arguing over the morning Sudoku.

Wait, why was Jojo here?

"Look, if you put a nine here, then this row will be off," my sister was saying. "And you can't use a three because of this block, here." She pointed out the square in question.

Dad pulled the paper away from her. "That block isn't even halfway complete yet. How do you know I can't use a three there?"

Jojo sighed. "Trust me, Dad. Look at the bottom row."

I rolled my eyes. It was like she could see the entire completed puzzle in her mind, without even writing anything down. She probably could, actually. Numbers were just like everything else for her—laughably easy.

"Hey, Jojo," I said. "What are you doing here?"

She was still examining the puzzle. "What, I can't come have breakfast with my family?"

"Joelle's going to shadow me at work today for one of her classes," Mom said. She was standing at the sink, rinsing dishes and loading them into the dishwasher.

I held my breath, waiting for the verdict—what had Mom and Dad decided after they'd talked last night?

Neither of them said anything.

I got myself a bowl of cereal, moving slowly, like at any moment I might trip a wire and a landmine would explode in my face. I sat down next to Nate. "Oh, Jojo, I have your sweatshirt. It's in my room."

"What sweatshirt?"

"Your University of Washington zip-up." The one I'd woken up in the morning after Appellooza played. It was still balled up on my floor along with the dress I'd worn that night.

Jojo was still studying the Sudoku. "I don't have a U-dub zip-up."

I frowned. "You must. Why else would it be in my room?"

"Maybe you have a secret college boyfriend." She looked up long enough to wink at me, then went back to the puzzle.

I rolled my eyes.

"And this square here is a two." Jojo thumped the page with her finger for emphasis. "My work here is done."

Dad frowned down at the puzzle, and Jojo turned her attention to something on her phone. For once, I was glad she was too busy to really look at me. Because if she did, she'd be able to read right off my face that I'd been kicked off the squad, and probably that I'd been reduced to ashes online. She'd always been able to tell when something was wrong with me.

Or, at least she had been until she'd gotten too busy to look.

I took a bite of my Cheerios and chewed slowly, letting the O's dissolve on my tongue while my mind spun back to the pile of clothes I'd thrown on the floor that morning. Where had that U-dub sweatshirt come from if it wasn't Jojo's?

My mom joined us at the table. "Aspen, can you get a ride home from cheer tonight? Joelle has another bout."

I stopped mid-chew. I couldn't tell her I'd been kicked off the squad without spilling the beans about finding Rhea cheating with Drake, the pictures that appeared the next day, and the rumor about me being pregnant. And if I did that (assuming my mom even survived hearing the word *pregnant* coming from my lips) she'd want to see the pictures, and then she'd insist on calling Chase's mom, and Rhea's mom, and probably the school, too, and that would just make everything a hundred times worse. So I said, "Um, sure, I can get a ride home."

Maybe I could use the time I usually spent at cheer to go back to the skating rink.

Jojo's head jerked up from her phone. "Wait, you're not coming to my bout?"

"I've been to a million of your bouts."

"But this one's with *Oregon*."

She said *Oregon* like one might say *The US Olympic Team*.

I stirred my now-soggy cereal, playing with the spongy bits. "Maybe Mom can take some videos for me."

"Ha!" my dad said in a burst. "It *is* a two!" He bent over the Sudoku, erased a number he'd previously written, and scribbled in a two. "Which means this, here, is a four." He wrote it in, his tongue peeking out between his lips. "And seven goes here."

Jojo leaned over his shoulder, apparently already over the fact that I wasn't coming to her bout. "See, I told you."

"Yes, you did." Dad folded up the paper and cleared his breakfast dishes.

He kissed my mom and I looked away. Sometimes it was physically painful how much they loved each other.

Neither of them said anything about me ditching school yesterday. Maybe it was a test. Or maybe they just couldn't decide on a punishment. Either way, I should leave. I dumped my cereal milk into the sink, then grabbed my backpack.

Time to go back to the war zone.

****

I needed to figure out what to say to Chase, and see if Coach would let me back on the squad once she heard my side of the story, but my walk of shame through the halls was interrupted by my guidance counsellor. He intercepted me before I made it to my locker, but I could see from a distance that the graffiti had been either cleaned off or painted over.

"Aspen, we need to talk about your locker." His tone of voice made it clear that I was the one on trial. As if I'd Sharpie the word slut onto my own locker.

"I don't know who vandalized my locker, Mr. Mead."

"Mmm hmm," he said, raising an eyebrow like he didn't believe me.

I mean, okay, this was not the first time he'd had to collect me for a talk. My terrible grades and habitual tardies, combined with the social protest some of us had launched last year to change the school dress code, had made me a regular in his office.

I tried ducking past him, but he side-stepped to block me. "I'd like to have a chat in my office."

"I'll be late for class."

"I'll give you a pass."

I huffed, resigned, and followed him to his office.

He shut the door behind us and indicated for me to sit. I did, and he settled in across the desk from me. He looked at me for a long moment, not saying anything, his fingers steepled together under his chin.

I shifted in my seat.

Mr. Mead finally cleared his throat. "If you know who vandalized your locker, it's important that you tell me. Our school does not tolerate this kind of behavior."

He waited.

But he hadn't actually asked me a question, so I waited, too. Anyone could have Sharpied my locker. For any number of reasons.

He sighed. "Ms. Heathrow, do you know who defaced your locker?"

"I don't."

"Has anything out of the ordinary happened outside of school lately?"

I eyed him. Was he so out of touch that he didn't know about the Photoshopped pictures? "Nothing besides the pictures," I finally said.

His gaze darted away from mine, and he swallowed conspicuously.

Yep, he'd known about them.

"The administration is aware of the rumors circulating online. Several students have been spoken to—the ones whose profiles we can identify—and we are dealing with them accordingly."

"The pictures are fake," I said, just in case there was any doubt. "I didn't really do that stuff."

He studied me, then said, "I believe you. If you really don't know who tagged your locker, I advise that you continue as you normally would. Don't let it get to you."

Yep, that was the plan. Hide behind my skating alter ego. Thanks for the stellar advice.

"But please come to me if you learn anything new," he said.

"Can I go?"

"Not quite yet."

"What else is there?"

Mr. Mead selected a pamphlet from a plastic case on the wall and slid it across the desk to me. Then he cleared his throat. "Have you spoken to Drake?"

I looked at the pamphlet. It was from a local women's clinic. Suddenly, I felt sick to my stomach. Not because I'd be needing these services, but because he thought I did.

Mr. Mead fidgeted, looking everywhere except my eyes. "The father has a right to know, whatever you decide."

I wanted to scream at him. I wanted to yell at the top of my lungs that I wasn't pregnant—that I'd never even had sex because I wanted it to be with someone special, and that I didn't feel ready to make that big of a decision yet. And that I'd never, ever, in a million years, give it up to someone I barely knew on a whim.

My voice shook as I struggled to keep my cool. "I'm not pregnant. Not that it's any of your business."

"I want to believe you, Aspen. But it's all over the school. Even the teachers have been talking about it." He flinched, like he knew he'd just crossed a line.

Super.

I got up and slung my backpack over my shoulder. "Yeah, that's how these things work. Rumors and all. You should read up on it."

I fumed out of his office and headed through the mostly-empty halls to my locker. I could almost hear the teachers in the breakroom: *Oh, did you hear about the poor girl who's pregnant? I hope she has some good support at home.*

Ugh, I was going to throw up for real. I stopped at the water fountain and took a long drink, then several deep breaths, trying to get control of myself, trying to cram my emotions into a box where they couldn't hurt me. I was going to be a skater girl—a Jetsi Girl—and I was tough. Too tough to let stupid gossip get to me.

There were still a few stragglers in the hall as I spun my locker combination. I unclicked the lock and flung my locker open. An avalanche of glossy papers—like ads from one of those coupon mailers—came tumbling out. I picked one up and read: **Enjoy 40% off your next purchase of Pampers diapers with this coupon.** A trio of fat, diapered babies smiled at me.

I crumpled it up and tossed it away, then saw a coupon for $100 off a breast pump. Then another for infant formula. And yet another for baby food. The coupons pooled at my feet, diapered babies and women with swollen tummies all laughing at me.

I slammed the locker shut, leaving all my books inside, and stalked down the hallway. My emotions roiled beneath a whisper-thin veil, threatening to spill over.

And suddenly, I didn't care. I was embarrassed and hurt, but I was also pissed. Let the world see it. I would not be one of those creatures who skulked away into a dark corner when they got hurt. I was a Jetsi Girl—a freaking lioness—and this cut, on top of all the others, had gone too deep.

Rather than making me cower, the little gift had lit my fuse and, I realized, given me the perfect skater name. I needed something with fire. Something that crackled and simmered and would help me harness my inner-fighter—because I'd need her in order to get through this day.

So.

Feline Explosion. My new name.

My tattoo would be cat eyes, with that wild look lions have just before a kill.

****

I found Coach Irina in the locker room office. Coach was tiny but fierce. She'd been a competitive gymnast in Russia and then immigrated to the US in her late-twenties, and had been coaching cheer for something like thirty years.

"Aspen, thanks for coming in," she said, her accent thick as always. "How are you feeling?"

"I'm not pregnant, so I'm feeling fine. Physically, anyway." I looked away.

"Wait," she said, getting up from her desk and hurrying over. "You're not pregnant? Rhea said you were really struggling with it and that you needed space."

"She lied." I almost told Coach about finding Rhea with Drake, but somehow that felt like a betrayal to Chase since I hadn't even told him yet.

Coach let out a breath. "Well, I'm glad you don't have to deal with that, at least. Don't worry, we'll get it all cleared up. Rhea submitted a formal report to the district stating you were being barred for behavior reasons, so it might take a few days to resolve. But I'll get you back to practice as soon as possible, I promise. I'm so glad you're okay." She pulled me into a tight hug.

I wasn't okay, but I didn't correct her. "Can I ask a favor?"

"Of course."

"Please don't contact my parents about this—I don't want them worrying over some stupid untrue rumor."

She nodded. "I understand. Remember I'm here for you if you need anything."

"Okay, thanks."

****

I didn't go back to my locker, so I was missing materials for almost every class, but the teachers seemed reluctant to talk to me, or even look at me, so I was mostly left alone. The one time I saw Zuri in the halls, she pretended not to see me. Maybe she really hadn't.

I spent the next few classes doodling cat eyes in my notebook so I wouldn't think about the baby coupons now scattered through the halls in every direction leading away from my locker. They were like a trail of bread crumbs, pointing everyone's attention back to me.

At least there was Marissa, the girl who'd pushed Tim away from me yesterday. "Do you want to talk about it?" she'd asked after the class we shared.

I was going to say *no*, of course, but she didn't actually wait for my answer before she started talking about a recent article she'd written for the school newspaper. She walked all the way to my next class with me, even though it was out of her way.

As nice as that was, it didn't stop Tim and his handsy friends from catcalling, bumping into me, and surrounding me while walking to class.

Finally, between fourth and fifth period, I grabbed the phone right out of Tim's hand as he tried to take a picture of me and tossed it into a trash can. Then I walked straight out a nearby exit as he cursed at me, his friends laughing as he dug through the trash.

Let them call my parents—I didn't care anymore. I'd made it a few hours longer than I had yesterday, so this was progress at least.

Someone followed me out the door and grabbed my arm. "Aspen, wait."

I flinched, ready for another fight. But it wasn't Tim.

"It's me, Summer," a girl said, her eyebrows popping up.

It took me a minute to place the face. Pixie-like features. Dark pile of hair on top of her head with a pencil stuck through it. It was the girl who'd found me sobbing over my newsfeed in the darkroom.

Then something clicked—this was also the girl I'd seen doing handstands and cartwheels in the park while I was pushing Nate on the tire swing.

"How are you?" Summer asked.

I shrugged. "My locker is a Coupon Cabin for pregnant chicks."

"Huh?"

"Never mind."

"Well. People suck," she said.

I nodded. "They sure do."

Summer stayed silent for a moment, scraping the toe of her shoe across the ground. Then she said, "Want some company walking to your next class?"

I shifted my bag to the other shoulder.

She must have taken that as a *yes* because she turned to go back inside.

I almost followed her, but something stopped me. Was this some sort of trick to get me back in the school so that someone could throw a bucket of pink and blue confetti on me or something?

I eyed Summer. I didn't know this girl at all. All I knew was that she spent time in a darkroom I hadn't even known existed and she did gymnastics at the neighborhood park in her spare time. Sure, she'd been nice to me once, and she seemed harmless enough, but I had no idea who'd been attacking my locker. Maybe someone had put her up to this.

"Um, actually, I'm leaving."

"Oh." Her shoulders slumped a little. "Some other time then."

"Sure. See ya." I got my bike and pedaled away as fast as I could, while my mind pedaled back to that night at the club.

I'd left Rhea and Drake in the bathroom, then ran up the stairs and back to the dance floor, almost bumping into a serving tray full of glasses on my way.

There were so many people on the dance floor, and a crowd surrounded our table, laughing and dancing and talking. But there had been no sign of Chase.

I'd headed over, pushing past people I knew and people I didn't. I'd just needed to get my bag so I could leave before Chase found me and asked about Rhea.

Then … nothing. That was all I remembered.

The end of the memory felt a little like a black hole—like there was a smudge on the reel of my mind that was clouding out the end of the night.

But what else would have happened? I'd grabbed my bag and gone home. The end.

My bike and I ended up back at the park I'd been to with Nate. The playground was mostly deserted. I left my bike on the ground by a tree, the front wheel still spinning, and sat on an empty swing.

I stared at my feet, digging them into that shredded rubber stuff they put on playgrounds, while I twisted my corded bracelet around my wrist. How was I ever going to go back to school and stay all day?

My phone pinged and I reached for it automatically.

Then I hesitated.

It was probably just more of the same. Pictures of my violated locker. Or pictures of me fleeing the scene of the crime. Or hateful comments about the cheerleader who got herself knocked up and barred from competing.

But maybe, just maybe, one of my friends was finally standing up for me. Maybe someone had finally posted something nice. Maybe Rhea had finally responded to my text. I took a deep breath and opened the phone.

I should have known better.

Someone I didn't even know had tagged me in a picture of my locker with its spilled contents, and there was a long thread of comments beneath it.

DanceIsLife451: **OMG, so embarrassing! id prob drop out of school**

Hiphopdontstop: **little whore was asking for it**

Jammer25: **Dude, she just wants attention. I bet she did that stuff to her own locker.**

And they just got worse from there.

I closed the feed and stuffed the phone in my bag. Feline Explosion didn't seem like the right skater name anymore.

I felt like I'd been blasted apart and pieces of me were slowly drifting away. Maybe a better name would be Bombshell Whimsy. Then I could change my tattoo, which would be good because I hadn't been able to get the cat eyes or the coiled up snake right. Maybe the tattoo could be a bombshell, breaking into pieces. Or, no, a bomb on a balloon string. Like the bomb *is* the balloon. Heavy, in danger of exploding, but also, at the same time, in danger of floating away.

Bombshell Whimsy. It was so poetic.

If I wasn't feeling so crappy, I'd be proud.

****

I sat in the swing until my legs started tingling from inactivity and the little kids went home for their naps. The skin underneath my bracelet was angry and red from how many times I'd spun it around my wrist. I really needed to stop fiddling with the cord. It was just so soothing, though.

When the elementary school kids started showing up, I was still sitting there, my legs now in full-on sleep mode. In fact, if I tried to stand up now, my legs would probably fall off, which really meant it would be best if I just stayed here forever. I could be a permanent fixture at the park. Kids would call me the Crazy Swing Girl.

Which would be way better than Has-Been-Cheerleader-Slut.

I sensed eyes on me and looked up.

It was Summer.

Ugh, of course she was here.

She looked away quickly and did a series of cartwheels. Then she went to the same bench she'd been practicing her handstands against the other day and leaned over, kicking herself up. Her feet stayed together, and her toes were perfectly pointed. She didn't wobble at all.

Good for her.

She stayed in the handstand for a long time. Then she moved away from the bench and tried it again. This one was shorter, but still decent. Her form was pretty good.

I stayed on the swing, picking the skin away from around my nails because my wrist hurt and I didn't trust my legs.

Then I felt eyes on me again. I looked up and locked gazes with Summer.

She frowned, then started walking over.

Oh, no. I pushed myself out of the swing and headed for my bike. Needles of pain shot up my legs, but I kept walking, pushing through it.

Summer adjusted her course and reached my bike before I did.

We looked at each other.

I opened my mouth and words came out. "It's you."

Okay, not the best words, but words.

Summer's gaze darted away from mine, and then back. "Look, I'm sorry. I can tell that you want to be alone. But once you saw me, it would have been awkward if I'd just left without saying anything."

Awkward, maybe. But also merciful.

Nearby, a toddler wrestled to get free of his mother. They were sitting on a blanket. The mom was holding a sandwich, trying to get him to take a bite while the kid screamed and writhed, trying to twist himself out of her lap. The mom ditched the sandwich and picked up a box of Raisinettes. "Okay, baby, how about some candies?"

The kid stilled, eyeing the box.

She shook a few into her hand and held them out.

The kid took one and popped it in his mouth.

"Now that's just gross," I said, eyeing the boy and his mom. "I'd take a sandwich over Raisinettes any day."

"Chocolate-coated fiber tastes better if you call it candy," Summer said with a little giggle. "That's a fact."

The boy was now happily eating, and the mom was sneaking bites of sandwich in between bites of Raisinettes.

"I guess Raisinettes make everything better," Summer said.

"Ew. Don't ever say that again."

She shrugged. "It appears to be true." There was a pause as she eyed me. "Have you been here all day?"

I felt myself clam up. I should grab my bike and pedal away. Summer didn't know me—why did she feel she could ask me that question? Catching me crying alone in a darkroom did not give her the right to pry into my personal life.

But…

Here was someone who was not icing me out. Someone who genuinely seemed to care how I was doing—assuming no one was paying her to be nice to me so she could learn all my secrets and use them to blackmail me or whatever. Which *probably* wasn't the case. And the truth was, having no friends was lonelier than I'd thought it would be.

I folded my arms across my chest. "Yeah, I've been here a while."

"Sitting on that swing?" Summer said.

I nodded.

"Sounds uncomfortable."

"It was. My legs are dead asleep." I made a show of shaking them out, wincing as pinpricks of pain worked through my muscles.

Summer chewed on her lower lip, hesitated, then said, "Do you want to talk about it?"

Why did everyone keep asking me that? Of course I didn't want to talk about it. My life was crap. The end.

I *did*, however, want to talk about the Jetsi Girls. "Do you know how to roller skate?"

If Summer was thrown off by the question, she hid it well. "Do people still do that?"

"Of course."

"I thought roller skates were extinct. Like jukeboxes and happy families."

I started to laugh at the happy family bit, but caught myself when I saw her expression twist. She hadn't meant that as a joke.

But this conversation needed to stay light, or the Bombshell Whimsy scenario would become a reality. Anyway, she probably didn't want to talk about her stuff any more than I wanted to talk about mine.

So I side-stepped the family comment. "Maybe skating was headed for extinction, but roller derby is bringing it back."

"Isn't roller derby that sport where people elbow each other off a track?"

"Well, you can't use your elbows, but yeah, something like that. So I take it you don't skate." I tapped a finger against my lips, thinking. "It's not hard to learn, so that's not really an issue." A pair of screaming kids ran by, one of them trying to tag the other. "How long have you been doing gymnastics?"

She raised an eyebrow, this time thrown off by the

shift in subjects. "Not long."

"Are you on a team?" I pressed.

"I'm self-taught. YouTube."

Huh, okay. Natural talent combined with inner drive. I could work with that.

"How does all of this relate?" she asked.

I looked at her, and waited, so she'd understand the importance of the moment. Then I said, "I'm going to be a Jetsi Girl. And I want you on my team." I held my breath, feeling my identity as a skater girl hanging on her response.

She blinked. "What's a Jetsi Girl?"

"I'm so glad you asked! A Jetsi Girl is a roller-skating gymnast." I pulled out my phone, swiping away several social media notifications, and found a Jetsi video. "Okay, Summer, get ready to have your mind blown."

I studied her face as she watched, and it was like her features were etched in marble. She gave no reaction at all.

I deflated a little. Maybe I'd been wrong about her.

But then her lips twitched up into a sort-of half-smile. "Wow." She reached over and clicked on the next video.

I released the breath I'd been holding. "The Jetsi Girls are in California, but I'm going to start a team here." I let her finish the video in silence, then said, "So … wanna be my first teammate?"

That's when her full smile appeared. "Um, definitely, yes. What do I need to do?"

Oh, if only I had some skates. We could've found a ramp and traded off skating and spotting each other. The tiniest little part of me wondered why she'd agreed so fast, but I was probably being paranoid. Anyway, I couldn't afford to lose my first teammate.

My phone buzzed with a call.

Oh, no, this was it—one of my parents had figured out I'd ditched school. I glanced at my phone's display.

Yep. It was my mom.

"Actually, I have to go," I said to Summer.

"Oh, okay. No problem."

"But why don't you meet me here tomorrow after school? I'll bring my skates and we can get started."

"Sure," she said.

I watched her walk away, feeling pretty good about myself. I should write a book: *How to remake yourself in ten easy steps.*

Step one: create an alter ego to hide behind.

Step two: find a sidekick.

Step three: evade parental figures long enough to complete the rest of the steps.

Also, I needed to figure out what the rest of the steps were.

My phone was still ringing. It would be so easy to just push the little *ignore* button. But, of course, my mom would call back. She would keep calling back until I picked up, and the longer it took her to get through, the more trouble I'd be in later. Plus, she could find me if she really wanted to—we had my phone's GPS enabled in case I ever lost it.

I sighed. "Hi, Mom."

Chapter Nine: Crazy Bread

"Aspen, where are you? Are you okay?" My mom's voice was pinched with worry.

"I'm fine." The lie was getting easier and easier to tell.

"Your school says you're not there. *Again*."

I hesitated. "I left early."

"Why? Where are you now?"

"I'm at the park, but I'll come home now. You can ground me or whatever."

"Aspen," my mom said. And her tone sounded … gentle. "Stay where you are. I'll be there in ten minutes."

"You don't have to come get me—I'm fine."

"I know," she said. "I'm coming anyway.

Great. So now my Mom was having to leave work to come rescue me. I sat back down on the swing, letting my head rest against the chain (worst pillow ever, btw). The grooves in the ground got deeper and deeper as I slid my feet back and forth.

Should I tell my mom what had happened?

She wouldn't understand, and she couldn't change anything or give me a rewind. If she couldn't fix it, what good was there in telling her? No, the best thing was move forward. Pretend it never happened and let it blow over. Be Feline Explosion or Bombshell Whimsy or whoever I needed to be in order to power through this.

But I needed to tell my mom *something*.

****

She brought food. A box of crazy bread from my favorite pizza place—with ranch dipping sauce—even though she always said crazy bread by itself wasn't a meal. She didn't even try to get me to eat some of her salad. And she didn't ask why I hadn't been at school or why I'd been acting like a psycho. She just handed me the crazy bread and sat on the swing beside me.

I pulled one doughy strip apart from the others and dipped it into the ranch sauce, realizing I was famished. The silence was comfortable, and I didn't feel like I had to talk. As the minutes ticked on, however, I found that I wanted to. At least, a little.

"I'm sorry I ditched school," I said between bites.

Mom speared a tomato with her plastic fork and stuck it in her mouth. "I know you are, baby."

"It's just ... my friends are being ... stupid." Or, I considered, maybe they were never real friends to begin with.

Which would mean that I'd never in my life had a real friend.

I sniffed. Jetsi Girls did not show weakness. I swirled my breadstick in the ranch, dipping and re-dipping, but not eating it.

Mom chewed thoughtfully. "Is that why you haven't been going to cheer practice? Because of your friends?"

My head jerked up. How had she—?

"No workout clothes in your laundry." She winked. "But I did find black fishnet tights and some of Joelle's old clothes."

Oh, wow, she was good. "There's been some ... drama."

My mom took a sip of her iced tea, then speared a bit of lettuce, but she didn't put it in her mouth. "Your father feels very strongly that we give you the benefit of the doubt right now. You are smart, competent, and old enough to start navigating complicated issues on your own. So you don't have to give me all the details right now—we're here when you're ready to talk. But you can't skip school. And you'll have to go back to cheer practice eventually so just remember it'll probably get harder the longer you wait." She put the bite into her mouth. She chewed, swallowed. "And don't you dare lie to me."

I nodded.

"I'll take you home. But you have to go back to school tomorrow, and this time you need to stay."

I nodded again.

Only, how was I supposed to go to school knowing I had zero friends? I'd never even seen Summer until that day in the darkroom—our schedules were probably so different that we wouldn't be able to hang out even if we tried.

Maybe Marissa would be my friend. I could give her advice for her articles so I wouldn't have to talk about myself.

When my mom had finished eating and I'd drowned all of my breadsticks in ranch, we put my bike in the car and left the park. Mom dropped me off at home, and then went back to work. "Your father is in charge of dinner tonight," she said. "He should be home in an hour or so. I'll see you when I get off."

"Okay. Thanks, Mom."

When I got up to my room, I opened my laptop and went to the Jetsi Girls website. On the contact tab, I typed out a message asking if it would be okay to start my own Jetsi Skate Team. I clicked submit, then flopped onto my bed.

My gaze caught on the shopping bag full of spray color I'd bought. Hmm…

I took it into the bathroom and lined everything up on the counter. Then I pulled my hair into two bunches and sprayed it all purple. The spray got on the shirt I was wearing, so I had to change clothes, and it made my hair crunchy like I'd just put in a gallon of hair spray.

But my hair was now purple, so … success!

I examined myself in the mirror. Honestly, I rocked purple hair—why had I never done this before?

My phone buzzed with a text.

Zuri: **will do**

Will do?

I scrolled up in the text thread. Oh.

I'd asked her to tell everyone I said 'hi' at cheer practice. Like two days ago. I'd been hoping for something more like, *Don't worry, we'll convince Rhea to let you back on the squad and it'll all be fine. I'll totally tell everyone you said hi.* And then there'd be a perfect meme for how sucky this all was.

But no. She'd just said *will do. Two days* later.

Scowling, I stuffed my phone in my pocket and went to scrounge up another outfit from Jojo's closet. It was skating time at the roller rink and my hair was purple—time to get my Jetsi on.

Chapter Ten: Open Skate

If I really wanted to be a Jetsi Girl, I'd need to find a skate park with ramps so I could learn some tricks. And, okay, figure out how to skate outside without tripping over stuff. First, though, my indoor skating had to be solid. So I spent the bus ride watching tutorials and running through the moves in my head.

When I walked through the doors of the roller rink, I stopped short. Because there, standing up from a bench in the lobby, was the guy from before—the beneficiary of my epically disastrous, first-ever impromptu kiss.

I whirled around, face flushing, while some retro song bee-bopped overhead. I'd completely forgotten to worry about who else might be here. Had he seen me?

Holding my bag up to hide my face, I turned just enough so I could see him.

He was wearing a black Twenty One Pilots t-shirt and the same gray beanie from last time. He skated across the lobby, awkwardly, since it was carpeted. But once he stepped into the rink, his skating didn't get any better, and I remembered I'd never actually seen him on skates.

Beanie Boy started jamskating. Or trying to, anyway. His skating was shaky, his turns off-balance, and he had no rhythm to speak of. He was basically wobbling around like a newborn colt.

I found a spot to sit and put on my skates, because Beanie Boy or not, I had purple hair and I wasn't about to waste it. I'd just have to stay away from him. Once he skated past, I entered the rink behind him, joining some shrieking kids—one with a birthday hat on—and a few couples.

I kept my distance from Beanie Boy as I practiced

the starts and stops I'd seen in the tutorials. There were also a few different ways of pumping. One method was called 'bubbles' where you push your feet apart from each other and then bring them back together, then apart again and back together, so you're making a series of 'bubbles'. This propels you forward without your skates ever having to leave the ground.

Once I got that down, I practiced turning by using alternating bubbles, and then I worked on some spins. Skating had always just come naturally to me—like walking, really. I'd had no idea there was so much technique involved.

Once I had everything down, I tried backward skating.

And almost fell on my face.

I got my balance and tried again, looking over my shoulder to see where I was going while making backward bubbles. But every time I built up any amount of speed, I lost my balance and my arms flailed.

Okay, now *I* was the one who probably looked like a newborn colt.

A rock song came on overhead, and it was one I actually recognized cause my mom listened to it on full blast whenever she deep cleaned the kitchen. I spun around and went back to something I was good at. The air whipped by my body as I sped around the rink, weaving in, out, and around the other skaters. I even threw in a few spins.

Okay, they weren't very graceful spins, but still. *Spins.*

Then I saw the gray beanie up ahead. Blast, he was going so slow! I couldn't stop in time, so I skated past him, keeping my head down so he wouldn't notice me.

Then I heard, "Hey, it's Phone Thrower Girl!"

Dang, how had he recognized me?

The way he'd said *Phone Thrower Girl* made it sound like some ultra-cool super hero name. There were a lot of other names he could have used.

Kiss-tastrophe came immediately to mind.

I sighed and jammed my left toe-stop down, spinning to face him. "Beanie Boy. We meet again." I said it like I was a villain greeting her arch-nemesis. Because I was no super hero.

He made his way over and did a wide, wobbly spin to stop himself. His arms flailed. Despite his lack of talent on roller skates, he had a great set of biceps.

I put a hand on my hip. "How did you know it was me?"

"Oh, I saw you come in," he said with a grin.

My face flushed. He'd known I was here this whole time?

"How's your phone?" he said.

"Still cracked." I couldn't look him in the eyes. I just couldn't.

"Man, that's a bummer."

Was he going to say something about that kiss? I deserved it, really. What had I been thinking, trying to kiss a total stranger? That was by far the dumbest thing I'd ever done.

We stood there, silence stretching between us.

He stuck his hands into his back pockets. "You never told me your name," he finally said.

Wait, what was *his* name?

I remembered him telling me, I'd just been too mortified by the kissing disaster to really listen. "I'm Aspen."

"That's a pretty name."

"Oh, thanks." I fidgeted. Was he really not going to give me a hard time about that disaster-kiss?

The silence stretched on until it became too much. Too awkward. Too big to fill. Trying at this point would just make things worse. "I should probably get back to practicing," I said.

"Oh, sure." He seemed to breathe a sigh of relief. Like I'd let him off the hook somehow.

Only, he'd been the one to let me off the hook.

I skated away, my thoughts tangling up in my head. This guy was a mystery.

Maybe it was time to start skating outside so I wouldn't run into him again.

Chapter Eleven: Saraya and the Dollar Flicks

When I got home, my family was stretched out on the couch watching Animal Planet. Mom was home and dinner was long over. Oops. Guess I'd lost track of the time.

"Did you decide to go to cheer?" my mom asked. Then she noticed my purple hair and her expression brightened. "Ooh, very hip!"

I cringed, wishing I'd thought to hide my hair under a hat or something. Not that I wore hats. Ever.

"Very hip is *not* the look I was going for."

"What about edgy, fun, or cool?" my dad said. "'Cause you're all of those, too."

I groaned and turned my attention to the TV. "Are you watching the predators one again?"

"Yep," Nate said. "The lizard is just about to get eaten—watch with us, Aspie!"

"I'm pretty tired. I think I'll just shower and go to bed."

"Yes, rest up so you can get in a *full* day of school tomorrow," my mom said, emphasizing the word full.

In my room, I stashed my cheer-slash-skate bag in the closet and set my phone on the bedside table, gazing at the cracked screen. I was afraid to turn it on.

My fingers found my corded bracelet, and I wondered what Jojo was doing right now. How would she handle it if people were spinning lies about her online?

The answer was that she'd fight back.

The Jetsi Girls would probably fight back, too.

In order to fight back, I had to know what I was fighting, so I opened my social app, avoiding my notifications and going straight to the current posts to see what people were talking about. Things were definitely buzzing.

But, this time, the gossip was not about me.

People were talking about a girl on the debate team—Saraya—and something about the local dollar theater. Some meme of a bandit jumping into a tub of popcorn was getting a lot of attention.

What?

I scrolled back through the posts, trying to find the first mention of Saraya. And then, there it was.

R33S: **You will never believe what just went down at the Dollar Flicks. Saraya Durban actually tried to rob the snack bar. She was baked out of her mind, but rumor has it that her supplier cut her off and now she's scrambling. Who would have thought the queen of debate could sink so far in so short a time?**

A picture accompanied the post, showing Saraya launching herself at the kid working the cash register.

Other posts included more pictures—an employee trying to pin Saraya down, a security guard rushing over, Saraya with a crazed look in her eyes. There was a meme of a badger getting thrown in prison (Or maybe it was a raccoon? It was something grumpy-looking), and a few gifs involving handcuffs.

Everyone, it seemed, had a take.

NatRBoy: **best thing I've ever seen at the dollar flicks, ever!**

kissU30: **saraya is so trashy, amiright?**

A+Ur: **I heard she takes speed before each of her debates. someone needs to take away her wins, like yesterday**

Jessisbae: **It's painkillers, people. she's hooked on painkillers**

Then, there were actually some posts from Saraya

herself.

DebateQuEEn: **@A+Ur that is a flat out lie. I won those debates fair and square.**

DebateQuEEn: **@R33S I was not *baked*. I've never smoked weed in my life.**

DebateQuEEn: **DESPERATION IS REAL, PEOPLE, ESPECIALLY WHEN YOU'RE FEELING IT FOR SOMEONE ELSE. NONE OF YOU TRASHBAGS EVEN HAVE ONE SINGLE CLUE WHAT YOU'RE TALKING ABOUT GO BACK TO WATCHING TIKT*K**

Oh, wow. I didn't know Saraya at all so I had no idea what to believe, but at least now people were talking about someone else. That was good news for me.

I should feel relieved.

I did feel relieved.

Then I felt guilty. Tomorrow, Saraya would go through the same thing I had. Maybe I should try walking into school with her so she wouldn't be alone.

I'd never even spoken to her, though—suddenly trying to be her friend would just be weird. Plus, tomorrow I had to figure out what to do about Chase and Rhea.

I went to Rhea's profile and froze when I saw the most recent picture—a selfie of her and Chase at the football game I'd missed, both of them in uniform. Rhea had red ribbons in her hair. Chase had his arm draped over her shoulder. He was kissing her on the cheek while Rhea grinned at the camera and snapped the picture.

I looked away. Chase had no idea she was cheating on him, but they were both my friends. Keeping Rhea's secret would hurt Chase, and telling the secret would hurt Rhea. Telling would also hurt Chase.

I twisted my bracelet around and around on my wrist until the skin beneath it burned. Jojo would know what to do. Why wasn't my sister here to give me advice when I needed it?

I took a chance and texted her.

Aspen: **hey, sis.**

I waited, but she didn't respond. She could be at practice. She could be studying. She could be out with friends or kissing a hot guy or doing a hundred other things more exciting than texting her little sister.

Then it was a new day. School loomed before me, and I was in my dad's car trying to come up with a tactical plan. He'd insisted on driving me because it was pouring, and when Chase had texted this morning—as he had the past couple of days—to ask if I wanted a ride, I'd said no. Of course I'd said no. Posting that picture of me—saying the things he'd said—was unforgivable.

But if I never forgave him, then I'd lose him forever.

Apart from the morning texts, Chase hadn't tried contacting me since that voicemail he'd left. I guessed he was giving me space or something.

Which I appreciated.

And also, not. Chase had always been someone I could talk things through with. Friend drama, parent drama, school drama, whatever. Chase had always been the neutral party. But if I saw him now—if I talked to him at all—I was afraid Rhea's secret would come popping right out of my mouth, and I didn't want to see the effect those words would have on him.

Even though he'd hurt me.

I turned my attention to Rhea. She'd had a few days to cool off, and a few cheer practices in which to realize that she needed me. It was time to convince her I hadn't hooked up with Drake.

"Are you okay?" My dad's voice pulled me out of my thoughts. We were almost to school.

"I'm fine."

"You're clearly not." Dad pointed to my bracelet, the one I was mindlessly spinning around and around my wrist. Again.

"You're going to give yourself rope burn." He put his hand on my arm to stop me.

Okay, my skin was burning a bit. I hadn't noticed until the spinning stopped.

"Do you have a test today or something?" Dad asked.

I gazed out the window, watching the trees blur as they slipped by. "Something like that."

Dad squeezed my hand. "Well, you'll do great."

I tried very hard to believe him as we pulled into the parking lot, but as I got out of the car and walked toward the school, my stomach flip-flopping all over the place, I wasn't so sure. I spun the bracelet around on my wrist. Just once. For good measure. I had one mission today, and one mission only: find Rhea and convince her I was not the bad guy.

And, okay, make it through an entire school day without leaving.

If Jojo were with me, this is how entering the school would go down: her hair would look especially wild—like a halo of flames—and if anyone tried to give me crap about anything, she'd get right up in their face and say, *Don't even think about finishing that sentence or I* will *go all derby on you.*" And then they'd back off and there would be no cat-calls and no grope-y guys for the rest of the day.

As it happened, there were no cat-calls or grope-y guys anyway. There was just a group of guys passing around a phone and laughing at something on the screen. One of them saw me. "Hey, nice—"

I opened my mouth to say something snarky and

fierce—like Jojo would—but all that came out was, "No." Nothing else. I put my head down and hurried away, the guys' laughter ringing in my ears as I went in search of Rhea.

Well, *no* was better than nothing.

I saw Rhea, standing by her locker, before she saw me. She was still just as beautiful as the day I'd met her, with her shiny black hair and golden-brown skin. Compared to her, I was basically glow-in-the-dark. With a mop of crazy hair that couldn't decide if it was red or brown.

Rhea was surrounded by our friends. Well, *her* friends now, it seemed.

I swallowed, fidgeting with my bracelet, and walked over.

"Look, the new routine may not be as good," Rhea was saying. "But it's unique. It'll get us there just as well as the old one would have."

"I don't see why Aspen can't compete with us still," Jasmine said.

"Aspen is *pregnant*," Rhea said. "You can't compete when you're pregnant. The rules clearly state—"

"But no one has to know," Jasmine argued. "By the time she's showing, states will be over."

Huh, they all still thought I was pregnant. Coach must be keeping her mouth shut until she resolved things with the district.

Bianca said, "But isn't that, like, bad for the baby, if its mom is doing flips and stuff?"

"And what about Aspen?" Zuri said. "She's probably not feeling great. Pregnancy makes you super sick, right?"

Well, at least Zuri was sticking up for me. Sort of. If I ignored the fact that she'd believed all the gossip just like everyone else.

No one noticed me standing on the outskirts of the group. "I'm not pregnant," I said, trying to sound bolder than I felt.

Almost as one, they whirled around to face me.

Zuri's face brightened. "Aspen!"

Rhea gave her a sharp look, then turned on me. "Of course you are. You're a little slut. Little sluts get pregnant."

I flinched. Rhea was not known for being mean. Smart, talented, and well-liked? Yes. But mean? No. So why was she being so nasty now?

I fisted my hands, summoning strength. "I'm not a slut and I'm definitely not pregnant. I would never hook up with Drake—unlike someone else I know."

Rhea's eyes flashed dangerously. She'd never looked at me like that before.

I pressed on, trying to channel my inner Jetsi Girl. "You had no right to kick me off the squad."

"Wait, you're not prego?" Jasmine said. "That's great! We can do the old routine."

"Of course she's pregnant. She's just a liar in addition to everything else." Rhea's eye twitched—her tell.

Wait. She was hiding something from me.

"Anyway, I've already told Coach you're pregnant. We reported it and you're officially suspended."

My jaw clenched as I studied my former best friend, but I had no idea what else she was hiding.

I made my tone as breezy as I could. "Yeah, she's working on reversing that. But I'm happy to watch you squirm for a bit. Go ahead and do regionals without me— see how far you get." I eyed her, then said, "You know, I actually missed you. Despite what you did to Chase, I thought we could still be friends."

Her expression softened, with something like regret tugging at the corners of her mouth. Suddenly, I saw my friend again.

Then Paloma said, "Wait, what did you do to Chase?"

Rhea's features hardened over, and she said, "Nothing." She silenced Paloma with a wave of her hand.

But I'd seen a crack in her amour. On some level, at least, Rhea missed me, too. As if to make up for letting me in, Rhea said, "You know, you only made it on the squad because of your sister. Freshman year when we tried out together, I heard the coaches talking. They said, *'That's Joelle Heathrow's little sister. Maybe we should give her a shot even though her technique is sub-par'.*"

I flinched.

Rhea continued. "Your sister is the only reason anyone even knows you exist."

My lower lip trembled, but I bit down on it hard. Then I opened my mouth and quoted Queen Taylor, telling Rhea exactly how awful she was with a line straight from the song "Mean".

She blanched.

Ha. That had done it. We never used that part of the song. Ever.

Watching her standing there, the words knocked out of her because of something I'd said, I couldn't help seeing the girl I'd grown up with. I saw the two of us singing "Mean" at the top of our lungs with hairbrushes as microphones as we laughed at ourselves in the mirror.

Calling each other mean had always been a term of endearment. But not today. Today I'd turned it into a knife.

"Good luck at regionals," I said. "You're going to need it." Then I walked away, refusing to look back even as my gut twisted at the words I'd just said to my best friend.

The school day was torture, but I made it through. I avoided Chase like the plague. Now that I knew Rhea had no intention of telling him she was cheating, it was up to me to break the news. I'd want him to do the same for me. But seriously, *how* do you tell a friend something like that?

And I couldn't forget what Rhea had said about me only getting on the squad because of Jojo. Even from college, my sister was needling into my life. She'd always been annoying like that.

So why did I still miss her?

Chapter Twelve: Skater Stares

When I got home, I raided Jojo's closet and dressed up as Feline Explosion—the Bombshell Whimsy thing was a little too melodramatic. Fueled by the prospect of slipping into a different life, I drew a cat-eye tattoo onto my skin just above my collarbone. I put my hair in braids—the only hairstyle I'd never worn before—and sprayed it a bright red that would put even Jojo's red to shame.

There. No one was going to recognize me.

I grabbed the U-dub sweatshirt of mysterious origins and shrugged it on, pulling the hood up to hide my hair-do while I biked from my house to the park.

I hadn't seen Summer all day, even though I'd been looking for her at school—she must be one of those smart kids, on a completely different academic track than me. She was doing cartwheels in the grass when I pulled up on my bike with my gym bag slung over my shoulder. Her form was getting better.

"Hey," I said.

She did a perfect round-off. "Hey."

"Ready to do it on wheels?"

She grinned. "I'm ready to *attempt* it on wheels." She pulled her hair out of its ponytail, which stretched all the way down her back, then re-tied it into a messy bun on top of her head.

"So, I scoped it out online, and there's a skate park a few blocks that way—" I pointed in the general direction. "Just past the community pool."

"Oh, yeah, I think I've driven by it before."

"Do you want to ride the bike or the skates over?"

"Bike," Summer said.

I sat down on a bench. Jojo's skates still pinched

when I put them on. Maybe it was time to finally spend the money I'd earned teaching junior cheer camp last summer and get my own pair.

Once my skates were laced up, I pulled off the hoodie.

"Whoa, cool hair!" Summer said.

I grinned. "It's my skater hair."

"It's edgy. But not overstated. I like it."

"Thanks." I put on my helmet—well, Jojo's old helmet—and some knee and elbow pads. The helmet mussed up my braids, and the kneepads felt weird—too bulky—but safety was something that the Jetsi Girls stressed over and over. Ruining a good hair day was a small price to pay in order to keep your brain inside your skull.

Skating on pavement felt a lot different than skating on an indoor rink—I could tell right away it was going to tire my legs a whole lot faster. But I wasn't nearly as bad as I had been that first day outside the roller rink. For one thing, the ground here was flat, plus the concrete was smooth. Still, every seam in the sidewalk tripped me up—until I realized I could just step over them. Eventually I got into a good groove as Summer pedaled beside me.

The real test would come at the ramps. Could I put skating and gymnastics together? Could I be more than Joelle Heathrow's little sister?

****

It was a Wednesday afternoon—not a busy time at the movies, or the mall, or any restaurant on the planet. But it was, apparently, a hot time at the skate park. We heard the scrape of wheels against pavement as we approached, and then the skateboarders came into view. None of them were wearing helmets.

There were a few guys with fohawks, and some

who were bic'd. Several of them wore beanies. But no safety gear was anywhere in sight. I saw a lone girl on the ramps, skating with the boys. The hair on one side of her head was shaved and the rest fell in loose waves over her shoulder.

Compared to these guys, I was like a bubble-wrapped toddler. I tugged at the chin strap of my helmet, fumbling with the clasp.

Summer grabbed my hand, stopping me. "Uh, uh. You have to wear it—Elasta said."

Elasta-grill was one of the Jetsi Girls. And, yes, she had said. More than once. My knees started to sweat beneath the knee pads, which now felt like oversized armor.

"Safety first," Summer said. "Seriously, just ignore those guys."

We both stood there staring at the skaters, who hadn't seemed to notice us. The atmosphere was gritty and exciting and just so *alive*. The boarders skated up and down ramps, slid on rails, jumped over gaps, and watched each other on a super scaled-down version of a half-pipe. It was some kind of wonderful, organized chaos.

One guy was surrounded by a group of onlookers. He wore a gray beanie and was doing some sort of jumping trick, kicking his board up in an arc and then landing on it over and over again. He kept going, the crowd getting more and more excited the longer he went. When he finished, to a chorus of whoops from his audience, he backed up several yards and skated toward a set of stairs going down.

When he neared the top of the stairs, he kicked the board up like he had before. But this time, instead of jumping on it so it went down in an arc, he kicked it all the way up to a rail that ran alongside the staircase. The board landed on the rail, and he landed on the board. He glided down, balancing. When he got to the bottom, he jumped the board off the rail, landed it on the cement, and skated in an arc. The crowd cheered.

Then he looked up, catching us watching him.

And I recognized him. It was Beanie Boy.

My face flooded with heat. Beanie Boy was *here*. *Why* was Beanie Boy here?

I dropped my gaze, willing myself to melt into the pavement. He'd been really, *really* bad on roller skates. Why had he spent time stumbling around at the roller rink when he so obviously owned on a skateboard?

I grabbed Summer by the arm. "Let's go skate over there." I pointed to the far end of the skate park, where there was a swimming-pool sized depression in the concrete. It wasn't far enough away that Beanie Boy and his crew couldn't see but hopefully far enough that he wouldn't recognize me.

Oh, please don't let him recognize me.

Summer parked my bike next to a spray-paint-tagged metal garbage can and walked with me while I skated to the edge of the concrete bowl. We stood together at the top and, as I looked down, my stomach dropped out from under me and I felt exhilarated and sick at the same time, even though I hadn't moved an inch.

Okay, skating at the roller rink was one thing. Standing at the top of a drop-off with a very large, very hard slab of concrete at the bottom was an entirely different thing.

But if I wanted to be a Jetsi Girl, I needed to take some chances—do something scary. Something that did *not* involve kissing a stranger.

I was Feline Explosion, and it was time to prove it.

"Do you know what you're doing?" Summer asked, her voice wavering as she glanced down into the skate bowl.

"Sure."

Actually, no. I did not.

In the videos I'd watched of the Jetsi Girls skating in empty pools similar to this, they just bent their knees and jumped over the edge. Then they pumped at the bottom of the ramp, using their bodies to gain momentum that would propel them back up the other side. Sometimes that was it. They'd just skate up and out of the bowl. Other times, they'd do some sort of trick that would turn them around and send them back across again.

Anyway, I had to start somewhere. Might as well start big.

I took a deep breath, my heart pounding in my chest. "Okay, here I go." I launched myself over the edge and into the bowl, leaning forward like I'd seen the Jetsi Girls do even though that felt like the exact opposite of what I wanted to do.

My stomach stayed at the top, while the rest of my body sped down the slope.

And then I was flying, the wind whooshing past my face. The only things that mattered were me and my skates and the ground beneath my feet. I was finally free.

It was exhilarating.

It was terrifying.

It was wonderful.

And then, suddenly, it was not.

I reached the other side and made it *almost* all the way to the top, but I hadn't built up enough speed to get all the way there. And the incline was now too steep to pump.

I started going backward.

But I was crap at skating backward!

I tensed up. My skates slipped out from beneath me and I fell forward, knocking my chin on the slope.

The concrete scraped my arms as I slid down the edge of the bowl and into the center, my limbs sprawling all over the place. One of my knees pulsed with pain, and I couldn't feel my chin.

Laughter sounded above me and I looked up, wincing.

Lining the edge of the bowl with Summer was Beanie Boy and a bunch of other skaters.

My body throbbed.

"Are you okay?" Summer yelled.

"Yeah." I peeled myself off the pavement, my body screaming in pain. Adrenaline coursed through me, not sure where to go now that I wasn't dead like I'd thought I was going to be.

Okay, so that hadn't gone according to plan. But, you know, it was fine. Surely the Jetsi Girls hadn't gotten so good without falling a bunch first.

I checked my injuries—my knee hurt when I extended my leg all the way, but nothing felt broken or torn or anything, probably thanks to my pads. Both my forearms were scraped up, and my chin was still throbbing. I touched it—no blood—but I was going to have a nasty bruise there. I felt shaky but tried really hard not to show it as I skated to the far side of the bowl where there was a ramp leading out.

"Are you seriously trying to skate our ramps on *roller* skates?" a guy with a fohawk said as I skated past him.

"Yeah, only skateboards are allowed at this park," another guy said. He pointed to a sign.

The sign said: *No bikes. No scooters. No Heelys.*

I rolled my eyes. "That sign says nothing about roller skates."

Beanie Boy was blocking my way to Summer and looking at me with his head cocked to one side. He snapped his fingers as I approached. "Phone Thrower Girl."

He'd said it quietly, so only I could hear, but I could see in his eyes what he was leaving unsaid. *The girl who tried to kiss me.*

And, for one crazy second, I wanted to try again. Kissing wasn't that hard. I could do it right, I just needed a do-over.

No. I shook my head. *No.*

"It's Aspen, right?"

I tried to hide the mortification rolling off me in waves. "I thought you were a jamskater."

He laughed. "Nope. You saw how terrible I am on roller skates."

I should just ignore him. Summer and I should go to another area of the park, preferably one with smaller ramps, and I should try again.

But now I was curious. If he knew he was terrible, why had he been on roller skates? Curse him and his mysterious Beanie Boy ways! I put a hand on my hip. "Okay, I wasn't going to say anything but, yes, you are terrible on roller skates. So why were you jamskating?"

"I wasn't jamskating. I was *trying* to jamskate."

"Um, those are the same."

"No, they're not," he said, grinning. "But now you're the neophyte, so we've swapped spots."

Oh, man, what was a neophyte? Was this guy hot *and* smart?

"Brogan, kick them out," a guy said, coming up behind us.

Right! Beanie Boy's name was Brogan.

Summer came over and planted herself by my side.

"Yeah, this park is for boarders only," someone else said.

The one girl joined in the conversation. "It's bad enough that the city won't fix this place up or build a better one," she said. "We're not sharing this old one with a bunch of wannabe skaters who don't have the guts to get on a real board."

Brogan eyed me, then turned to the girl. "Aren't you even a little curious to see what a roller skater could do on these ramps?"

Oh, crap. What I wouldn't give to be a full-blown Jetsi Girl right now. If I was, I'd show these boarders who should really rule the ramps.

But I hadn't learned anything yet.

Should I show them a video?

"We just started a roller-skating gymnastics team," Summer said. "Give us a month, then we'll show you what we can do."

Some of the boarders actually laughed.

But Brogan said, "Gymnastics on roller skates, huh? I'd like to see that."

A guy said, "You can't be seri—"

Brogan held up a finger, cutting him off. "But a month is too long. You have a week."

Summer gasped. "A week? That's not enough time."

"You have a week," Brogan said. "We'll move aside, let you have the ramps for a few days. Then we'll have a skate-off to decide if you belong."

I elbowed Summer. This was our in. We'd have free reign of the ramps for a whole entire week. Sure, it would be hard. But at least we had an in. "A week is great."

Brogan said, "Come on people, let's go." His crew dropped their boards to the ground and skated off. Brogan winked at me, then joined them. "Good luck."

Once Brogan's crew cleared out, there were only

three skaters left. Two were younger boys—maybe age nine or ten—practicing kicking their boards up and landing on them again. The third was a guy our age sitting on a bench on the far side of the park. He was watching us, but he didn't get up.

"Are you insane?" Summer said, tearing my focus away from the other people in the park. "We can't learn enough to impress those guys in a week."

"Sure we can."

"Why don't we just go to a different skate park?"

"This is the only one."

"No way that's true," Summer said. "Seattle is huge."

"Well, sure, there are other skate parks in Seattle. But none within biking distance of our houses. I don't want to spend all my practice time on public transportation, do you?"

"No ... I guess not."

"Then this is the best spot. And we're going to have the same problem anywhere else we go, with the regulars—the *boys*—not wanting us there."

Summer chewed on her bottom lip.

"Anyway, we're here now, and the ramps are clear. Want to look up *'how to skate backward without falling on your face'* and give me some pointers?"

I went to the smallest ramp I could find and skated the tiniest way up, keeping my skates parallel to each other, and then let gravity pull me back down. I looked over my shoulder to spot where I was going, but I didn't pump. I needed to get comfortable moving backward first.

"Okay," Summer called out, reading from her phone. "Start off slow, and don't look down at your feet. Knees bent, chest forward, butt out. Make sure you don't lean back when you're glancing over your shoulder."

I practiced until I could skate backward on flat ground without straightening my legs or flailing my arms. Then I noticed a series of small ramps, like humps on a camel's back, that looked really fun. So I spun to a forward skate and sped toward them, crouching low at the bottom of the first ramp and pushing with my quads to launch myself up. I zipped down the opposite side and back up the next hump, leaving my stomach behind. I came off the last one out of breath but happier than I'd been in days.

I skated back over to Summer and shook out my quads. "Ready for your turn?"

"I guess now's as good a time as any to eat some concrete." Summer pulled the elastic out of her hair and re-tied the bun at the nape of her neck so the helmet would fit.

I passed her the skates and gear, flexing my toes before putting my shoes back on. Once Summer had everything on, I said, "Ready to stand up?"

She pushed herself up from the bench, wobbling a bit, but stood.

"Okay, now pick up one foot at a time and just let the other glide forward."

She started skating. After a few wobbles, she gained her balance and kept it. Taking short strides, she skated away from me on the path, turned in a wide circle, and then skated back. She was smiling. "It's like ice skating. Only way easier cause the ground isn't slippery."

"Right?"

Summer skated away from me again, doing a loop around the park. My phone buzzed with a new mail notification. I pulled it out and saw an email from the Jetsi Girls.

No way, they'd actually responded!

Hi Aspen!

Thank you so much for your note. We're thrilled you've seen our videos and like what we're doing. Go ahead and start your own team—just always use the right safety gear. And don't get discouraged when you fall, because falling is part of the gig. Always get back up and try again. You've got moxie!

Happy skating!

--Elasta-grill, Jetsi skate team

P.S. Check out my Skate The Planet channel for some skating tips—link below

I couldn't believe Elasta-grill had actually emailed me. These girls were so cool!

Summer had ventured off the flat path and was now skating up and down the smallest ramps. Overall, she looked pretty darn good. She was probably one of those people who were good at everything they tried, like Jojo.

Skating was one thing, though. Adding the gymnastics would be something else entirely, and we only had a week to get it down.

I clicked on the link Elasta-grill had included, and called Summer over. We watched the first episode of Skate The Planet together, practiced a couple of the basic moves Elasta-grill taught, and then watched the second one.

Before we knew it, the sun was low in the horizon and we'd watched four episodes of Skate The Planet.

"Oh, shoot, I have to go," Summer said, pulling off the skates.

"Same time tomorrow?"

"You know it!"

I watched her walk away, then put the skates back on. My feet were sore and the skates rubbed in all the wrong places, but I stood anyway and started working on the moves from the video we'd just watched.

Then a voice said, "You're letting your right foot drift out when you spin."

I bristled, turning to face Brogan. "I thought you left."

"I forgot something." He skated to a stop, picked up a water bottle I hadn't noticed sitting beneath one of the benches, and held it up like some sort of prize.

"My spins are just fine," I said, demonstrating one for him. "Not that I asked you."

"Why are you still here?"

"Well, see, there's this guy who challenged me to a skate-off, but only gave me seven days to get ready, and if I flop then I'm banished from the ramps forever and I'll have nowhere to skate. So, you see…" I skated away from him, did a perfect set of spins, and then skated back. "I don't really have time to talk to you."

Brogan clapped. "Nice. Four full spins. Good job."

I huffed. "Thank you."

"But your right foot is still drifting out. If it weren't, I bet you could have done a few more. Look, I took a video." He pulled out his phone and proceeded to play a video of me skating.

I felt my face go hot. "You videoed me without my permission?"

"Well, yeah, that's the best way to get a candid shot. Seriously, just watch it. Watching yourself skate is the best way to get better." He held his phone out. "Don't throw it at me or anything."

He laughed, but I was not in the mood for playful banter. "You can't just go around videoing people without telling them." My voice sounded shrill. Hysterical, even. I reached for the phone, where a tiny me was spinning on his screen, and deleted the video without watching it.

"Why'd you do that?" Brogan said.

"You should have asked me before taking that video." I crossed my arms over my chest, breathing hard.

He opened his mouth to say something, then seemed to reconsider. Eventually, he held up his hands in surrender. "Okay, I'm sorry. It won't happen again."

"If you know so much, why don't you just show me how it's done?"

He shrugged. "I can't. As you pointed out earlier, I suck on roller skates. But I've watched an awful lot of tutorials, and I can spot a drifting toe when I see one. I'll leave you to it."

He tipped his head, like he belonged in a different century wearing a fedora, hopped on his skateboard, and dropped into the bowl. He skated away from me without a backward glance, his gray beanie bobbing in the light from the streetlamps.

Ugh.

I did not need him, of all people, telling me how to skate. But, just for kicks, I tried the spin again and made a conscious effort to keep my right toe turned inward.

It felt different right from the start. Tighter. Better. Faster.

So fast that I lost my balance and fell on my butt.

"Ow," I said out loud, even though there was no one there to hear me. As much as my tailbone hurt, it hurt even worse to admit that Brogan had been right, but that one test spin had confirmed it—if I kept my right toe pointed inward, my spin would be light years better.

Curse him for being so cocky and so right! And for only giving me seven days to become a skating gymnastics master.

Chapter Twelve: Skating Mash-Up

If my life were a movie, this was where they'd insert one of those training montages. It would show me and Summer becoming roller skating gymnastics pros, forgetting about friend drama and online rumors and every other stupid thing. Sure, we'd fall. But it wouldn't hurt much, and before the end of the montage, we'd be full of Jetsi skating awesomeness.

Unfortunately, my life was not a movie.

And doing gymnastics on roller skates was freaking hard. Even harder when it rained, but we skated rain or shine—we only had seven days, after all. Plus, this was Seattle, and if we let a little rain stop us, we'd never go anywhere. At least the ramps were less crowded when it rained.

It had been three days since the boarders called us out, and one week since I'd caught Rhea with Drake. I'd gone into each and every one of my social media apps and turned off notifications so I could ignore what was happening online and instead focus on my skating. This was the best way to forget about the rumors, and the fact that I still hadn't told Chase about Rhea.

My parents had noticed the nasty bruise that appeared on my chin the morning after my humiliating spill in the bowl, but my mom had just said, "Looks like you took an elbow to the face at practice last night. Is the squad working on a new move? I thought the routine for regionals was all set."

Which I'd been able to evade with a simple, "I thought so, too."

Hey, it wasn't technically lying.

She'd smeared some special trauma cream on my chin and said, "There—that bruise will be gone by tomorrow." Which it was. Well, almost—the bruise was way faded by morning and gone by day two. The cream worked so well, I stopped by the drugstore later and bought a tube to keep in my gym bag. Sometimes it was handy having a nurse for a mom—she knew all the tricks.

The skateboarders had been around, but they'd given us space. Brogan didn't talk to me again, though, and every time I saw him, he was wearing the gray beanie.

My hips and butt were tender and bruised from all the times I'd fallen over the past three days, but I had a brand-new pair of roller skates so at least my feet were comfy (even if my bank account was now empty). The skates were the prettiest shade of purple I'd ever seen— like a mixture of pulled taffy and the sky just before a summer storm.

Summer skated over and did a t-stop, without even the tiniest hint of a wobble. Jojo's skates fit her better than they fit me. "Did you get that?"

"Yep." I pressed end on the video I'd been taking. If Brogan found out I'd taken his advice and was now videoing everything, he'd probably rub it in my face.

Summer smiled as she watched the replay of herself. "I think we're ready for episode nine."

We'd been churning through Elasta-grill's Skate The Planet series, adding new moves to our arsenal every day. The earlier episodes had been pretty basic, while the later ones got more complicated.

So far, we'd learned the proper body position for skating, which was knees bent and butt to the ground like you're doing a squat—the lower the better when you're just starting out because it's easier to keep your balance. Plus, if you fall, it's a shorter distance to the ground. We'd also learned several methods for moving forward and backward, and a few different ways to stop. We'd learned how to spin while keeping our body weight centered on a straight axis, how to pump at different times while skating up and down slopes to either gain momentum or slow down, how to navigate hills, and even how to go up and down stairs.

Most of it felt pretty intuitive, except for the backward skating thing, but I was slowly getting better at that. Summer didn't seem to be having trouble with it at all.

The tutorials didn't break down any of the Jetsi Girls' actual tricks, though—the cartwheels, handstands, and flips. The handstand turned out to be straightforward enough, given my gymnastics training. You just had to use your toe stop to kick yourself up, and then be ready to skate backward for a bit when you came out of it.

Their other gymnastics moves were more complicated, though. I'd started watching the Jetsi promo videos in slow-motion so I could pick apart the moves, but I wished there were tutorials for those.

"Hey, the next video is on jumping!" Summer said.

I perked up. Jumping was a step in the right direction. We watched the whole thing, then went to the nearby tennis courts to practice, since Elasta said a large flat surface was best for learning.

It turned out that catching air wasn't as hard as it looked, if you did it right. You had to use your body like a spring, crouching way down low into a squat, and then launching yourself upward. When you landed, you had to crouch back down to absorb the shock of landing so you wouldn't fall when your feet hit the ground.

Summer and I skated back to the ramps after our jumping practice and flopped down on the bench where I'd left my U-dub hoodie. Sure, I didn't know where it had come from, but at least now it had a purpose—I wore it whenever I left the house with colored hair, only taking it off once I'd reached the skate park to make sure my alter ego stayed separate from my real life.

I did a quick scan of the area, but the boarder with the gray beanie was gone.

"You know, Brogan's probably bald underneath that hat," Summer said.

"No, I've seen his hair sticking out," I mused dreamily, biting my bottom lip. I did wonder, though, what he looked like without his signature headpiece.

Summer leaned into me, nudging me with her shoulder. "I knew you were looking for him."

Oh, shoot.

"No crushing on the enemy!" Summer said, picking up her water bottle and twisting off the cap.

Gah, Summer was right. "Fine."

Then a guy's voice said, "So, you're the crazy roller girls."

I jumped, thinking it was Brogan.

Summer dropped the cap to her water bottle.

But it was not Brogan. It was the guy who'd stayed to watch us that very first day after the rest of the boarders left. I'd noticed him watching us on and off over the past couple of days but hadn't thought much of it. Most of the boarders watched us on and off.

The guy bent down to pick up Summer's bottle cap. He handed it back to her, holding her gaze a little longer than necessary.

Summer made a move like she was going to tuck a strand of hair behind her ear, forgetting she was wearing a helmet. She ended up just patting the helmet and then putting her hands in her lap.

The guy was wearing jeans two sizes too big for him, and he held a skateboard in one hand. "Everyone says you're nuts and that you're gonna get creamed at the skate-off."

"We might be nuts. But we're not gonna get creamed." I narrowed my eyes at him. "Why do you care?"

He dropped his skateboard to the ground and skated in a slow circle around us. "Your stuff is pretty sick."

"Um, thanks?" I said.

He completed his circle, then kicked the skateboard up, dragging the tail along the ground into a stop. "Is your team open to guys?"

I glanced at Summer. She looked as shocked as I felt, her mouth hanging open in a little O. Technically, the Jetsi Girls were an all-girls skate team. That was kinda their thing. I tried to picture this guy on roller skates, baggy jeans and all. The image almost made me laugh.

But ... we needed more teammates, and he looked comfortable on wheels—maybe he could teach us some tricks.

"Can you roller skate?"

"Not sure. But my parents put me on roller blades when I was little—they said I had too much energy—and I got pretty good on those."

I'd never been on roller blades, but how different could they be?

Summer was suddenly extra-focused on picking at her cuticles. I tried unsuccessfully to catch her eye.

"Okay," I finally said. "You're in—on a trial basis."

His smile brightened. "Nice!" He dropped his board and started skating circles around us again. "My parents were right, by the way."

I raised an eyebrow. "About what?"

"I do have too much energy."

Summer's gaze finally darted up, and then back into her lap when she saw him looking at her. Okay, seriously, it was like she'd never spoken to a guy before.

I refocused on him. "So, do you have a name?"

He grinned, kicking his board up into an arc, flipping it with his toes, and landing on it again. I really needed to learn what all these cool skateboard moves were called. "I'm Dylan. And it's a good thing you let me join." He started skating around us again.

"Why?"

He slid to a stop, just short of running me over.

I almost stepped back, but for some reason, I didn't. My helmet, my knee pads, my skates—they now made me feel safe.

Dylan was all up in my personal space, but I stood my ground. He said, "You're gonna need my help. Brogan's intense. And he doesn't fight fair."

"What does *that* mean?" I said.

Dylan ran a hand through his hair, which was sandy colored and hanging in his eyes. I couldn't tell if it was shaggy on purpose or if he just needed a haircut.

"Brogan didn't tell you about the promo opportunities at the skate-off, did he?"

Summer finally looked up from her nails.

I studied Dylan. "What do you mean?"

"There are going to be some important people there—reps looking for good skaters to sponsor. If you want to make it in skating, sponsorships are everything, and Brogan's been trying to get one for years."

"What, exactly, does a sponsor do?" I asked, trying to figure out why it was such a big deal that Brogan didn't tell us about them. *We* weren't looking for a sponsor.

"Well, it depends," Dylan said. "A basic sponsor would be like a brand of shoes or a skate shop or something, and they would do things like giving the skater stuff to wear with their brand on it, and sometimes covering event fees or new equipment."

Okay, free roller skates would be cool.

"At the highest level, though—the pro level—a sponsor would actually pay the skater a salary, or cover living expenses, so the skater can skate full-time for the company. Think Tony Hawk or Sean White. Once a boarder gets that famous, people will buy anything with their name on it, and the skater can just keep doing what they love."

Hmm, maybe we *should* be looking for a sponsor.

"With Flipfezt coming to Seattle this year, the whole city is buzzing. Brogan invited a bunch of brand reps to the skate-off, and he's already got a few local news outlets lined up to cover the event. If you flop, you'll flop big."

I rolled my eyes. "What the heck is a Flipfest?"

"Uh." He raised an eyebrow like I'd just asked who Beyoncé was.

When neither Summer nor I responded, he said, "Okay, wow. You're serious. Well, if you're gonna hang at the skate park, this is essential—first of all, it's Flipfezzzt. With a 'Z'. Not Flipfest. Say it."

Summer and I repeated the name, emphasizing the 'Z'.

"Good," Dylan said. "Secondly, it's not *a* flipfezt, it's Flipfezt, and it's huge—right up there with the X-Games. Only Flipfezt is just for skateboarding. They're coming to Seattle this year, so everyone around here is going a little nuts."

"Okay, so, Brogan wants to compete in Flipfezt?" I asked, trying to understand.

Dylan laughed. "You can't just compete in Flipfezt. It takes years of practice and making a name for yourself before you even have a hope of getting invited. And then there's the dozens of qualifying competitions in the months leading up to it."

"So why is everyone so excited if none of you will get to compete?"

"Look, if Harry Styles set up in your backyard, you'd be excited even if he didn't invite you onstage, right?"

I shrugged.

But, okay, yeah. Point made.

"Anyway, the first step is getting a local sponsorship," Dylan continued, "which is what Brogan and the other boarders are working on right now. So, like I said, if you flop, you'll flop in front of everyone who's watching. And there are a lot of people watching right now."

Dylan paused to check something on his phone, and his lips quirked up in a smile. "But, actually, you might not need to worry. I posted a video of you two skating and it's already getting a bunch of hits. I tagged it #FlipfeztPrep to pull in traffic from boarders and other Flipfezt fans."

A jolt of panic pulsed through me.

Nobody at school could know what I was doing. If they found out, it would ruin everything. My school life and my skating life could not touch. Not ever. Summer knew that. But I hadn't even thought to worry about something like this.

My voice came out in a squeak. "You posted a video of us? What video? When did you take it?"

I reached up to make sure my helmet was still in place. It was, but I hadn't been wearing a mask or anything like I had that first day at the roller rink. At least I'd put my hair in braids and used some blue hair spray before practice this morning. But still. Any close-ups of my face and it would all be over.

"Chill," Dylan said. "I took it a few minutes ago and you both looked awesome." He held out his phone. The video was a mash-up of the practice moves we'd been doing all afternoon—jumps, spins, and even some handstands, which, I had to admit, looked pretty cool with roller skates on. And the shots were from far enough away that you couldn't really see my face.

But still.

My mind flashed back to the last image someone had posted of me, and the same helplessness I'd felt then thickened my throat. My voice came out low, simmering with barely-controlled emotion. "You can't just go around posting videos of people without their permission."

"It's no big deal," Dylan said.

I pressed my hands to my head and squeezed my eyes shut. *Deep breaths*. There were words that needed to be said, but I couldn't quite find them. "Just don't post videos of me, okay?" I snapped.

Summer pressed her lips together, like she knew what I was referring to and was debating saying something.

I continued quickly. "You should have asked before you posted anything."

"But the world needs to see this," Dylan said, "and I didn't think either of you would post it. You're good, and I can tell you're just going to get be—"

I cut him off. "We're not trying to get a rep or a sponsor or whatever it's called, so it doesn't matter. And it's not okay to post videos of us without asking. Don't ever do that again." I wrapped my arms around myself, breathing hard.

Dylan's gaze darted to Summer and then came back to me. "Okay. I'm sorry." He ran a hand through his hair. "It won't happen again, I promise."

My phone buzzed with a text, making me jump.

Oh, no. Someone had seen the video. They must have zoomed in and recognized me. My secret identity was going to be blown wide open, and I'd have to start all over again.

Again.

I fumbled to get out my phone, dreading for the first time all week seeing a text from one of my friends. Or one of my former friends.

But the text was from a number my phone didn't recognize. It offered a suggestion.

Maybe: Sara: **Thought you should see this. It's Sara, by the way. Not sure if I'm in your phone.**

Sara. She was the senior who was new to squad this year. She'd stayed at our table the night Appellooza played, with her nose in her phone, while the rest of us danced. Really, all I knew about her was that she drove a pickup truck and hated her parents for making her switch schools just before her senior year—she'd had to try out for the squad with the incoming freshman.

She'd included a link with her text. I pressed it and a post appeared, along with a picture. It was Zuri, up on a stage in a tiny strappy dress, clinging to a pole. In the background, someone else was visible.

I caught my breath. Because that someone looked a lot like me. Or, the me in the fake picture Chase had posted, with the red bra and panties.

But Zuri and I had never been at what looked like a nightclub, dressed like … that.

So this was another Photoshopped picture. The caption said:

R33S: **Zuri Tyrell, people, slutting it up for your enjoyment. Since Zuri lacks any actual skills, she's stooped to groveling for your attention any way** she can.

The post already had dozens of comments.

Faebae: **she's not even pretty how'd she get on the cheer team?**

Tim.the.man: **id bang her**

$tar78: **shes cheap, and there's enough to go around #freeZuri**

Who the heck had posted this? One of Chase's stupid friends?

"Is something wrong?" Summer said, peering at me. "Aspen?

I could show her the picture and maybe, finally, talk to her about everything. I could spill all the gory details, right here, right now, and just leave my bleeding heart on the concrete for Summer and Dylan to clean up.

But my friends had turned on me before—friends I'd known better and longer than these two—and I couldn't risk that happening again.

"Everything's fine." I turned my phone off. My fingers found my bracelet, and I spun it in a slow circle around my wrist, irritating the skin that had just begun to heal.

Chapter Thirteen: Learning

Zuri didn't respond to any of my texts asking if she was okay. I even tried calling her.

As for Rhea, I'd given up trying to get a response. Honestly, after what she'd said to me about Jojo, she didn't deserve my friendship or my forgiveness.

But I couldn't forget the look on her face when I'd used Taylor against her.

So I threw myself into my alter ego, waking up early so I could skate in the mornings before school and meeting up with Summer and Dylan every afternoon.

I'd ordered an arsenal of temporary hair color products and tried a new one out each day. So far my favorite was the purple hair putty—it was easy to apply and vibrant in color. It didn't make my hair crunchy, *and* it didn't run when my hair got a little rain on it, unlike the sprays and chalks. I now had it in every color available and used it each day with my braids. Nobody was going to recognize me by my hair, that was for sure.

Eventually, I gave Dylan permission to post more skating videos of us, since it might help intimidate our competitors before the skate-off, as long as he blurred out our faces in anything he posted. Having an alter ego was the only thing keeping me going.

"Let's work on the handstand-bowl-backskate," I said one afternoon. It was a rare sunny day, so I was in a good mood. Plus, my hair was silver and I was kind-of digging it.

The handstand-bowl-backskate was one of the moves I'd picked apart by watching the Jetsi Girls in slow motion. I didn't know what the move was officially called, or if it even had a name, so I'd made up my own.

The handstand-bowl-backskate consisted of

skating up the side of the bowl, grabbing the top lip and doing a handstand on the edge, then lowering your body back down and skating backward into the bowl. It was tricky, especially given the fact that backward skating still threw me off sometimes, but it was easier than some of their other moves. I hadn't worked up the nerve to try any flips yet.

So far I'd perfected a handstand on roller skates on flat ground, a cartwheel/roundoff thing where you do a cartwheel and land on both skates in a backward skate, and a move we called the jump-and-grab. In the jump-and-grab, you used a ramp to catch some air, then tucked your knees and grabbed your skates. Then you just untucked and landed on the downward ramp, bending your knees as you touched down to absorb the shock. Overall, our skating was solid, and both Summer and I could catch some air and land without wiping out.

Well, we could land without wiping out *most* of the time.

But we were improving quickly, and my backward skating was getting better—almost perfect on flat ground. It was just on a decline that I still had trouble.

I skated to the edge of the bowl to start the handstand-bowl-backskate. Summer got her phone ready to video while Dylan stood close by, looking over her shoulder at the screen.

Summer gave me a thumbs up and I launched myself in. The exhilaration was the same as it had been that very first time—my stomach stayed at the top and the wind tugged at my hair and clothes as my body sliced through the air. I pumped a few times when I got to the bottom, picking up speed for my trip up the other side.

I reached the top with plenty of momentum and grabbed the edge with both hands. The extra momentum carried my body up into a handstand. I made it *almost* all the way up. I felt my legs as they moved—compared their position to where my gymnastics training said they should be for a perfectly straight handstand. They didn't quite get there, so I wasn't able to hold the move, but that was okay. I'd get it next time.

The drop back into the bowl came next. I focused on that, my heart speeding up as I anticipated the backward decline skating. Gravity pulled my legs down and I tucked my knees up toward my chest, angling my feet so my toe stops wouldn't get in the way of my landing. My front wheels touched the ramp just before the back ones. I glanced over my shoulder to spot where I was going as I skated backward into the center of the bowl.

Come on, Aspen, you can do this.

My arms lifted as I tried to keep my balance, but my body tensed. I was flying backward. It was not natural. I wobbled, and then overcorrected the wobble by leaning too far forward just as I reached the bottom of the ramp. My right toe-stop touched the ground, breaking my fall, but also killing my speed. My arms flailed at the sudden change in velocity.

I did a quick one-eighty spin and felt my balance come back as I returned to forward skating. I'd kept myself from falling, and kind-of saved the move. But, man, why was it so hard for me to just let go and skate backward?

I picked up speed, returning to the deepest part of the bowl. I let my muscles work, propelling me forward, and skated around the bowl like it was nothing more than a heavily banked roller-derby track. The sun warmed my face, and the wind kissed my cheeks as it whipped passed my body.

This was freedom.

This, right here.

"That was great," Summer called down to me. "You just need a little more speed next time ↑ get that handstand all the way up."

"It's better every time you do it," Dylan added.

I decided to try something I hadn't done before. When I finished my loop around the bowl, I started another, speeding up even more. Then, when I got to the far side where my friends were standing, I zoomed up the incline, with speed to spare, and let myself catch some air as I launched myself out of the bowl, doing a quick skate grab before landing next to Summer.

She raised an eyebrow and pressed end on the video. "Wow. What was that?"

"I don't know." I was breathing hard. "Just having fun."

"Well, it was cool. It can be our jump-and-grab bowl exit."

"My backward skating totally killed that move," I said.

"Nah, you saved it by spinning at the last minute," Dylan said. "No one would even know that wasn't supposed to be part of it."

"*I* knew."

"Still. It looked really cool." Summer played the video back.

I watched, but cringed when I saw myself wobble and almost fall.

They were right, though. All I needed was more practice. I'd get the backward skating down if I had to spend every freaking minute at the skate park until the day of the skate-off.

"I'll add the jump-and-grab bowl exit to our list." Summer pulled out the notebook she'd been using to catalog all our moves, complete with stick figure diagrams showing how each move was supposed to look in case we forgot any of them.

Dylan attacked a set of stairs, running up them on his toe stops and doing his own jump-and-grab at the top.

Summer's bag lay open on the bench beside her, leaving the contents partially visible as she added our new move to the notebook.

"Is that a camera?" I asked, pointing at what looked like one of those bulky professional deals.

Summer tugged the bag to her side. "Yeah, it's for one of my classes."

"Can I see some of your pictures?"

"No!" Her hand flew to the bag, like she thought I might try to snatch the camera without permission.

I eyed her. "Jumpy much?"

She gave a stale laugh, stuffing the notebook back in her bag and tugging the drawstring closed. "It's just that the camera belongs to the school. I can't afford anything happening to it. Plus, I'm pretty new to photography, and my pictures aren't very good."

"I'm sure that's not true."

She stood. "I should get going."

"Already?"

"My mom needs me to watch my baby sister."

I stood, too, but had no intention of going home. There were still so many practice hours left in the day.

****

I stayed long after Summer left. The sun went down. Dylan and the other boarders went home. And, still, I practiced. When I took a break to rewatch some of the videos Summer had taken of me, a shadow fell across my phone screen, blocking out the light from a nearby street lamp.

"What's your deal?" said a voice from behind me.

My heart skipped a beat, because I knew exactly who it was.

Brogan and I still hadn't spoken since that day he'd given me the tip about keeping my toe in during my spins. I tensed as he settled on the bench beside me. Were we finally going to talk about that kiss fail? Or were we going to talk about skating? Or … wait, had he asked me what my *deal* was? "Excuse me?"

"You know, your deal. What is it?"

I gawked at him. "What's *your* deal?"

"Nope. I asked you first."

"Well, I don't have a deal, so there's nothing to talk about."

"Everyone has a deal." He leaned in closer, like he was going to tell me a secret. "I've seen you, you know—practicing every morning. I live right across the street." He pointed out his house. "And I've seen your video, along with everyone else in town."

I scowled. Dylan's video of us had spread—around town and around my school—and now everyone was talking about the two fearless roller-skater girls. He hadn't posted a second one yet, but I knew he was working on it.

Luckily, no one had figured out I was one of the girls in the video. Keeping my hair braided and colored when I skated had done its job—no-one recognized Aspen without her signature giant hair. The helmet helped, too.

Brogan interpreted my scowl wrong. "Hey, everyone loves you. You all should start an actual channel or something." He paused. "But you're here all the time—almost seems like there's more to it than a skate-off. Like maybe you're hiding from something?"

My face went hot. So what if skating was the Band-Aid holding me together? My secrets were keeping me safe, and I had no desire to talk about them. Especially with him. I fingered my bracelet but tried not to spin it—the skin underneath was raw, and spinning it hurt.

"How come you didn't tell us about the sponsors?" I said, turning the spotlight on him.

His face went blank. "Huh?"

"Dylan says there are going to be sponsors at the skate-off. Is that true?"

"Well, yeah."

"And were you planning on telling us?"

He shrugged. "Why? Do you want a sponsor?"

"Well, no … or maybe, yes. I don't know," I spluttered. "It doesn't matter. You're using us to get sponsors here so you can make fools out of us and make yourself look better."

"Um no, I'm not. First of all, there's nothing I could do to make you look like a fool. You're a good skater. And secondly, there's nothing wrong with wanting a sponsor—I figured the skate-off would be a good way to get them out to see us skate. You could benefit from it just as easily as I could."

"You were just trying to get them here to watch us flop."

His eyebrows shot up. "That's not true."

"Whatever, Brogan. I don't know you at all. And I certainly don't trust you." I got up from the bench, grabbed my bag, and left the park.

Chapter Fourteen: Will The Real Aspen Please Stand Up

I paced around my bedroom in the dark, my skating equipment in a heap on the floor.

Brogan thought he knew me, but he didn't.

Summer and Dylan thought they knew me, but they didn't. Not really. Not yet.

And the internet claimed to know me.

But it didn't. I had to keep reminding myself of that.

Contrary to the comments on Chase's picture of me, I was not a slut. I was not a fame-seeking whore who'd tried to sabotage football season, and I did not deserve to die.

Also, contrary to the comments on the skating video Dylan had put up, I was not a superhero. I was not fearless, and I did not have gravity-defying skates.

Lastly, I was not stupid. Being photographed in a skimpy outfit, even if it *had* actually been me, did not give people permission to attack me. The online storm was still raging, despite the fact that I'd been ignoring it, and I could no longer pretend it was okay.

I pulled up the recent picture of Zuri and examined it, trying to figure out how the Photoshop expert had created it. Because it had to be fake. It just had to be.

But it didn't look fake.

Zuri hadn't called or texted—or even looked my way at school—since the day I got kicked off squad. I texted her again.

Aspen: **can we plz talk?**

I studied the picture of Zuri. In it, she was on a stage in some dimly-lit night club. What I'd initially thought had been a pole was actually just a microphone stand, though she had one leg slung around it as if it were a pole. Her dress was skimpy—more like lingerie than an actual dress, and a red bra strap was visible beside the spaghetti strap of her dress—but sometimes she wore stuff like that on purpose. Actually, what had she been wearing the night we'd gone to the music club?

I couldn't remember.

I shifted my focus to the background of Zuri's picture, where I stood on the same stage wearing nothing but a red bra-and-panty set. I zoomed in on the picture— on the red underwear—with the lacy details and delicate straps. The color exactly matched the red on our cheer uniforms—Bulldog red.

Wait ... bulldog red...

The ground tipped beneath me as a memory came back with horrible clarity. That lacy bra-and-panty set— the one I'd taken a single look at before and dismissed as being Photoshopped in—was actually mine.

My phone slid off my lap as I scrambled from the bed and yanked open my underwear drawer, pawing through it. Maybe the thread of memory was false. I upended my laundry hamper and dug through the dirty clothes. I went to the closet and tackled the pile on the floor beneath the hangers, throwing shoes, pajama bottoms, and rumpled t-shirts I hadn't seen in weeks out of the closet. I dug all the way to the bottom, until my knuckle scraped against something hard. My fingers wound around the object and I pulled it out.

Oh. It was an old roller skate. A *little* roller skate that had once belonged to me.

I shoved it back where it belonged. No need to dredge up *that* memory right now.

The mess I'd made had not revealed the object in question. Had I imagined the whole thing?

And then I saw it—a shock of red, tangled up with the dress I'd been wearing that night—and I knew the memory had not been a dream. I tugged the bra free as my mind jumped back to the day of the Appellooza concert.

A bunch of us had gone to the mall after school. We'd popped in and out of stores, not really buying anything, just wandering. But in one of the stores, Rhea had gasped and plucked up a Cranberry-red pair of lacy panties.

"O.M.G." she said. "It's the perfect shade. Bulldog red. We have to get these for states!"

Jasmine put a hand on her hip. "What, like some sort of good-luck charm?"

"Yes, like a good luck charm. We'll all wear them." Rhea grabbed a matching bra and held it up to her chest, admiring herself in a nearby mirror. "What better way to get lucky than with sexy underwear?"

One by one, the girls on the squad grinned. They were on board.

I'd been on board, too. It had seemed so fun. So innocent. We were prepping for states. I'd grabbed my size and gotten in line with the others, holding my secret good-luck charm.

Only mine had not stayed secret for long.

My stomach lurched as the ground seemed to crumble beneath my feet. That picture Chase had posted had not been Photoshopped at all. None of them had.

Which meant there were some very big chunks missing from my memory.

****

I needed answers, and I needed them more than anything else. So the next morning, I got to school early and waited in the parking lot. A group of girls walked past, and I overheard one of them say, "—new skater video—" and then they were out of earshot.

A new skater video.

Wait, had Dylan posted again?

Before I could get my phone out to check, Chase's car pulled into the lot. He turned down the aisle and headed for his spot, then slammed on the breaks when he saw me standing there.

I moved out of the way so he could park and watched him carefully as he got out of the car. His expression was guarded.

"Aspen, I'm so sorry," he started. "I don't know what happened. You're one of my best friends—I never wanted to hurt you." His voice broke on the last word. His eyes were dark and watery—a bottomless well. In them, I saw the boy I'd climbed trees and built sand castles with. I believed him. He hadn't wanted to hurt me.

And yet, he had. He'd hurt me so deeply.

Chase stayed a few feet away, but his eyes were intensely focused on mine. "I know this isn't a good excuse for posting what I did, but I was wasted."

That, right there, cracked me. One simple statement called up a flood of angry heat that overpowered all other things. "Being wasted does not give you a free pass. There is *no* excuse for what you did to me." I stepped toward him, a dammed-up river finally busting through. "Taking those kinds of pictures is not okay. *Posting* them is definitely not okay, and doing nothing to try and make it right is inexcusable."

His expression went slack. "I haven't done nothing. Haven't you seen my posts?"

I had not seen his posts. I hadn't seen anyone's posts—I'd been off social media.

He scrambled for his phone and pulled something up, then turned it around so I could see the screen. All his latest posts were visible, starting the day after those pictures of me had shown up:

What I did to Aspen Heathrow was messed up. It's not okay to post stuff like that about girls. #respectforwomen

Aspen is not a ho. She's my friend and all this online hate needs to stop. #stopthehate

Seriously, everyone needs to chill. Football season is not in jeopardy, I promise. #relax

The posts went on. Begging, placating, pleading words. In my behalf.

Each post had a string of comments attached, but I didn't click on them. Instead, I said, "So, how are people reacting? Are they listening to you?"

Chase ducked his head but didn't say anything.

"So that's a *no*." My fingers found my bracelet, and I started spinning it around and around on my wrist. When I spoke, my voice was small. "Do you have any idea what it feels like to be sliced wide open for everyone to see?"

He shook his head but refused to meet my gaze. "If I could take it back, I would."

I studied him, softening. At least he'd tried to make it right. That's what I'd wanted him to do, wasn't it? He'd made a mistake—a giant, monstrous mistake. But he was my friend, and he was trying to make it right. And, honestly, I needed his friendship right now.

Chase finally met my gaze, and the hope in his eyes was almost comical.

I laughed, breaking the tension. "I'm still mad at you. I think I will be for a long time. But I also think we can be friends again."

He smiled and moved to close the distance between us, but I held up a finger, stopping him. "And because we're friends, I need to know something."

"Okay."

"What happened that night, Chase? What *really* happened?"

Chapter Fifteen: The Facts Don't Add Up

Chase started on his version of the story. "I was looking for Rhea."

I froze. He still didn't know about me finding her with Drake. "But you sent me to look for her," I said carefully.

"You came back and said you couldn't find her."

I frowned. I didn't remember that part. "Okay."

"I thought maybe she'd gone out for some air, so I went outside to look for her. You said you were going home but wanted to find Zuri first."

I searched my memory. I *had* intended to tell Zuri I was leaving—she was my ride—and then I'd intended to go home. So why hadn't I?

Chase continued. "When I came back in, you and Zuri were onstage, pretending to be groupies or something. The band was taking a break."

What the heck? What had possessed me to go onstage after finding Rhea with Drake? I searched my memories, but after going back to our table, my mind was blank.

"What was I wearing?" I held my breath, waiting for the answer.

Chase shifted uncomfortably. "You still had your dress on, if that's what you're getting at."

"It is. What happened next?"

"The deejay put on some music. Zuri got really into it and started dancing. She was yelling at you to loosen up. She grabbed the mic stand and started some sort of pole dance. And you, well..." His neck colored. "You ditched your clothes."

"And you decided that would be a good time to take pictures?" My voice was shaky.

His head jerked up. "No. I did not decide to take pictures. Seriously, I have no memory of that part."

"How can you remember everything else and not that part?"

He stuffed his hands in his pockets. "I don't know, Aspen. I really don't. I've gone over this a thousand times in my mind."

My hands were fisted at my sides and my cheeks burned. I felt so ashamed. So humiliated. And more confused than ever. What I'd thought had been a simple prank was so, so much more. I'd actually done those things in the pictures. I *was* a slut.

What on earth had gotten me there? How had my decision to go home so I wouldn't accidentally tell Chase about Rhea cheating turned into a public striptease?

The school parking lot had mostly emptied, with just a few stragglers left. First period would start soon.

I took a steadying breath. "What happened next?"

Chase glanced toward the front of the school. "What do you mean?"

"Chase, come on. I don't remember any of this."

His eyebrows shot up. "You don't?"

"No, I thought the whole thing was a joke—that you'd Photoshopped a picture of me just to be a jerk. But if you didn't do that, then—"

"You think someone drugged your drink?"

I stared at him, my mind grinding to a halt. "You were at the table with Sara when I was looking for Rhea. You were watching our drinks, right?"

Chase pushed a hand through his hair. "Not really. I had my head down on the table most of the time."

"And Sara was buried in her phone," I said, remembering, spinning my bracelet around my wrist. "But who would have drugged our drinks? Who else was there that night?"

Chase blew out a huff of air. "Who wasn't there? Almost the entire football team, the baseball team, your cheer squad, friends of the band, a bunch of other people. Honestly, half the school was there. And half of East."

I jerked my head up. I hadn't noticed our rival school there. "East was there?"

"Yeah, a bunch of the football players, at least."

My heart sank. "And their cheerleaders?"

Chase caught on. "You think East's cheer squad messed with your drinks?"

"Well, it totally fits. Who else would try getting us suspended from squad for drug use? Then if our own classmates decided to start a smear campaign against us, all the better for them. It would tear the squad apart, and we'd be weakened right before regionals."

Which is exactly what had happened. I was off the squad, and the routine would have to be dumbed down without my tricks, giving East a clear advantage.

"There *were* a lot of people hanging around the table," Chase said.

"East's cheerleaders?"

"Probably."

I chewed on my lower lip, thinking. If I were able to get some sort of proof that East's squad deliberately sabotaged us, that might convince the district to hurry things up and let me back on the squad sooner.

But … did I *want* to be back on the squad?

I'd started skating in order to hide until my friends took me back. But, somehow, things seemed to be shifting. What about Summer and Dylan and my roller skating? I couldn't rejoin the squad and keep skating—I didn't have time for both—but I loved roller skating. I felt freer on the ramps than I'd ever felt before.

If I walked away from cheerleading, did that make me a coward for running away, or did it make me strong for finding something new?

Chase's voice pulled me out of my thoughts. "Rhea's wondering where I am."

Ugh. *Rhea.*

Chase was typing out a text.

I wiped my hands—which suddenly felt all clammy—on my jeans. "Hey, there's something else."

He shouldered his bag and took a step toward the building. "Maybe we should get to class?"

"Oh. Yeah, we totally should." I fell into step beside him. What was I thinking? I couldn't just tell him, right here in the school parking lot, that his girlfriend of two-and-a-half years had been cheating on him for who knew how long. And I definitely couldn't tell him that I'd known for over a week and kept it from him.

"What is it?" Chase said, side-eying me.

"Huh?"

"Just now, you said there was something else. We can talk on our way in."

"Oh. Right." I tucked a curl behind my ear, searching my mind for something else I could tell him. The curl stayed put for about point-one seconds and then popped free. "Um, when I woke up the morning after that night at the club, I was wearing a U-dub zip-up. It was kind-of big on me—is it yours?"

"Nope."

"Huh. Okay."

I still had no clue whose sweatshirt that was, but I had bigger things to worry about. Like the fact that Chase and I were back on speaking terms, and I didn't know how I'd ever be able to tell him about Rhea.

"Hey, Chase," I finally said as we neared the school entrance. "You should talk to Rhea."

He laughed. "I talk to Rhea every day."

"I know, but … you should *really* talk to her.

Like, look into her eyes and talk to her."

"*Okay*," he said, stretching the word out as he studied me.

My phone buzzed, saving me from having to meet his gaze. I had a text from Summer.

Summer: **did you see the new video dylan put up?**

Oh, no. My mind scrolled back to the girls in the parking lot who'd been talking about a skating video. What had Dylan posted? Most of our practice sessions ended with us falling on our butts, and even if he'd gotten something good, had he remembered to blur out our faces?

I texted her back.

Aspen: **im scared**

Summer: **dont worry, he made us look really good**

What did *that* mean? That we weren't actually good? Or that he'd taken out all the wipe-outs so it looked like we never fell? I wasn't sure I liked either of those options.

I realized I'd stopped walking.

Chase was a few feet ahead, holding the door open for me. "Is everything okay? You're acting weird."

"I'm fine."

****

We got inside and Chase went one way while I went the other. I prepped myself for the snarky comments and lewd gestures that had become the norm at school. To my surprise, none came. In fact, everyone seemed a bit distracted, either on their phones or huddled in groups.

I pulled out my phone and started scrolling through my social feed. It only took me a few seconds to find what everyone was talking about—a video of two girls doing tricks on roller skates.

My stomach lurched. I couldn't handle anymore online infamy.

I clicked on the video, holding my breath. I'd seen our practice videos, of course, but I hadn't seen what Dylan could do to them with some editing. As I watched, though, a smile stretched across my face—the girls in the video looked amazing.

We looked amazing.

My artificially-colored braids and helmet did a good job of disguising my hair, and Dylan had blurred out my face in a few of the closer-up shots. But most of the shots were from far enough away that our faces weren't really visible anyway.

I watched the video again. Dylan had taken out all of our falls and strung together only the times we'd nailed the moves. Which didn't exactly tell the complete story, since we spent a lot of time falling on our butts. The video was not a lie—it just didn't tell the whole truth.

Kind of like that picture of me onstage in my underwear.

I bit my lip, trying to convince myself this was not a big deal—that the two situations were different. Everyone who posted skating videos edited out the fails. That was what you were supposed to do.

I clicked on the comment thread and started reading.

Jax0n5: **This is mind blowing**

its.sheriz: **Crazy cool**

TheRealPaloma: **these chicks are so fierce! #girlpower**

abby.lane: **Roller skates for the win. Its so retro, I love it!**

DnDfan: **how do they jump so high?**

magic8rulz: **more videos plz!!!!**

And the comments went on.

People loved it. People couldn't believe it. People wanted more.

The same people who'd called me a slut and a poser and a fame-seeker.

It was messed up, but the praise got to me. Boosted me. Lifted me out of my sad little funk and dusted me off.

During my next few classes, as people talked about the amazing skater girls, I felt myself smiling again—walking down the halls with more confidence, even though no one knew it was me in the video. When I saw Marissa in the bathroom halfway through the day and she asked how I was doing, I actually smiled and said, "Great!"

She got an odd look on her face and walked away. Off to find someone new to pity, probably.

By the end of the day, I'd decided one very important thing: Aspen the cheerleader was dead and I didn't miss her. If I never had to feel as crappy as I had this past week, I was happy being a faceless skater for the rest of my life.

Just to make it official, after school I went in search of Coach Irina. "Aspen, perfect timing," she said when she saw me. "We just got word from the school district that everything's been cleared up. You can start practicing with us again tomorrow!"

"Actually, I just came here to let you know that East sabotaged us at the concert last week to lower our chances of making it to states. Also..." I took a deep breath and, before I could reconsider said, "Thank you so much for clearing things up with the district, but I won't be rejoining the squad."

She sucked in a breath. "But we need you."

"I know. And I'm really sorry. But I need friends who will stand by me no matter what."

Irina was silent for a moment, her eyes going watery as she studied me. At length she smiled and said, "Okay, Aspen. I understand. Good luck to you."

"Thank you." Then I left, cutting the ties to who I used to be and leaving the old me in the past. Aspen the skater was so much stronger than Aspen the cheerleader had ever been, despite having to hide her face.

On my way out, I got a text from Summer.

Summer: **where r u?**

I checked the time. Crap, I was supposed to meet her at the skate park. My little detour to the locker room had made me late.

Aspen: **on my way**

Summer: **get here quick. the skaters upped the game**

Chapter Sixteen: Fan Base

The ramps were swarming when I got to the skate park. Summer hurried over, her face pinched, with Dylan right on her tail. She'd gotten less shy around him but still blushed every time he looked her way. And with good reason. Even I felt inclined to look away when he gazed at her. It was so obvious he'd joined because of her.

I didn't care, though, 'cause he was good. He'd caught on to the roller skates fast (though he still wore his giant jeans with them), and he'd taught us some cool skateboard tricks we were now trying to adapt for skates. Plus, this morning's video had given me back my self-respect.

I could forgive him for crushing on Summer.

"The skaters are saying we have to bring our own crowd to the skate-off tomorrow," Summer said, twisting her fingers together. "But I barely know anybody—I kind-of keep to myself at school, you know. And my mom can't come because—" She bit her lip, then turned to me. "How many people do you think you can get here?"

"Um…" She knew full well I didn't have any friends these days other than her and Dylan. And I couldn't tell my family I was skating—there would be way too many questions—plus, skating was Jojo's thing. "Why do we need to bring a crowd?"

"The skate-off is going to be crowd-judged," Dylan explained. "So the more people we can get here, the better. They'll be on our side, yeah? If the crowd is just boarders, then obviously the boarders will win."

"Why don't we just post another video and ask people to come see us live?" I said, without thinking.

Then I realized that was the worst idea ever. Sure, people hadn't been able to tell that the random skater in a standard-quality video was me, especially with Dylan's editing, but how would I hide my identity if they saw me in person?

But Summer's face had brightened and Dylan was grinning.

"That's a great idea," Dylan said. "And I can put out a blast to my channel subscribers—I have a decent local following."

"Wait, are you, like, an influencer or something?" Summer said.

"No, but I posted a bunch of tutorials for some guys I met skating a few years ago, and those got enough shares that my sub count grew. Mostly word-of-mouth fame, you know? My followers are friends of friends. But I bet some of them would show up if I asked them to."

It was too late to take back what I'd said, but there had to be a way to skate anonymously.

That first day at the roller rink, I'd worn an eye mask from a kid's superhero costume and it had worked just fine. If I did that again, colored and braided my hair, kept my helmet on the whole time, and chose an outfit that Aspen the cheerleader would never have worn, there was a good chance no one would recognize me. They'd never expect to see me on the ramps—maybe that would keep me safe.

But if I was the only skater wearing a mask, that in itself would draw attention.

"Hey, what if we all wear masks while we skate?" I blurted out. "Like we're going to a masquerade or something—so we can keep our identities a secret."

Summer frowned. "Look, I know you're afr—"

I cut her off, not wanting Dylan to know about my sordid past. It was bad enough that Summer knew.

"Come on, alter egos are cool. It could be our thing."

Dylan said, "It *would* be an interesting gimmick—something unexpected to make us stand out. We could be the secret skaters or something."

I held my breath, waiting to see what Summer would say.

Her face was unreadable. "Won't it be hard to see if we're wearing masks?"

"Not if it's a small mask," I said. "Or you could use face paint, I guess. Then it won't get in your way at all. We just need something to hide our identities."

Summer studied me, chewing on her lower lip. Whatever she saw in my expression made her soften. "Okay. Secret identities it is."

"Ah, thank you! I'll set up a profile for my alter ego tonight and put out some social media blasts. Let's make another video today for Dylan to post. And you two should work on your skater names."

Wait. What was my skater name these days? Feline Explosion? Or was it still Bombshell Whimsy?

A voice cut into my thoughts. "You all ready for tomorrow?" Brogan kicked his skateboard up into a slide-stop, a move that I'd finally looked up and found the name for.

Were we ready?

My handstand-bowl-backskate was finally feeling strong after all those hours of early-morning practices. (And, okay, after I'd figured out that I was glancing over my shoulder too early. Apparently, you're supposed to wait until you're most of the way down before turning your head during a backward decline skate.)

Our catalog of moves in Summer's notebook now filled several pages and included cartwheels on skates, handstand back-walkovers, moves where we pinwheeled our legs around a center axis with our hands on the ground, different types of jumps, and several dance-type moves we'd borrowed from jamskating and modified to shine on the ramps. We were strong, and we'd grown a ton in just a week, but we still had a lot to learn. Flips, for example. The Jetsi Girls were all about flips, but even I wasn't crazy enough to believe I could do an actual flip on roller skates after a single week of training and not die.

Still, I said, "We're ready. What do you intend to prove, anyway?"

Brogan smiled—a Cheshire grin that revealed nothing. "I don't have anything to prove."

"Then why the whole charade? Give us another week. Or, better yet, call it off. We can share the ramps."

He shook his head. "What fun would that be?"

A skinny guy with an ear spike skated up to Brogan. I wasn't sure if I'd seen him before or not. "Man, let's go," the guy said. As he skated circles around us, he muttered, "It's about time we kick these flipping *roller* skaters off our ramps."

Okay, so the skateboarders still wanted us gone. Or, at least, Ear Spike Guy did.

Brogan hopped on his board and followed the guy. "See you in the morning, Aspen."

I liked it when he said my name.

Brogan skated away, jumping his skateboard up onto a rail and sliding on the trucks.

"He's very consistent," Summer said, watching Brogan skate.

I said, "Yeah," but I was thinking about what Ear Spike Guy had called us.

Flipping roller skaters.

Hmm…

****

While my family slept, I looked up '*How to make*

a website for free' and got to work. Soon, I had a decent page dedicated to our skating gymnastics crew, with pictures that hid our identities and made us look all tough and mysterious. Summer, Dylan, and I were now, collectively, the Flippin' Skaters. Which I loved because we actually did flips on our roller skates. Or, at least, that was what we were working up to.

The name was just too perfect—thank you, Ear Spike Guy.

I settled on Skate-or-Dye as my own new name— a tie-in to my newfound love of temporary hair color— and set up some social profiles exclusively for Skate-or-Dye.

Once I had the website ready, I added our latest skating video with an invite to the event tacked on at the end and shared it to Skate-or-Dye's pages. Then I opened my own social pages so I could share the link there, too.

When I got on my feed, though, I noticed a new thread of frenzied gossip ... with a marching band theme and some mentions of open world video games.

Okay.

I scrolled through the posts. Where the heck had this started?

There were a few tuba memes. Some stuff in Spanish. And then, there. A picture of a dough-faced boy I didn't recognize, with the words:

R33S: **I have the juiciest news for you all. @RonaldHenkins, fourth chair tuba in the marching band has a secret crush, and you'll never guess on who ... okay, okay the suspense is killing me, I'll tell you. It's Senorita Morales. Yep, you heard right. Little sophomore Ronald is in love with a grown woman. His Spanish teacher, no less! And since he knew he could never have her in real life, he created a virtual world where they could be together. You** should see the booty on his fictional lover. Ronnie has a pretty twisted imagination.

GamR5119: **ooh, which game is this in, I want to find them**

L00kie8: **virtual love: the fate of losers everywhere**

LucyLuvs: **he's a band geek and plays rpgs—this tracks**

Ronald Henkins … I didn't know him at all. I clicked to go to his profile, but got an error message.

The page you are looking for no longer exists…

Oh. Ronald must have deleted his social account. Was it because of this?

My gaze caught on the name of the poster of this "dish." *R33S*. That combo of numbers and letters looked familiar, but I couldn't put my finger on where I'd seen it before.

Then I saw a meme of a kitten wearing a sombrero and playing a tuba, and immediately thought of Rhea. Not that she would have posted it. It just made me think of her.

Fun fact: Rhea loved cat memes. Well, she loved cats in general, but especially cat memes. Not very many people knew that about her. I wanted to type a caption into the picture and send it to her, but that was something friends did. So I just stared at the picture and didn't share it with anyone at all.

Okay.

Moving on.

I put Rhea and Ronald out of my mind and worked on spreading the news about the skate-off. I used my own profile to share Skate-or-Dye's video with my former friends. They may not like me anymore, but people didn't usually care where their news came from as long as it was good. They probably wouldn't even notice who posted it—they'd just see another skating video and click to watch it.

There.

Hopefully everyone would see this and get tired of gossiping long enough to come vote for us. For better or for worse, this was about to get real.

Chapter Seventeen: Flippin' Skate-off

Brogan and his gang were already there, tearing it up on the ramps, when Summer and I got to the park after school the next day. There was no sign of Dylan. My stomach was a tangle of nerves, just like the laces on my skates as I fumbled to get them tight enough.

Summer worked her skates on, gazing at the boarders in dismay. "How did they beat us here again?"

We'd come as fast as we could, hoping to warm up in private before the boarders arrived. "Maybe they don't go to school," I said, thinking out loud. "Maybe they're dropouts. Or drug dealers."

"Or college kids," Summer said.

No way, Brogan couldn't be that much older than me. Could he? It was hard to tell—I'd still never seen him without his beanie.

"There is that community college nearby," Summer said. "Maybe they come here between classes?"

"I'm not in college," Brogan said from behind me.

I whirled around, giving Summer the evil eye for letting him sneak up on me, but she was focused on lacing up her skates.

"Okay," I said, gliding toward him, "then how do you always beat us here? I know you live across the street and all, but assuming you go to school, you'd need time to get home first."

"We go to East," he said.

Oh.

East, as in East High—our rivals. They got out a half hour before we did due to a shortage of school buses.

But… "Why do you go there if you live here?"

"My mom's the art teacher there."

"Oh." I couldn't think of a good response to that,

so I just said, "Well, good luck today."

He peered at me from under the shadow of his ever-present beanie. "You, too."

"Thanks." We stood there, face to face.

He eyed me.

I looked everywhere except his eyes.

Summer said, "We should probably go find Dylan."

"Right. We should." People from school were going to start arriving soon, and we needed to get our looks ready. "See you on the ramps," I said to Brogan.

We skated away. I didn't look back, even though part of me wanted to. Brogan was my rival. And Skate-or-Dye was going to crush him. Not crush *on* him.

Summer and I skated behind the cinderblock structure that served as the park's only bathroom. Nobody ever used it because it was so nasty, but it was there in a pinch.

"Did you bring a mask?" I asked.

Summer nodded, pulling out a piece of fabric that looked similar to what I'd worn that first day at the skating rink—something that had once been a part of some little kid's superhero costume. At least hers was red and not boring black like mine had been.

Summer handed it to me. "Help me put it on?"

"Sure." I positioned it so the eye holes were just perfect and then knotted the fabric in the back. "Tight enough?"

"Yeah. Let's see yours."

I grinned. I couldn't help it. The mask I'd ordered online after that first day at the roller rink had finally arrived, and it was perfect—like Venetian masquerade meets steampunk pirates.

I pulled the mask out of my backpack, fingering the silver-gilded edge and purple fabric.

Summer drew in a breath. "Oh, Aspen, it's beautiful."

It was all swirls, arches, and cat-eye lines. It looked like it belonged on some exotic bird. Paired with the electric green I'd colored my braids with that morning, it was going to look amazing.

"Can you tie it on? And put in some bobby pins, too?" I pulled a few out of my pocket and handed them to Summer. When she was done, I fit my helmet on, taking care not to upset the pins holding everything in place. "This disguise is not going to budge."

I eyed Summer's mask, and how the knot was already slipping toward the nape of her neck. "Let's anchor yours, too."

Even with a few bobby pins in, Summer's mask ties still drifted toward her neck—her sleek hair didn't hold things in place as well as mine did. I pulled an extra hair tie out of my bag and gathered her long hair into a ponytail, catching the mask ties along with the hair and securing them in place that way. "There. How's that?"

"It feels good." She swiveled her head around. "And I can see, too."

I laughed. "Seeing is a plus! Now all we need to do is find Dylan."

Summer eased her helmet on. "I haven't heard from him all morning. He said he was meeting us here, right?"

"Wait, do you usually hear from him during the day? Like, while we're at school?"

A blush crawled up Summer's cheeks and disappeared beneath her mask. "Well, sometimes, yeah. A little more lately. He'll text me when he's between classes and stuff, but it's always when I'm in class."

"Wait, does Dylan go to East, too?"

"Yeah. I thought you knew that."

Okay, maybe I'd been a little self-absorbed lately. I'd thought he was homeschooled.

"I'll try calling him." Summer dialed while, together, we headed out to warm up.

The first thing I noticed when we emerged from behind the bathrooms was the crowd. It now stretched away from the ramps and up a grassy hill beyond. "Oh, wow."

Summer pressed her phone to her ear while I scanned for familiar faces. There was Chase and his football crew. And Jasmine, Zuri, and Rhea, laughing and flirting and gossiping. Chase had an arm slung casually around Rhea's shoulder—clearly, he hadn't gotten the hint when I'd told him to talk to her. Watching her just stand there—letting him dote on her like she'd done nothing wrong—well, it made bile rise in my throat.

I swallowed and let my eyes rake over the rest of the crowd, trying to ignore Rhea and Chase. Tommy Appell and his band were there, looking a little lost without instruments in their hands. I even saw pothead Drake, standing with his friends apart from the crowd.

Then, with a jolt, I spotted Jojo. She was sitting on a blanket with a group of her roller derby friends, holding a hand-painted sign that read: *Metro Roller Derby hearts the Flippin' Skaters*. The other derby girls held similar signs. I picked out: *Skater girls rock!* and *Conquering the world eight wheels at a time*.

Wow. Jojo was *here*. How had she even heard about this? Did she still read my social media posts?

Now extra grateful for my disguise, I ducked my head and skated toward the ramps, reminding myself that no one had ever seen me in braids, no one had ever seen me skate, and no one, including my sister, had any reason to suspect Skate-or-Dye might be me.

A squeal—like the kind made by a microphone

placed too close to a speaker—made the crowd cry out. Several peoples' hands flew to their ears. Then a voice came over the loudspeaker. I hadn't even known there was a loudspeaker.

"All right, everybody, give it up for deejay Simms." A pulsing, rhythmic music track started, instantly transforming the event into a party.

I craned my neck, searching for the deejay booth. It was set up beside the bowl, nowhere special, just on the ground like everything else. One of those pop-up awning things was beside the deejay, providing shade for two rows of empty chairs. Were those for the sponsors, maybe?

Brogan and several boarders were already on the ramps—skating, doing tricks, and generally just showing off. The skate-off would start in twenty minutes, right at five o'clock.

Summer and I really needed to warm up. I grabbed her arm and tugged her toward the ramps. "I'm sure Dylan's on his way. We need to get moving."

She put her phone away and, together, we skated through the course, going up and down the smaller ramps, pumping at the bottom like Elasta-grill had taught us, and letting our legs weave around as we skated, mimicking the loopy strides from episode two. I let myself go, ignoring the crowd. The breeze felt cool on my skin as I flew without wings.

When we got to the top of the bowl, I glanced at Summer. We didn't want to give ourselves away by showing off our best tricks now, but since this was a crowd-judged event, it couldn't hurt to have them on our side from the start.

Summer eyed the bowl, biting her bottom lip. She looked at me. "Drop in together and do handstand-bowl-backskates on the other side?"

The handstand-bowl-backskate was now one of my favorite moves. "Let's do it."

Together, we stood at the edge. And, together, we dropped into the bowl. My stomach did the same flip it always did at the start of a drop-in and, for a moment, I was flying. At the bottom of the bowl I pumped, gaining speed to get up the other side. I timed it perfectly. We both did.

Summer and I reached the opposite edge, kicked up into side-by-side handstands, held them for a second or two, and then dropped back into the bowl.

"Wow!" the deejay exclaimed, talking over the music thumping in the background. "Did you all see that? A little pre-game sneak-peak from the Flippin' Skaters. If they've got more where that came from, this will be one epic show-down."

I crouched into the landing, keeping my knees bent and my center of gravity low, waiting until I reached the bottom before glancing over my shoulder to spot where I was going.

Just as we reached the bottom, Summer yelled, "Let's add a cross-hand-pinwheel."

"Okay!" I yelled back.

We separated and skated in opposite directions, staying in the backward skate. We'd tried this move yesterday, where we skated around once backward, passed each other and grabbed hands to do a pinwheel spin in the center of the bowl.

I was halfway around the perimeter of the bowl, still in a backward skate with Summer across from me, when I spotted something in my path. A branch? Or … maybe it was just a leaf?

I didn't want to risk running over it and having it trip me up in case it was something substantial, so I skated up the side of the bowl to avoid it. But I'd never skated backward up the bank and … well …

My body tipped and my feet started to slip out from under me. I flailed and spun around, trying to save the move. But then I was on my butt and sliding into the bottom of the bowl.

The crowd hooted.

The deejay exclaimed, "Ouch, guess you don't have this in the bag yet, Flippin' Skaters."

My face burned. I'd done plenty of falling and getting back up over the past week, but none of these people had seen that since Dylan cut all our wipe-outs from the videos he posted. My tailbone throbbed, but I jumped up.

Summer was finishing her loop around the bowl. She mouthed, "*Are you okay?*"

I nodded, heading for the exit. Summer skated out first. I followed, doing a little jump at the top as I exited, and then drifted into a spin to stop.

So. My backward skating still left something to be desired.

And, okay, now the crowd thought I sucked.

But, overall, the run had felt good. I'd just have to nail everything once the skate-off actually started. The viewers didn't know how often I fell, but *I* knew. I knew I could still get up and skate a perfect set. I just needed to focus.

"There was something in the bowl. I was trying to skate around it," I said to Summer.

"I'll go get it," she said. "You rest for a minute."

My gaze caught on Brogan, who was sitting on the edge of a rail with his legs dangling below him. He held his board in one hand, and he was looking at me with a sort-of half-grin. It was a look I'd seen on him before, but not in a while. The last time had been at the roller rink after he'd chased me down to return my cracked phone. Right before I'd … you know … tried to kiss him.

My stomach fluttered, and not in the same way it did when I dropped into the bowl. These feelings were bigger—too big to wrap my brain around.

I took a sip of water, trying to get my head back in the game.

The deejay spoke up again. "I hope you're all getting pumped, because this showdown is about to go down!"

There was a whoop from the crowd, and the volume of the music cranked up. It was all thumping bass and wild dance beats. I glanced toward the booth and noticed the seats under the awning starting to fill up—and not with teenagers.

Yep. Those were the sponsors.

"Okay, seriously, where is Dylan?" Summer said, holding up the thing she'd retrieved from the bowl—a piece of a Twix wrapper—and then tossing it into a heavily-tagged garbage can. "We're starting in, like, ten minutes."

My gaze caught on a figure skating toward us. A figure wearing baggy jeans and roller skates. I nudged Summer and she followed my gaze.

"Dylan!" She skated toward him, running up a short set of stairs on her toe stops instead of going up the nearby ramp, to get to him faster. "Where have you been?"

When I joined them, Dylan was out of breath. "Sorry I'm late. Aspen, I saw the page you created last night."

I frowned. "You were up that late?" I hadn't finished it until close to two A.M.

"No, I saw it this morning. I love the name you picked—Flippin' Skaters—it's perfect."

"It was something one of the boarders said—not in a nice way, of course—but I thought it would make a cool name."

Dylan continued. "Well, my head just filled up with all sorts of sick logos. I drew up a few, and realized it would be cool to get some tattoos made up." He pulled several tiny squares of temporary tattoos out of his pocket and held them out for us to see.

My jaw dropped. The artwork was a close-up colored pencil drawing of a pair of roller skates, upside down, as if the person wearing them was doing a backflip, with our name stretching in an arc along the bottom. The whole thing was bordered by a circle, drawn to look like the wheel of a roller skate—like the logo was enclosed in a wheel. And, just like my mask and our name, it was perfect.

"I emailed the design to a friend of mine and he said he could get them made up for me today, I just had to go downtown to pick them up after school. That's why I'm late." He handed one of the tattoos to Summer, and another one to me. "Sorry, again."

"Why didn't you answer your phone?" Summer said. "Or text or something?"

"My brother stole the charger out of my car again, and my phone died during school. But I'm here now. We have time to put these on, right?"

I glanced at my phone. "We have three minutes. And you still need to warm up."

"Nah, I'm good. Tats are more important." He grinned.

"Where should we put them?" I eyed Dylan, with his baggy jeans and loose-fitting long-sleeve t-shirt. Other than his face, the only bare skin was his hands.

Summer was right with me. "Hands it is."

We put the tattoos on the backs of our hands, then

snapped a pic of our fists together in a triangular fist-bump sporting our new Flippin' Skaters logos. I posted it to Skate-or-Dye's social feed.

"I've got a buddy handing them out in the crowd," Dylan said, taking his helmet off and tying on a black face mask.

"These are so cool," Summer squealed, grabbing Dylan's arm.

Then the music faded and the deejay's voice echoed around the park. "All right, all right. You all ready for this?"

The crowd whooped in response.

I focused on the ramps. We were ready. Ready to fight for our right to skate.

"This is how it's gonna go down," the deejay said. "The teams will take turns skating, in five minute intervals. What each team does with their five minutes is up to them. They can send out a single skater, they can skate a few in succession, or they can all skate together. But by the five minute mark, when they hear this sound" —a foghorn blared from the sound system— "their time is up and they have to exit the ramps. There will be a thirty second break and then the next five minute block will start. We'll do six rounds, and then *you*" —he paused for emphasis— "will decide the winner!"

The crowd roared.

Adrenaline coursed through me. I clenched and unclenched my hands. Despite my flop during warm-ups, I felt ready for this. I could do this.

"Newbies are first," the deejay said. "That means you, Flippin' Skaters."

"Who wants to go first?" Dylan spoke over the noise of the crowd. "Or should we all skate together?"

"We haven't choreographed anything and I'm afraid we'd get in each other's way," Summer said with a glance at me, no doubt thinking of my warm-up fail.

I hadn't fallen because she was in my way. But maybe my focus had been split between what I was doing and what she'd been doing.

I fingered one of my braids. "Yeah, let's showcase our individual talents. Less room for error that way."

"Sounds good," Dylan said.

Summer glanced at the ramps. "Can I go first?"

"Really?" I peered at her, trying to decipher the expression beneath her mask.

"Yeah, I'd just like to get my part over with."

I looked to Dylan.

"Fine by me," he said. "I think I should go in the middle, though—you two started this thing. You should get to be the bookends."

"Yeah, okay," I said. "I'll go last."

The deejay's voice boomed from the speakers. "Flippin' Skaters, your time starts in ten, nine, eight..."

"Eep!" Summer fingered her face mask.

"Your mask is perfect," I said. "You've got this, girl!"

"Go crush it," Dylan echoed.

"Oh, I plan to." Summer grinned and skated to the edge of the bowl.

And crush it, she did. She used the entire skate park, starting in the bowl but moving straight to the rails and jumps. Watching her, I couldn't help feeling like a proud parent. We'd learned together, of course, but she was here because of me.

Once the skate-off began, time flew. Before I knew it, Summer's turn was over and a group of boarders I didn't really know took over the park, their skateboards scraping the pavement in a sort of music that had become my favorite soundtrack. Then it was Dylan's turn. As always, he tore it up like he'd been born to skate.

The next group of boarders featured the girl with the half-shaved head who'd been there that first day at the park. I had to admit, she was good. I told myself not to watch—to close my eyes and get into some sort of Zen state where I pictured myself skating my own perfect set—but I couldn't tear my eyes away. The way this girl skated—like she held some deeply personal grudge against gravity and was just daring it to keep her down—was mesmerizing.

Instead of letting it intimidate me, I let her fire fuel my own, and when it was my turn to skate, I was ready. The fierceness I felt as I dropped into the bowl was unlike any I'd ever felt before. The world melted away until the only things that mattered were me, my skates, and the pavement beneath my feet.

I did rail tricks, ramp tricks, jumps, spins, handstands, and cartwheels, and it was like I'd taken some performance-enhancing drug. Or like I'd suddenly found my superhero mojo. Because I nailed every single trick. When it came time for my handstand-bowl-backskate, I wasn't nervous at all. I knew I'd hit the trick—and I did—without even the tiniest little wobble.

Brogan skated last, while I was still flying high from the rush of skating a perfect set. Of course he was amazing. The way he moved was almost animalistic, and I watched with a fascination that felt forbidden.

Despite the boarders' awesome skating, by the time it was all over, I still felt like we'd done better. What we were doing had never been done before. It was freaking gymnastics on roller-skates—how could the crowd even for one second think of giving the victory to the boarders?

When it came time to vote, I knew we had it in the bag—I could feel it deep inside my bones. We'd come here to prove we belonged, and we'd done it. Dylan, Summer, and I stood in a row at the top of the bowl, with the skaters facing us on the opposite side.

We clasped hands and held on tight as we waited for the results.

Chapter Eighteen: Not What They Seem

"All right, all right," the deejay called, turning the music way down. "How about those tricks? The Flippin' Skaters pulled out all the stops, didn't they?"

The crowd cheered.

Summer squeezed my hand.

"And they did it all in masks, no less. I wonder if they'll let us see who they are."

More cheers.

I shook my head and made a sign with my hand like I was karate-chopping the air beside my shoulders. That was the universal gesture for *No Flippin' Way*, right?

The deejay chuckled. "Another time, then, Flippin' Skaters. And how about those boarders? They really tore it up."

Another cheer came from the crowd.

"But only one group will walk away today with the right to rule the ramps."

I vaguely wondered who had hired this guy and who had told him the rules. Was it normal to have a deejay at a skate-off?

Actually, was it normal to even have a skate-off?

I caught Brogan looking at me, with that same grin he'd had before the event started. He needed to stop looking at me like that—it made me feel so bare. So seen. But, also, I never wanted him to stop looking at me like that.

"Now for the moment of truth." The deejay paused dramatically, putting on a low, pulsing sort-of music. It almost matched the rhythm of my heart. "If you think the Flippin' Skaters deserve the right to rule these ramps, let's hear it for them. Right here, right now! Give it up!"

The crowd cheered, clapped, shrieked. The sound reverberated around us, coming from everywhere and nowhere all at once.

My heart soared. We'd done it. We'd gotten all these people here, they'd seen us skate, and they thought we deserved to win. We'd shown our Jetsi-skating awesomeness to the world, and they'd loved it.

The clapping kept going. And going. On and on. I could not contain the smile bursting off my face.

Finally, the deejay said, "Yo, let's bring it back down."

The crowd stilled.

He put on a different soundtrack. It was a lot like the other one, with the beating heart, but this one had an added sense of urgency to it.

Immediately, I was on-edge. This was the kind of music you played right before a big reveal or an epic showdown. It was the kind of music that stirred a crowd into a frenzy. It almost made me want to scream.

The deejay said, "If you think the boarders deserve the right to rule these ramps—the ramps they've ruled since our first parents decided to put a board on wheels and defy gravity with it—if you think they deserve to keep their territory, let's hear it for them. Right. Now."

Before he'd even stopped talking, the crowd exploded into a thunderstorm—a frenzy of cheers. The applause, the whoops, and the cheering went on and on, raining down on us, the boarders, the whole park.

And right then, I knew.

We'd never even had a chance. The boarders had known it, too.

The applause went on forever.

Summer's expression mirrored the tragedy of my

own thoughts. Dylan's jaw flexed as he gazed across the divide at the boarders, who were eyeing us triumphantly. Well, everyone except for Brogan, who still had that little half-grin.

I wanted to punch it off his stupidly attractive face.

The deejay's voice cut through the crowd. "I think that's pretty clear. Sorry, Flippin' Skaters, better luck next time. Because this competition goes to the boarders!"

The crowd cheered again. The deejay put on some EDM, which pulsed into my brain like a worm. I struggled to push it out, to think above the noise that was this music.

Summer looked like she was going to cry. "What just happened?"

"We got served, that's what," I said.

Dylan said, "I was afraid of this."

"Of what?" Summer said.

I answered for him. "It wasn't a fair fight, clearly. We did awesome—we did not deserve to lose like that. The deejay totally influenced the crowd."

"It wasn't just the deejay, though he definitely didn't help," Dylan said. "I told you before—Brogan doesn't fight fair. This crowd already had their minds made up, before they even saw us skate. It was a rigged deck."

I started to crumble inside. Of course it was a rigged deck. *Life* was a rigged deck.

Only then, instead of crumbling, I got pissed. That tattoo on my hand—it was an emblem, and I'd *earned* the right to wear it. If the deck was stacked against me, I'd just have to demand a new hand.

I dropped into the bowl with a fury I'd never felt before. It fueled my legs as I pumped, fueled my body as

I jumped out of the bowl and hopped a rail on the other side, causing the boarders to scatter. I whirled to a stop and got up in Brogan's face.

"Nice mask," he said, fingering the edge of my disguise.

I slapped his hand away. "I demand a rematch." The music pulsed around me, matching my anger beat for beat. "That was not a fair fight and you know it."

Boarders closed in around me, pressing on all sides and shoving me closer to Brogan. His face was all edgy lines and dark stubble, topped with the ever-present gray beanie.

I pressed my hands against his chest, trying to create some space between us. The fabric of his t-shirt clung to the muscles beneath.

Still, he wore that smirk. And his eyes danced as he gazed at me.

"Will you please say something?" I had to scream to be heard over the dance music. "Seriously, what is with that stupid smirk?"

Finally, *finally*, his smile died. "You're right, it wasn't a fair fight."

My anger should have left—he'd just admitted I was right—but his statement only fueled the fire. Dimly, I became aware of Summer and Dylan elbowing their way through the crowd to me.

I opened my mouth to respond, but Brogan held up a finger to silence me. And then he had the gall to press it against my lips.

I smacked his hand. "How dare y—"

He cut me off. "It wasn't supposed to be a fair fight. You didn't think that was an actual contest, did you? That we were really going to leave the ramps if you won?"

My anger hissed and boiled over. I yanked off my

helmet, not even caring that my lime-green hair was matted to my skull.

But Brogan was still talking. "And you didn't think we'd actually kick you off the ramps if you lost, right?"

Wait.

"What?" The fight bled out of me, leaving my limbs feeling all cold and shaky.

The girl with the half-shaved head said, "The contest was just so we could see what you're made of."

"What do you mean?" Summer asked.

Brogan grinned. "We can't let just anybody skate our ramps. But now you're not just anybody. You're skaters and you've proven you belong here."

All I could say was, "What?" Only this time it was with a sense of awe. Did this mean we could stay? That we could skate here whenever we wanted?

Beside me, Summer squealed. "Aspen, we did it!"

I heard myself saying, "That was *such* a jerk-wad move."

Dylan punched one of the skaters in the shoulder and said, "Man, that's messed up."

Still, Brogan stared at me. As the skaters parted and the spectators danced, I became aware that I was standing too close to him.

He didn't back away. Neither did I.

One of my skates slipped forward and I steadied myself, now closer to him than ever. I could smell whatever faint scent was left over from his shampoo. Or maybe it was aftershave. It was something musky and manly.

I finally found my voice. "What you did—faking a freaking skate-off. That's really messed up."

"Admit it, you had fun."

I nodded toward the deejay. "How much did you

have to pay that guy to throw the competition?"

"Nothing. He's one of us; he just spins on the weekends."

The intensity of his gaze was too much. His eyes were too bright—his breath too hot on my face. I looked away. "Again, so messed up."

"Maybe." He paused.

Was he waiting for me to look at him? I wanted to. Also, I didn't.

He said, "But worth it, right? I mean, this crowd, this energy—it's electric!"

Yes, it was. I could almost feel the sparks flying between us.

But what he'd done—it didn't help me trust him. Anyway, he knew nothing about me—had no idea I'd been out-of-control dancing on a stage in my underwear barely a week ago. If he knew what a wreck I was, he wouldn't be looking at me like that.

I pressed my hands against his chest and pushed, letting my skates take me backward, away from him. "Electricity can kill you."

His expression crumpled—just a little bit—as I opened the space between us.

Playing with fire was a risk I just couldn't take.

****

Summer and Dylan were handing out Flippin' Skaters tattoos and chatting with fans—still with their masks and helmets on. I joined them, thinking of nothing but putting some distance between me and Brogan.

Then I noticed who they were talking to. Too late.

My heart skipped into my throat as Jojo's eyes locked on mine. I jammed my helmet back onto my head and felt to make sure my mask was still in place. It was.

My sister's face lit up. "Oh my gosh, your skating!" she said. "It was so raw—so fierce. You skate like it's the only thing there is." Jojo was looking at me in a way she never had before, her eyes dancing with excitement. Her face was even a bit flushed. "You go by Skate-or-Dye, right? I'm Red Thunder—with the Metro Roller Girls?"

I stared at her. Did she really not recognize me?

A girl wearing a pencil skirt and white blouse approached Dylan and started talking to him. Her dark brown hair was highlighted red and pulled into a messy up-do, revealing a punk rock crisscross undercut at the nape of her neck.

Summer eyed her, but said to me, "We've been sharing skating tips with the derby girls. They invited us to the rink to learn some of their moves if we'll teach them some ramp tricks."

Still, I couldn't speak. My two worlds were colliding and nobody knew it but me.

Jojo put a hand on my arm like we were brand new BFFs. Her nail polish was chipped, as always. "How do you separate yourself from the rest of the world while you're skating? Because that's always where I have the most trouble. I love to skate, but there are just so many other things going on, it's hard to turn my brain off and just be all in it, you know? But you—I could tell—during your runs, it was just you and the skates and nothing else."

My sister was actually asking me for skating advice. If only I could travel back a decade with a recording of this moment. Then those child-sized skates in my closet might actually have some wear on them.

I started slowly, trying to figure out how to answer her question. "Skating is the best thing I have." I stopped—why *was* it so easy for me to get lost in skating while everything else went to crap?

Jojo's grip on my arm tightened.

"I guess it's easy to focus when you're doing the only thing that feels real," I finally added, meeting her gaze.

"Your voice…" she said, her eyes narrowing. "Have we met?"

Crap. I backed away, dropping my gaze to the ground. "Nope. I would have remembered meeting you."

Summer added, "This is the first time we've met any of the Metro Roller Girls."

I risked a glance at my sister.

A tiny grin appeared on her face. One eyebrow lifted as she studied me. "Okay," she said slowly.

Oh, man, she knew. She knew it was me. The few words I'd spoken had given me away. Why hadn't I thought to try and disguise my voice too? Talk lower or something. My face burned beneath my mask, and I studied a nearby garbage can like it was a work of modern art.

What should I say? How could I spin this? I couldn't have her telling Mom and Dad—if she did, then everything would come out. I couldn't deal with any more drama—the faster everyone forgot about those pictures of me the better, and if my mom got involved, there would be no forgetting for a very long time.

Before I could come up with a game plan, Jojo said, "Well it's such an honor to meet you all. I hope you'll come to one of our bouts soon—we'll get you front row seats." Then she melted back into the crowd with the rest of the roller girls, but not before she winked at me.

Gah!

"She was nice," Summer said.

My voice went soft. "That was my sister."

"What?" Summer screeched.

"Shh!"

"Your sister is one of the Metro Roller Girls?" she

whisper-hissed. "How come you never told me?"

"Because she's in college and we basically never talk anymore. I didn't think it was relevant."

"Um, the fact that you're related to skating deity is definitely relevant."

"Okay, but that's just it. I don't want to be Red Thunder's sister, you know? I want to be Aspen. Or ... Skate-or-Dye or whatever." I was breathing heavily, and suddenly, inexplicably, felt close to tears.

Summer snapped her mouth shut. "Right. Of course, I'm sorry."

Dylan interrupted us. "Hey, come over here." He was standing with the girl he'd been talking to before. She looked young—mid-twenties, maybe—but like she was trying to dress older. And that undercut—wow. It took her look from business casual to business punk.

We joined them. He held an arm out toward the girl and said, "Summer, Aspen, this is Mollie. She's a brand rep for Skateopia magazine."

It took a minute for his words to sink in. My mind stuck on the word Skateopia, trying to figure out where I'd heard it before, and I almost missed the words *brand rep.*

Dylan's eyebrows were raised expectantly, and he was putting obvious effort into trying to tame the biggest, goofiest grin I'd ever seen on him.

Summer recovered before I did. She stuck out a hand. "It's a pleasure to meet you, Mollie."

"Skateopia—like the store in the mall?" I said, finally placing the name.

"That's the one," Mollie said. We launched a skate magazine a couple of years ago and recently became an official sponsor of Flipfezt. We're expecting exponential growth this year, and we're looking for some fresh talent to represent our brand."

My mind whirled.

Flipfezt. That was the competition Dylan had told us about—the one that was coming to Seattle this year.

Wait.

Was this woman saying she wanted *us* to be the fresh talent to represent the Skateopia brand?

"Who better to represent Skateopia to the nation than our own local skaters?" Mollie continued.

Summer's brow furrowed, like she was trying to work out some equation. "Does Skateopia sell roller skates?"

"Historically, we've been a skateboard shop, as you probably know," Mollie said. "But with the crowd you've drawn here today, and the buzz your videos are getting online, there's clearly a gap that needs to be filled. We're looking into expanding into roller skates, and would love to sign the Flippin' Skaters to our brand."

I felt my expression mirror Dylan's. We were receiving an offer of rep, after a single public event! This was huge. Sure, Skateopia was small beans compared to the big names like Zumiez and Monster Drinks, but if Skateopia grew and we'd been there from the start, it could mean huge things for us.

I wondered how Brogan would feel about that. Had any sponsors approached him?

Mollie was watching us carefully. "We love your idea of skating under secret identities. The mystery of who you are in real life will drive our readers wild. Of course, one of the stipulations of the contract would be that you not reveal your true identities, under any circumstance."

Okay, this was just getting better and better. A contract that would guarantee my Skate-or-Dye identity would stay separate from my real-life one? And I'd get paid to keep the secret? Sign me up!

"Here's my card," Mollie said, handing each of us a chunky, square business card. "Why don't you discuss it and get back to me. If you'd like to proceed, I can email you the contracts." She shook each of our hands and then withdrew back into the crowd.

As soon as she was out of earshot, Dylan pumped a fist into the air and let out a whoop. He grabbed Summer and kissed her—and from the look of surprise on her face I could tell it was the first time. Then he pulled us both into an awkward, three-man bear hug and yelled, "This is so awesome!"

Then one of us lost our balance—I couldn't even tell who, since we were all still on skates—and together we tumbled to the ground in a laughing pile of amateur skaters who'd just been given a once-in-a-lifetime opportunity.

On my way home, sitting in the backseat of Dylan's car, I got a text from Jojo. She hadn't texted since she'd left for school.

Jojo: **umm, got anything you wanna tell me?!?!?!?**

I didn't have to think twice.

Aspen: **nope**

She started and stopped typing a couple of times. Finally, she said:

Jojo: **fine keep your secrets. but I'm here if u need anything. for real.**

Jojo hadn't paid any attention to me in years and, suddenly, now that I was on skates, she wanted in. I ran my fingers along the cracks in my phone screen and stared out the window, trying not to think about my sister.

Chapter Nineteen: Just Sign Here

The boarders made good on their promise to share the ramps, and they were surprisingly cool with the fact that we'd gotten a sponsorship offer so fast. Lia, the girl with the half-shaved head, said that having sponsored skaters at our park would boost everyone else's street cred. *Success breeds success*, she'd said. The skaters who'd been around from the beginning (and knew our true identities) agreed to keep our secret after Mollie offered them new equipment in exchange for signing something.

But today marked day four that Brogan had been M.I.A. from the ramps.

Not that I knew what I'd say to him anyway. Or if I really even wanted to see him. But I also didn't *not* want to see him. For all my fear of playing with fire, I had to admit—fire might be better than ice.

As I put on my skates and adjusted the laces, I turned my focus to the bigger problem at hand: we'd decided to sign with Skateopia—obviously—but the contracts Mollie had emailed required an adult signature. If I told my parents I was skating, they'd want to know where I'd found the time and I'd have to tell them I wasn't doing cheer. Then they'd want to know why and the whole rancid story would come out.

Not happening.

So then how would I sign the contract?

When Dylan and Summer arrived, the first words out of Dylan's mouth were, "Have you signed yet? I thought it would be cool to make a video today announcing our sponsorship, but we can't post 'til it's official."

I sighed. "It requires a parent signature."

"So?" Summer said. "It's digital—you just have to type their name in."

"Oh." I eyed her. "Is that what you did?"

"No, I had my mom do it. But I was watching over her shoulder. It never asked for any sort of identification—she just had to type her name in and click submit to electronically sign."

"Anyway, it's just a formality," Dylan added. "Even with a parent's signature, a minor can back out of a skating contract whenever."

"Really?" Summer said.

"Yeah. A friend of mine went pro a few years ago and he told me about it. It's the same for any talent contract with a minor—so like models and actors and stuff can void their contracts whenever. It's to make sure companies don't take advantage of someone too young to understand what they're getting into. Once you turn eighteen, though, if you don't re-negotiate then things get real."

"Then why have us sign at all, if it's not legally binding?" I asked.

"Well, there's still power in making a commitment, you know? Skateopia knows we'll take this more seriously if we've signed something first. Plus, our reputations as skaters are on the line. This isn't a very big industry. If we back out of a contract for some stupid reason, word will get around and we'll have a harder time getting a sponsor in the future. Skateopia knows that. Just because we *can* void the contract doesn't mean it would be a smart thing to do, as long as Skateopia keeps their end of the bargain."

"Just tell your parents," Summer said. "They'll understand."

I shook my head. "Nope."

"Then sign it yourself," Dylan said. "Pull it up on

your phone—we can do it right now."

I hesitated. "Hang on, I need to think. You two go warm up."

"Sure." Dylan took Summer's hand. "But I swear it's not a big deal." They skated away and I pulled up the contract I'd started filling out last night, clicking through the various checkboxes to initial what I'd already read. When I got to the field labeled *Parent/Guardian Signature*, I clicked on it. That was one step further than I'd gone last night. I skimmed the page—lots of legal-sounding stuff—and then, at the bottom, there was a field to type in a signature.

I started typing in my mom's name, then stopped, chewing on my lip. Okay, maybe I needed my sister after all.

Aspen: **hey I have a question for u**

I fired off the text and then waited, staring at my phone. She probably wouldn't text back. She was probably busy wi—

Her reply appeared.

Jojo: **k**

I thought about how to word my question, then started typing.

Aspen: **when it comes to skating contracts, are they legally binding for minors?**

I hit send, then added:

Aspen: **asking for a friend, obvi**

Jojo: **ha ok**

Jojo: **tell your friend—wink—the short answer is no. they're not legally binding for minors**

Then she sent a link to an article that basically said everything Dylan had, only with bigger words.

Jojo: **having a contract protects u—makes sure the sponsor does everything they promise. u should definitely have one. but yes, since you're a minor, u** can void it anytime. that's pretty standard

Jojo: **the sponsor will probably hold back on how much they invest in u until ur old enough to sign a legit contract, but having one before that time will fast track u once u turn 18**

Jojo: **ok, kinda freaking out rn, ngl!!!!**

She added another winky face and the emoji with its lips zipped shut, then a confetti popper.

I sent an upside-down smiley face back.

Okay, so, Dylan, Jojo, and the internet were all saying the same thing, and if the contract wasn't hardcore anyway, what difference did it make who typed my parent's name into the box? If they really cared about it being a parent, they'd have made us come into the office and sign it in person with ID's or whatever.

I tabbed back over to the contract on my phone, finished typing in my mom's name, and continued to the next step.

Oh, wait.

It was asking for an email address. Was it going to send my mom a confirmation or something?

I texted Jojo again.

Aspen: **can I use ur email? and if u get something about me, can u pleeeese not tell mom and dad?**

Jojo: **of course!**

Okay. I took a deep breath and typed in my sister's email, then clicked through to the next page, which was a final review of all the information provided. I scanned through it and pressed *Submit*, then let out the breath I didn't realize I'd been holding.

I opened my social feed to start composing a post announcing our sponsorship—I'd wait to post it until Summer and Dylan had weighed in, of course—but it couldn't hurt to get a little head start right now while I was excited.

My smile died when I saw the top post.

R33S: **Let's talk about Keir Harless, aka @star.pitchR. He's the heartthrob of the baseball team, and he's driven more than one girl mad with those curls. But do I have a juicy dish for you! Keir is a closet D&D nerd and can't find a single person willing to play with him. He's even offered to pay people. But his real-life friends are too cool for nerd games, and real-life nerds don't trust him. So he plays by himself every Thursday night, shifting seats around a table in his basement and playing all the parts alone like a sad loser.**

There was a picture of Keir with some sort of wizard hat on, sitting at a table by himself. It looked like this had been taken from outside a window, which was just … creepy. Still, the comments were spiraling fast.

TaQita53: **what a loser I can't believe I thought he was hot**

DollaBilz: **When people won't spend time with you even if you're paying them, you KNOW something's wrong with you.**

star.pitchR: **you mindless sheep will believe anything. this is CLEARLY a LIE. we have practice on thursdays**

star.pitchR: **that pic was taken at my little brother's birthday party, btw, and whoever took it is a STALKER and should be put in JAIL**

Baseballislife: **he's boring as hell, we only keep him around for his killer arm**

Jayce.eats: **practice ends at 9:00pm. plenty of time after**

Ugh. Seriously, why was this a dish? Even if the part about the birthday party was a lie. So what if the guy wanted to play nerd games in his spare time? That was nobody's business but his. And there was that name again: R33S. It was the same person who'd posted the stuff about the tuba guy. And … had that also been the person who'd posted about Zuri?

Wait, maybe there was more going on here. Some connection I was missing.

My phone dinged with a text.

Jojo: **i confirmed for u. ur all set!!!!!**

Aspen: **confirmed what?**

Jojo: **I got an email asking me to confirm I was the parent who'd just signed ur contract!!!!!! I still cant believe u didn't tell me u were skating, but don't worry, ur secret is safe with me**

Oh. I stared at my phone. I'd totally just lied my way through an official contract.

"Aspen, seriously, are you done yet?" Summer's voice pulled my attention away from my phone. She and Dylan were skating over, flushed from the workout they'd already gotten in. I'd still done zero skating today.

"Is it official yet?" Dylan said.

I forced a smile. "Yep, the Flippin' Skaters are sponsored!"

Dylan let out a whoop and launched himself into the air, jumping higher than I'd ever seen him jump before.

Summer was eyeing me. "Why aren't you happy about it?"

"I *am* happy about it."

"Then what's wrong?"

Geez, it was like she could read the emotions right off my face. Was I really that transparent? I gave my bracelet a single spin around my wrist before remembering I was trying to quit.

Okay, feeling guilty over forging my mom's signature was my own issue, and I could deal with it on my own. Later.

What I really wanted to talk about right now was the post I'd just read. "There's another victim." I tilted my phone screen to show her.

"Oh." She sat down on the bench beside me.

"Victim of what?" Dylan said, settling down on my other side.

I'd lost track of how many days it was since my social plunge. The cheer squad had eked by at regionals (which I'd convinced my parents not to go to, claiming I was feeling nervous and didn't want them to watch, which was technically not a lie). The squad had made it into states, proving they didn't need me. So while my life as Skate-or-Dye had rocket-launched into awesomeness, my life as Aspen had spiraled out of control.

Only, it was becoming clear that I wasn't the only one going down, and that fact made me feel even worse. I'd been the very first subject, and I couldn't help feeling like, somehow, my actions had started it all.

I looked at Summer and Dylan. Was there a way to help them both understand why I was upset now without going into all the gory details of my own embarrassing social plunge?

They're the last friends you have, a voice in my head reminded me. *Don't risk it.*

"Okay, seriously, what's wrong?" Summer said.

They're the last friends you have, the voice said again, more insistent.

But Summer and Dylan were the real deal—friends who would stand by me no matter what. I knew that now.

So I shushed the voice in my head, swallowed my pride, and started slowly. "You've seen all the social media victims, right, Summer? Saraya and Ronald and my friend Zuri?"

"Yeah, I don't live in a darkroom."

"Again, victims of what?" Dylan asked.

I explained. "Some cyber bully keeps attacking people at our school—leaking secrets, exposing private aspects of their lives, and splashing it all over for people to comment on and debate over. There was another one today." I held my phone out so they could read the stuff about Keir together.

"Are you friends with this guy or something?" Dylan said when he'd finished reading. "Like, it sucks and all, but I don't get why you care."

I hesitated, then said, "I was the first victim. It started with me."

He sucked in a breath.

"I have no idea who's behind it. They must have some sort of objective—like, massive social takedown or crusade against … *something*. I just can't figure out what a tuba player, a baseball pitcher, a debater, and two cheerleaders have in common. It sounds like the start of a bad joke."

"What did they say about you?" Dylan asked.

Summer eyed me meaningfully, wordlessly asking if I wanted her to deflect Dylan's question. I could stop right there and Dylan would never have to know the whole truth.

But I needed to tell him. I wanted him to know the whole me.

The sound of wheels and boards scraping the pavement soothed me. "A few weeks ago, someone posted pictures of me at a club—onstage, in nothing but my bra and underwear. I don't even remember doing that—I thought the pictures were fake at first. But, apparently, they weren't and…" I couldn't finish. And, what? I was a loser slut with no friends? Even the school guidance counselor thought I was pregnant with a

175

pothead's baby?

Dylan said, "Is that all?"

Summer punched him.

"Um, have you ever had people saying horrible things about you that aren't true? It sucks." I pulled up the original posts about me, and shoved my phone at Dylan.

He took it, scrolled through the pictures and some of the comments, and then handed the phone back. I held my breath, cringing as some of the comments came back word-for-word to my mind.

Attention-seeking, back-stabbing slut.

What kind of friend goes after her bffs man like that?

Just as ugly inside as she is outside.

For one crazy second, I thought I'd just blown everything. Dylan would never want to skate with me again. The Flippin' Skaters were over—I wasn't worthy of having friends as cool as Summer and Dylan. He'd talk Summer into ditching me, and I'd go back to being Bombshell Whimsy, sitting alone on a kiddie swing at the park.

Then Summer said, "Aspen, you know those comments are a load of crap, right? Whether the pictures were fake or not."

"Well, I don't know," I said. "When I'm not pretending to be Skate-or-Dye, I do kind-of suck at being human." I'd meant it to come out light—a joke. But the bitterness in my tone made the words heavier and exposed the truth.

That was how I really felt about myself.

"You do not suck at being human," Dylan said. "And I can say that with confidence because I know some truly sucky people. You are not one of them."

Summer took over. "Aspen, seriously. You are so

much more than what a bunch of idiots say about you online. You're seeing through a false lens—it's acting like one of those funky mirrors at the fair, making you think something that's not true."

I wasn't sure I believed them, but I knew arguing wouldn't get me anywhere. "The worst part is, I still don't understand what, exactly, happened that night. I thought the East cheer squad got us drunk because they wanted to take us down before regionals, but with these other people going down, now I'm not so sure."

Dylan frowned. "Wait, you think someone messed with your drink? That's serious stuff."

"Why else would I have gotten onstage in my underwear and not remember it?"

I suddenly felt like skating.

No, I *needed* to skate.

"Let's make a list of clues." Summer scrambled for her phone and opened her notes app.

"Clues to what?"

"Help you figure out what happened that night. Talking through everything might jog your memory." Summer started typing and muttered, "Acting weird onstage." She looked up at me expectantly. "What else?"

"Oh, you're writing it down?"

"Yeah, we have to be scientific about this. Right, Dill?"

Dylan was gazing at her like she was the cutest thing he'd ever seen. I wished someone would look at me like that. "Right, bae."

Bae? Dill? Since when had they started using nicknames?

"Aspen?" Summer prodded.

Right. I thought back through the night. "I don't remember anything after getting back from the bathroom, really. There were a lot of people at our table—people who hadn't been there before. But after that it's kind-of blank." I frowned. "But the next morning I woke up wearing a U-dub sweatshirt, and I can't figure out whose it is."

Summer was typing furiously.

"And then there's that rumor about me and Drake—I still don't know how that started."

"Who's Drake?" Dylan said.

"My supposed baby-daddy. I'm not really pregnant," I added quickly. "I've never even spoken to the guy, let alone…" I trailed off. "But, anyway, yeah."

Actually, maybe I should talk to Drake. He seemed like a person who would know stuff.

"Do you have any ex-boyfriends who might be jealous?" Dylan asked.

I snorted. "There seems to be an unspoken agreement between all guys in the universe to get tired of me before I get tired of them." And that's all I wanted to say about that. One could only take so many times of getting friend-zoned before deciding it wasn't worth it to even try anymore.

Summer took a breath, like she was going to press for more information, but Dylan said, "Sounds like we've got a good start. Aspen, wanna skate?"

I jammed my helmet onto my head. "I've never wanted anything more."

Then, despite the embarrassment of letting my friends in on my dirty little secret, I had the best run of my life. The air parted around me like I was a demigod. I flew, feeling like my skates were sparking beneath me.

Summer and Dylan joined me on the ramps.

Brogan never showed up.

Chapter Twenty: Logos

I found a new normal, powering through school each day with the least possible amount of human interaction and spending all my free time at the ramps with Summer and Dylan. We announced our partnership with Skateopia and released some more videos.

Today had been like all the other days—survive school, then head straight to the ramps. We were taking a water break when Summer pulled her helmet off and readjusted her mask. Our contracts stated that whenever we skated in public, we had to wear our masks to keep our identities hidden. I didn't even notice mine anymore, but Summer was always fiddling with hers and pressing the fabric down around her eyes just before she started skating.

"Maybe you need one with bigger eyeholes," I said.

Summer tore her gaze off of Dylan, who was working on a rail trick. "Huh?"

I pointed to her mask.

"Oh. No, the eyeholes are fine. It's just annoying—I really wish we hadn't agreed to the face masks."

"Really? I thought that was the best part of our deal. We get a clean slate to build ourselves up however we want."

"I just kinda wish people at school knew it was me under here."

"Trust me, you don't want that much attention, even if it starts out good. These masks will keep us safe."

Summer fiddled with her mask a bit more, tying it at the nape of her neck right under her massive bun, then untying it and trying above the bun, just under the lower edge of her helmet.

"Here, let me help."

I crossed the ties above her bun and then wound them around it and tied it all up underneath. "There. Now it's acting as an extra hair tie, too. Your mask won't fall off unless your hair does."

"I still wish we didn't have to wear them."

Dylan finished showing off and skated over to us. "Look who I found!"

Behind him, walking quickly to try and keep up, was Mollie. She wore heavy black combat boots, jeans, and a polyester jacket I could only describe as Hillary Clinton gone to the dark side. "Hey, Flippin' Skaters! How's my favorite new trio?"

"Mollie's got some merch options to show us," Dylan said.

"Ooh, merch?" Summer said. "That sounds so official."

"Well, you're definitely official. We're working on putting together a schedule of events for you—I'll let you know as soon as I have the final version. We loved your announcement video, and we did one as well, which you're free to use for promotional purposes however you wish. Also, we have a stylist working on your signature looks—we'll set up a photo shoot once we have everything settled. But for now, which products do you like best?"

She pulled a tablet out of a studded canvas shoulder bag. We gathered closer so we could all see. She scrolled through a few pages, showing different items we could have made with our logo on it—t-shirts, water bottles, headbands, tote bags. There were even things like makeup mirrors and phone chargers.

We pointed out ones we liked and she marked them.

Then she pulled up another page. "Okay, here are your logo mock-ups. Our artist started with the drawing you all were handing out as tattoos at the skate-off. She made a few different versions—some were embellishments or alterations of the original and some are brand-new. Keep in mind these are just mock-ups. Once you pick your favorite, the artist will clean things up and add some finishing touches."

She tapped a few times on the screen and, suddenly, there were our logos.

I drew in a breath. "They're beautiful."

Summer squealed.

Dylan said, "Those are sick!"

We all peered closer. They were amazing. Each version featured roller skates, but the color and number of skates varied. The name *Flippin' Skaters* varied in font, color, and placement but was on every version.

"I love them all! I don't even know how to pick a favorite." I studied them. "Like, this one here is bright— eye-catching and, like, somehow happy." I pointed out another. "But this one is edgy and captures the fierceness of skating. And this one feels really retro—roller skating is retro, so that fits too, you know?"

"I like that one," Summer said, pointing to the bright one.

"I think I'm leaning toward the retro one."

Dylan pointed out another I hadn't noticed. It was a pencil drawing, with splashes of color subtly worked in. Actually, it was pretty similar to the original drawing Dylan had made.

"I like this one—it's understated, but when you really look at it, it's got everything. The pencil lines have that raw edge—like skating itself—but the color adds emotion to mirror the way you feel when you're skating."

Summer and I gawked at him.

181

He tore his gaze away from the tablet and looked at us. "What?"

"That was just very…"

"Poetic." Summer finished for me. "I always knew you were a big softie."

I gazed at the logo, trying to picture it on t-shirts and water bottles and stuff. Dylan was right. It was edgy, raw, and beautiful, all at the same time. It was perfect. "I love it," I said.

Summer grinned up at Dylan, taking him by the hand. "Me, too."

"Okay," Mollie said, tapping on the chosen logo. "I'll have the artist clean it up. We'll send you the finished version and get some merch ordered. I've got a great feeling about this partnership!" She shut off the tablet and tucked it away. "I'd like to stay and watch you skate for a while, if that's okay."

"Sure," Dylan said.

"Would it be all right if I take some video as well? Maybe post a live-stream?" She glanced around the group.

Summer and Dylan looked to me. I checked to make sure my face mask was in place—it was. "Yeah, that's fine."

"All right," Mollie said. "I'm gonna sit on that hill over there. It looks pretty chill." She headed for the grassy hill where the spectators had gathered to watch the skate-off.

We did a quick warm-up and then hit the ramps.

****

I saw Mollie's post later that night when I opened my social app. She'd done a livestream of us skating, from Skateopia's official account, with the words, *'Just signed these amazing new skaters! Here's a sneak peek at what they can do. Go follow them!'* I checked our

Flippin' Skater account and, sure enough, we'd gained a ton of new followers.

But being on social media reminded me that I had some work to do. Well, *Aspen* had some work to do.

I went back to my personal account and started combing through old posts to see if I could find any links between the five recent social media victims. Because I still felt like I was missing something—some connection between the targets that should have been obvious but wasn't.

I found the post about Zuri and, sure enough, the poster was R33S, just like it had been with Ronald and Keir. I went back further to the stuff about Saraya, and ... yep, that bombshell had been posted by R33S, too.

Okay, there was definitely something deeper going on.

I took screenshots of each of the posts and compared them. They'd all been put up by R33S, but each one had a different profile picture—like the user had set up multiple fake accounts to attack people with. Which was just ... I mean, w*hy?*

What did that combo of letters and numbers stand for? Were they scrambled up coordinates? Some secret coded language? And how did I fit in? Chase had been the original poster of that stuff about me, not this R33S person.

Right?

I searched back through the threads of gossip. It took a long time to get through it all. But, yep, there it was—the picture Chase had posted of me was the very first one. Though, other people had jumped in with their own pictures and memes pretty quickly. I scrolled through the flood of posts.

And then I spotted it—a picture posted by R33S. It showed me onstage—shocker—and there was a caption.

R33S: **Aspen Heathrow sure put it all out there. Can anyone say cheerleaders gone wild? How's this little diva going to react when she learns how the crowd really feels about her? Get off the stage, NOBODY wants you there.**

Ouch.

Only now that I was a Flippin' Skater, I knew that wasn't true. People *did* want me on stage. Or, at least, they wanted Skate-or-Dye. Which was also me, even though nobody knew it.

Anyway, this proved we were all connected—me, Saraya, Zuri, Ronald, and Keir—by R33S. But what the heck did that mean? Who was R33S? There'd been so many people at the club that night—too many to even start trying to narrow the suspect list down.

I peered closer at the picture R33S had posted of me. It showed the same scene that Chase's picture had—me onstage at the music club—but it had been taken from a different angle, so some of the crowd was visible.

And, was that…?

I zoomed in, focusing on the face that had just jumped out at me.

It was Drake. Looking right at whoever had taken this picture.

Chapter Twenty-One: Glass Castle

I stood across the street from Drake's house, checking the address on my phone to be sure I had the right place. The house was small, with a sagging awning that looked as tired as I felt after a day on the ramps. It was late, but there was a light on inside. I left my bike in his driveway and knocked on the front door—three solid knocks.

From inside, a woman's voice said, "Drake, dear, the door." Then, a moment later, she said, "Drake!"

"Coming, Ma," said a male voice.

The door opened to reveal a frail-looking woman sitting on an armchair with too many blankets piled in her lap. The TV was on, and the remote sat on a table beside her.

Drake's expression was surprisingly tender as he looked at the woman, but I only caught a glimpse of his face before he saw me and his expression soured.

"Who is it, dear?" the woman said.

"No one," he answered. "I'll be right back." He advanced onto the porch, forcing me to step back. His gaze caught on my polar bear pajama bottoms (yeah, probably should have changed out of those) and he rolled his eyes.

There was really no way to do this that wouldn't be awkward—it was already awkward, me standing on his front porch in my pajamas—so I just jumped in. "Can we talk about what happened at the club?"

"I haven't seen her since then, if that's what you're getting at."

I frowned.

"Rhea," he said, clarifying. "We haven't spoken since that night—ho won't answer my calls."

"Oh. That's not why I was … look, I just came to ask you abo—"

"Why everyone thinks I knocked you up?"

My face flushed. "No, as it happens, I've moved passed tha—"

"It's because of Rhea. She's the one who started that rumor about us."

Hold up. *Rhea* started the rumor about me and Drake? "Why would she do that to me?"

Drake shrugged. "She's your friend, not mine—I just made out with her. She said it would be funny to tell everyone you got knocked up—see what you'd do if you got taken down a few rungs. Of course, I didn't know *I'd* be part of it. Anyway, you didn't just fall a few rungs, you crashed through the floor, didn't you?"

So that's what Rhea had been hiding that day by her locker.

My thoughts circled, trying to make sense of this new information. I'd seen Rhea with Drake at the club. Rhea had begged me not to tell Chase, but I'd said I would if she didn't. And she clearly hadn't planned on fessing up. So maybe she'd invented the rumor to throw everyone off in case I started talking. The fact that the lie would get me kicked off squad was probably just a bonus.

I mean, her plan had basically worked. If I'd accused her of cheating on Chase those first few days, especially with Drake, it would have just looked like a pathetic attempt to take someone down with me.

I waited for the rage to hit—to feel the pain of such a sharp betrayal from my former best friend—but I just felt numb.

Drake pulled a pack of cigarettes from his pocket and lit up. "Why are you here, anyway? I know it's not to apologize for your trash friend starting rumors about me."

He blew out a puff of smoke, right in my face.

I stepped back, coughing. "You know those can kill you, right?"

He laughed. "The friends or the cigarettes?"

My mouth twitched up into a tiny smile. "Both, I guess." I sighed. "Actually, I'm not here about Rhea. I came to ask if you saw anything that night that would help me figure out why I don't remember getting onstage."

"Girl, you don't remember that? Really?"

I shook my head.

"That's messed up."

"I know. But in one of the pictures posted of me, you're looking right at the camera—or, at the person taking the pic. I was hoping you'd remember who it was."

"Wasn't everyone taking pictures of you?"

There was a beat of silence. "I don't remember. But yeah, I guess evidence would suggest that. Still, can you walk me through what you saw?"

Drake frowned. "There were a ton of people at your table when Rhea and I came upstairs. Chase wasn't there, though—Rhea was watching for him."

"Who was at our table—people you knew?"

"Not really. I mean, some of your teammates or whatever. And that new girl—the one who's always with you but kind of alone, too?

That would be Sara. She was usually around, but no one really talked to her. I mean, she was always on her phone so it was kind of hard to. But, come to think of it, where had she moved from? I didn't know—in fact, I didn't think she'd ever said. If she'd left a squad we'd be competing against at states, maybe she'd jump at a chance to take us down. And it was possible she'd made some enemies at school since moving in. Could Sara be

R33S?

But, no. Sara had been the one to tell me about that picture of Zuri when it went up. She wouldn't post something like that and then tell me about it right away. Would she?

Drake's voice broke through my thoughts. "Other than your friends, there were just a bunch of guys."

"What guys?"

Drake shrugged. "Guys I didn't recognize. They looked older."

I froze, thinking of the U-dub sweatshirt. "Like, college guys?"

Drake glanced up at the night sky, the butt of his cigarette glowing a faint orange-gold as he took another puff. "Maybe."

"Did you talk to any of them?"

He shook his head. "We saw how crowded the table was so we went to another one. We didn't stay very long."

"Do you remember anything else?"

"Nope." He threw his cigarette on the sidewalk and smashed it under his boot. "But, hey," he said.

When he didn't continue, I said, "What?"

"Okay, don't take this the wrong way, but can I give you some advice?"

"Um, I guess?"

"Get over yourself."

I bristled, but he continued.

"Stop caring what everyone thinks of you. You're upset because your glass castle shattered, and now you're trying to tape it back together. But glass can't be taped together, blondie, so stop trying."

"My hair is *red*, not blonde. Well, it's red-*ish*. Auburn, really, I guess you could say. But I prefer re—"

He cut me off. "You wanna know what's messed

up? You look down on me—I can tell—because my life isn't as polished as yours. But, news flash, your polish is wearing thin—I can see it right there." He gestured toward my wrist. "You are just as broken as I am."

I followed his gaze. And froze.

My fingers were tangled up in my bracelet, which was twisted into a knot around my wrist that I was pulling tight. So tight it was drawing blood.

I didn't even remember touching it, let alone hurting myself. That's how it usually was these days. I hadn't been able to stop fiddling with it since I saw those pictures of myself online—they'd left me feeling exposed and out of control, but the motion of spinning my bracelet around and around made me feel better. Like I was back in control. But that also left the flesh beneath the leather band red and raw. Truthfully, I barely noticed anymore. It was a price I was willing to pay.

I said nothing, just grabbed my bike, hopped on, and pedaled home as fast as I could.

Drake was wrong about me. I was fine. My life was fine—good, even. I had a skating contract, a team, and friends. And once I figured out who R33S was and stopped them, life would be perfect.

Then I'd feel better about being me.

Chapter Twenty-Two: Events

It was a rare sunny day at the skate park and, for once, Brogan was there. I tried catching his eye as I entered the park, but he didn't look my way.

Dylan did, though. As soon as I was within earshot, he said, "Did you see the schedule?" He was wearing his new face mask—earthy colors to match the look Mollie had created for him. Summer had her new teal mask on and a pair of second-hand skates (with better ankle support) to replace the ones she'd been using. They were skating together.

I joined them on the ramps, barely noticing my own face mask, which felt like a natural extension of my helmet. "No, what schedule?"

"Mollie sent it," Summer said, doing a Jump-and-Grab. "We have a photo shoot in the morning, and then our first gig is tomorrow night!"

"Wait, we have a skating gig?"

We were skating around the park in a pack, hopping over or jumping on or spinning around whatever obstacle came up. It felt oddly creative, figuring out what trick best suited each obstacle and making that decision in the milliseconds between them.

Dylan hopped over a low beam, while I did a one-handed skate grab at the top of a practice mound. "It's at some small-town state fair two hours south of here," Dylan said. "We're the pre-game event for a demolition derby."

"Ooh, a demolition derby! We are moving up in the world." I spun to a stop.

Summer and Dylan circled back to join me.

We were all breathing hard, but the energy coursing through our little pack was electric.

"We have a bunch of other events, too," Dylan said. "Mollie's got us scheduled out for weeks."

"Oh, and Skateopia bought Dylan's logo," Summer said, beaming at him.

Dylan looked like he was trying not to smile. And failing.

Summer continued, breathless, "Mollie said it was so similar to the one we ended up picking that they decided they needed to buy the rights to Dylan's image before moving forward. Skateopia has started handing out bumper stickers, and Mollie says soon they'll have a whole section of Flippin' Skaters merchandise for sale in the store. T-shirts, drawstring bags, water bottles, even some retro knee-socks."

"Seriously? That is so cool!"

"Face it, Aspen, you created a monster," Summer said. "Flippin' Skaters is going to be huge." She adjusted her face mask. "I just wish I didn't have to wear this."

Dylan lifted her mask slightly, kissed her, and then patted it back in place. "A small price to pay for fame," he said, tweaking her nose.

She giggled.

Ugh, they were too cute.

Without entirely meaning to, I scanned the park for Brogan. He was watching Lia do a rail trick. The hair on the side of her head that wasn't shaved had been put into a bunch of tiny braids, which took on a life of their own when she caught air.

Summer nudged me. "He'll catch you staring if you're not careful."

I tore my eyes away. "I wasn't staring, I was thinking." Half-truth. I'd been staring *and* thinking.

"Liar."

I scrambled for a safe subject. "I talked to Drake. He was in the background of one of the pictures of me, looking at the camera. I thought he might remember who took the picture."

"Wait, do you think he's R33S?" Summer said.

"No, the person taking the picture of me was R33S, and Drake was looking right at them."

Dylan said, "So, did he remember who it was?"

My shoulders slumped. "No." I started fiddling with my bracelet, then caught myself and stopped.

"Well, *we* learned something at the party last night," Dylan said.

My head jerked up. "What party?"

Summer waved a hand dismissively. "I don't know, it was at someone's house. But we overheard your friends talking about the club and about Rhea."

My friends had all been at a party without me, and no one had thought to tell me—not my former friends *or* my current friends. I swallowed, wrapping my arms around myself.

Summer continued as if it was no big deal. "Apparently, Rhea's been acting super strange lately— like hardcore focused on states one week, running double practices and working everyone really hard, and then missing practice herself for days in a row. And Sara, the girl who took you home that night, has been running practices in Rhea's absence. The coaches made Sara co-captain."

My brain snagged on multiple things at once: Sara was co-captain, Rhea had been missing practice, and Sara had taken me home after everything went down at the club. "Wait, how do you know Sara took me home?"

Summer frowned. "Oh, um. I think she was talking about it?"

Dylan jumped in. "Yeah, she was telling one of the girls that when she took you home, you were so out of it that she had to walk you all the way up to your bedroom. She said you were acting really strange and maybe it was good you weren't on the squad anymore."

Summer elbowed him.

"What? That's what she said."

I ignored them, still processing the fact that Sara had been the one to take me home.

If she was R33S, maybe she'd helped me home and told me about the picture of Zuri just to throw me off. It was possible she was a really good actress. Maybe the zip-up sweatshirt belonged to her. Maybe she really was trying to sabotage us from the inside. I chewed on my lip, trying to make sense of it all.

My gaze wandered to Brogan. He was looking at me.

I looked away, but peeked back in time to see him hop on his skateboard and jump a gap. I watched him skate, wishing I could go back to that moment after the skate-off and stop myself from pushing him away.

If only I could go back to that moment.

If I could go back...

Suddenly, I knew what I needed to do next. Not about Brogan, but about everything else. "Hey, what are you all doing tonight?"

Chapter Twenty-Three: Scene of the Crime

Summer was sitting on a stone wall outside the music club. When she saw me walking toward her, she hopped down, brushing her palms off on her jeans.

"Is Dylan coming?" I asked.

"Yeah. He said to get in line without him." She jerked a thumb toward the club. "Ready to fish for answers?"

I took a deep, stuttering breath. "Yes. And you are here to keep me from chickening out."

"Got it," Summer said. "Absolutely no chickening will happen on my watch. I swear it, on the mother of all half-pipes."

Summer didn't seem to notice that my upper lip was breaking out in sweat. Or that my right hand had gone to my left wrist to fiddle with my bracelet even though the skin was still raw from my conversation with Drake.

We crossed the street, heading for the club. The slap of my flats against the pavement didn't feel momentous enough for what I was about to do—I should have worn combat boots. We got in line and waited. And waited. And waited some more. So much for striding confidently back to the scene of the crime.

"Geez, whoever's on the bill tonight must be big," Summer said, eyeing the number of people still in front of us.

"It's not a local garage band, that's for sure."

We edged up in line, inch by measly inch, both of us scrolling through our phones. My legs grew tired and my feet started hurting—I could feel every crack and bump in the pavement through my thin shoes.

Maybe we should just come back another day.

But when? I needed to get to the bottom of this. How had I gone from catching Rhea and Drake in the bathroom to standing onstage in my underwear? Why didn't I remember any of it? And who was responsible?

I'd been chickening out long enough—it was time to get some real answers.

I'd texted a picture of the mystery sweatshirt to Sara and asked if it was hers. She said it wasn't, but she could be lying.

We inched closer to the front. With every step we took, my stomach got a little tighter.

Then I started worrying about Dylan. If he didn't get here before we got to the front of the line, he'd have to wait in the whole thing. "When did Dylan say he was coming?" I craned my neck, looking for him.

Summer glanced up from her phone. "He didn't say. I'll text him."

More waiting.

I fingered my bracelet. And shifted from one foot to the other.

We moved up in line.

"He's not responding," Summer said.

We were almost to the front.

"Should we try calling him?" I said.

"I'm sure he'll be here soon. He's probably trying to find a place to park."

I fidgeted. "But if he's that close, maybe we should let some people go in ahead of us, you know?"

"Aspen. We're going in. Stop trying to stall."

I wasn't trying to stall.

Was I?

"Dylan is perfectly capable of standing in a boring line by himself." Summer grabbed my arm. "Come on."

The group ahead of us went in, and Summer and I moved to the front.

The bouncer said, "IDs and cover charge."

My throat went dry. I was so close to getting answers.

I forked over the ten dollar cover charge and handed him my bag for inspection. After examining my ID, he fastened an orange wristband onto my arm and stamped both of my hands with the word: *UNDERAGE.*

Once Summer and I were both through, we went down the staircase leading into the venue. The walls and stairs were painted black, with track lighting along the floor. The bass thumped in my ears. The lower we went, the louder the music got.

We reached the bottom and the band came into view. Dozens of tiny round tables surrounded the dance floor, and behind those were a semi-circle of low-backed booths. I gazed at the booth my friends and I had been crowded around that night and had a sudden memory.

I'd gone back to the table to get my bag and find Zuri, but I was worried Chase would be there and ask about Rhea. I'd taken a sip of my Coke, hoping it would calm me down before the inevitable conversation. There were so many people at our table. But I didn't see Chase anywhere.

"Aspen's back!" Zuri yelled. She clunked her glass with mine and took a swig of her own Coke, diet in her case. "This is so good!" she said. "Aspen, you really should switch. All that sugar isn't good for you."

I just looked at her. The sugar verse aspartame debate seemed so inconsequential given the fact that I'd just found my best friend cheating on my other best friend.

Zuri nudged me, misjudging the distance and knocking into me. Her drink sloshed over the sides of her cup, but she didn't seem to notice. "This Coke is new— it's, like, not diet and not regular. It's ... I forget what it's called. But it tastes just like regular, I promise. Try it, babe, try it!"

She thrust the drink in my face and, just to get her off my back, I took a sip.

And she was right. It was good. Sweet, with a little something extra that I couldn't put a name to. I took another swig, then handed it back to her. "I'm gonna go home."

"No," Zuri whined, tugging on my elbow. "Stay, the party's just getting good. Don't you love the band? I'm going to go meet the drummer—he doesn't go to our school. Did you see the size of his biceps?"

More people joined our table.

Zuri started up the stairs to the stage.

I went after her, trying to tug her back. "You're going to meet him right now? They're still playing."

She giggled, her laugh sounding like wind chimes on a summer breeze. "What better way to get his attention?"

"Aspen, are you all right?"

Summer's voice tugged me back to the present, and I realized I was staring at a couple making out. I shook my head, like maybe the pieces might rattle around and give me more details. But that was it. I couldn't remember what had happened after I'd chased Zuri up the stairs. But I could guess.

So, was that it, then? Had someone messed with Zuri's drink? Was that why the Coke had tasted different?

I'd only taken a sip or two, though. Definitely not enough to get me so drunk that I'd go onstage in my underwear and not remember it the next day.

Summer's voice came again. "Aspen, what's wrong?"

"I think I was right—someone messed with my

drink. Well, Zuri's drink, but then I had some."

"Okay, think hard—who else was hanging around you that night? R33S has to be somewhere in your memory." Summer frowned at her phone. "I am starting to think it's weird that Dylan hasn't responded to any of my texts. I'm going to call him."

As Summer tried Dylan, I gazed at the bar. Bartenders scurried this way and that, pouring drinks and taking money. I walked over, elbowing my way through the crowd, and got the attention of the nearest bartender. "Were you working the night Appellooza played? It was a couple of weeks ago."

He ignored me, filling up a glass and handing it to a guy beside me.

I tried again. "I really need to talk to someone who was working that night—can I speak to your manager?"

He barely glanced at me. "I *am* the manager. Who's asking?" Then, to a girl beside me, he said, "What'll it be?"

The girl gave him her order and he started making her drink.

"I'm Aspen. Something weird happened to me that night—I'm just trying to get some answers."

The bartender handed the girl her drink and then cocked his head at me, really looking for the first time. And then something clicked behind his eyes. He remembered me, I knew it.

But he only said, "That was a long time ago. Can't help you." He shifted his focus to the next customer. "What can I get you?"

"Please," I said, leaning farther across the bar. "I need your help."

Summer came up behind me. "Dylan's on his way."

The bartender made the next person's drink, handed it off, and then said to me, "Get out of my bar. Go home."

I flinched at the fire flashing in his eyes. It was almost like he was mad.

Or, that wasn't quite it, exactly. But there was something there.

When I didn't move, he added, "Do I need to call security?"

"Seriously?" Summer said. "She hasn't done anything wrong."

"She's taking up space at my bar. We're busy tonight—I can't have you kids annoying my actual customers."

"We have every right to be here," Summer said, her chin jutting out in defiance. "We paid our cover charge just like everyone else."

"The cover was for the band, princess, not the bar."

"Well, then I'd like a Shirley Temple, please." She slapped some bills down on the counter.

The bartender sneered. "We don't do Shirley Temples. Now get out before I call security." He was shouting now, and there was still that fiery look in his eyes that was not quite anger or annoyance … what was it?

I looked at him again, studying his features. Then it clicked. I grabbed Summer's arm and tugged her away from the counter.

"Wait, I'll order something else," she protested.

"We'll go," I said to the bartender. "No need to call security."

Summer frowned, but she followed me—away from the bar, up the stairs, and out of the club. As we walked, my mind circled, trying to figure out what had

just happened. Because that look in the bartender's eye—
it was fear.

Summer waited until we were outside before
turning to me. "Why did we leave? I could have just
ordered a soda. Now we'll have to wait in line all over
again."

"That bartender was afraid of something. Of me, I
think. He wasn't going to talk to us."

Summer chewed on her lower lip. "You think he's
hiding something?"

"He must be. Why threaten to kick us out just for
asking a few questions?"

Summer's phone rang, and it was a ringtone I'd
never heard. Her cheeks went pink as the singer crooned
about a moonlit sky and a starry night.

"Who's that?"

"Dylan." Summer sounded like a schoolgirl
caught leaving a tack on the teacher's chair.

I laughed. "Really?"

She ignored me and answered the phone. "Hey,
where are you?" She paused. "Awesome, we just left—
we're outside by the streetlamp." There was another
pause. "Me, too." She hung up.

"Me, too, what?" I teased.

Her cheeks went pinker still. "They'll be here in a
few minutes."

"They?"

She put a hand on my arm. "Don't be mad,
okay?"

Uh oh. "Don't be mad about what?"

"Dylan's bringing reinforcements."

Chapter Twenty-Four: Skaters Unite

Dylan could have been walking down the street with the Channel 8 news team, led by Rhea, or Chase, or even Drake, and I wouldn't have felt as mortified as I did when I saw who he'd actually brought.

Brogan, with his ever-present beanie, was walking toward us. He wasn't smiling.

Beside him was Lia, who'd only recently started being nice to us. *She* was smiling. She sidled up to me like we'd been skating together for life, her braids brushing my shoulder.

"Aspen, girl, we are going to get to the bottom of this." She marched up to the bouncer, who smiled and gave her a fist bump as she walked by—right into the club. When she realized we weren't following, she turned and said to the bouncer, "They're with me."

We followed Lia into the club, dodging evil glares from the people in line.

"Dylan, *what* is going on?" I hissed.

But Dylan was whispering something to Summer. He hadn't heard me.

Brogan came up beside me and said, "Lia's dad owns the place."

Oh, great. If the manager was afraid of me, imagine how thrilled the owner would be to see me here.

Brogan continued. "And my brother was working that night. Lia got him the job. He'll talk to me."

I stopped walking. Brogan had said *that night.* How much had Dylan told him?

Brogan caught my elbow, lightly, and nudged me forward. "They told me what happened. I'm sorry—I know you don't like me, and you don't want me here, but ... I thought I could help."

Wait, he thought I didn't like him? That was so not why … argh, I'd really messed things up with him. "Look, I don't not like you—" I started.

He cut me off. "It's okay. You don't have to explain, I get it."

"No, you don't. I was just in a bad place after the skate-off. I'm sorry I pushed you away." I caught and held his gaze.

A slew of emotions crossed his face.

A voice shouted out to us, breaking our brief connection. "Brogan, Li!"

One of the bartenders—not the one I'd talked to before—was making his way over. He looked like an older version of Brogan, with just a touch more stubble and hollower cheeks. Also, he had dark, wavy hair.

Was that what Brogan's hair looked like under his beanie?

The guy reached over the bar and clapped Brogan on the shoulder. "Sorry, man, you're still not old enough. You might be taller than me, but I am not going to give you booze."

Brogan shrugged him off and, with a wry smile, said, "When have I ever asked you for booze?"

"There's a first time for everything, little bro."

Lia spoke up. "Hey, Slate, how's the bar treating you?"

"It's great—thanks for hooking me up."

"We miss seeing you at the park."

"Yeah, I know. Community service takes time."

Lia made a pouty face.

Slate said, "But maybe I'll be able to swing by sometime this weekend." There was something pinched about the way he said it.

Lia lowered her voice. "Xander's doing time— there was a bust. You don't have to worry about him anymore."

Slate glanced at me and Summer, probably wondering why two strangers were being allowed in on this conversation.

"Can I get a Coke?" Brogan said with a sideways glance at the manager we'd spoken to earlier, who was now eyeing Slate.

I ducked my head and shifted out of view.

Slate followed Brogan's gaze. "Yeah, man."

When he handed Brogan his drink, Brogan said, "Do you have a break coming up? We need to talk."

"I don't know, it's pretty busy right now. This band has some serious groupies."

Dylan was eyeing a booth, where a group was just leaving. "It's all right. We can wait." He and Summer made a beeline for the booth, and were sliding into it before all the glasses were even cleared away.

Brogan turned to his brother. "We'll be right over there whenever you can get away." Then he nodded toward the manager, who was still eyeing us. "Better keep that guy happy."

Slate nodded, then turned to a group of girls in slinky dresses and super high heels. "What can I get you ladies?" He flashed a smile at them, and I saw an echo of the carefree Brogan I'd first met at the roller rink.

We joined Dylan and Summer at the booth, Lia, Brogan, and I sliding in across from them. I was crazy-aware of how much space was between me and Brogan. It was not enough. And, also, it was too much. Way too much.

But, apparently, he thought I hated him and he'd only come tonight to … actually, why had he come if he thought I hated him?

Summer and Dylan were whispering something, but they looked up when I turned to Brogan and said, "Do you remember the first time we met?"

Summer laughed. "You mean at the skate park when you wiped out in the bowl?"

I shook my head.

Brogan tensed up beside me. He didn't say anything, but the way his gaze pierced mine said he was trying to figure me out.

Actually, no, that wasn't quite it. He was grasping, struggling, banging his head against the wall, trying to figure me out.

Wait, did he think I was referring to the fact that I'd tried to kiss him, but had actually bitten him instead? I felt my cheeks go pink and clarified what I was getting at. "Why were you teetering around on skates at the roller rink when you were already a skateboard deity?"

Lia laughed. "Brogan doesn't roller skate."

When Brogan didn't say anything, Dylan raised an eyebrow.

Summer stifled a giggle. "Wait, did you two meet before that day at the park?"

"We did," Brogan said. "Sometimes I like to try new things. Prove to myself that I'm still alive, you know? That week it was roller skating. The week before, it was BMX biking. I've gone cliff diving, surfing, even salsa dancing. But that day at the roller rink was the most dangerous by far. I almost lost my head thanks to some crazy girl with a traitorous phone and a killer arm."

He grinned, shifting in his seat so he was looking straight at me. "And then, later, I lost my head for real when…"

He trailed off but kept his gaze locked on mine, and I knew he was referring to my botched kiss. But was it possible that, to him, I hadn't botched it? That it had actually been this life-altering, earth-shattering thing?

"That day, my life made sense," he finished.

My body filled with heat—a roiling, maddening thing that made me want to laugh and cry and just stay in this moment for all of time. A smile crept onto my face. I became hyper-aware of Brogan's thigh beside mine. And his hand, resting on top of his thigh, right beside my hand.

His pinky twitched and brushed my skin. The tiniest hint of a question. He was asking, apologizing, hoping. Maybe we could start over.

I slid my hand into his.

An answer, an acceptance, and an apology.

He grabbed on, winding his fingers through mine like he was drowning and I was air.

Fireworks went off in my chest.

Dylan said, "Wait, I'm confused. You lost your head for real when what? And how did losing your head help you make sense of your life?"

Dylan, Summer, and Lia were all waiting for the conversation to continue. But Brogan and I had just finished it, silently, on our own.

Then Slate slid into the booth beside Dylan. "Okay, I've got fifteen minutes. What's up?"

Chapter Twenty-Five: That Night

Brogan squeezed my hand under the table. "Slate, this is Aspen. She's a skater, and she needs your help."

Everyone turned to me. I took a deep breath.

Knowing we only had fifteen minutes, I spoke quickly, giving as many details as I could about that night. When I mentioned the pictures and vulgar comments, Brogan tensed beside me.

"I don't remember anything after taking a sip of my friend's drink and following her onstage. But even if someone spiked her drink, it doesn't make sense that a few sips would have made me do the stuff I did without remembering anything. I was hoping you might have seen or heard something that would help me figure out what really happened that night. And why does the manager seem scared of me?"

Slate leaned forward, his voice quiet and low. "This club is real strict about not serving booze to minors. Another bar was shut down recently after authorities found out a date rape drug was being dealt in the bathrooms, and Mike, the manager, has been worried about it coming here ever since. We saw you and your friend go onstage, and we all knew you were drunk, but nobody fessed up to serving you alcohol. That's probably why he was being cagey."

"So, did you see someone tampering with our drinks?" I pressed.

"I didn't see anything," Slate said. "I was working the bar, not waiting tables."

His words sat in the air, heavy with meaning.

Duh, we needed to talk to one of the waitresses. Slate was on it before I'd even said anything. He slid out of the booth and came back a moment later with a girl.

She had short black hair, cut in a severe downward angle that stopped at her chin. Her nametag said *Genny.*

Slate said, "I've got to go back on, but this is Gen. She was on that night, and you can trust her. Plus, she owes me a favor." He winked at her. To me, he said, "I hope you find what you're looking for."

I didn't have it in me to tell the whole story again, so I gave Genny a condensed version, then said, "So, did you see anyone messing with our drinks?"

Genny scrunched up her nose. "There were a ton of people at your table, and not all of them were underage."

I sat up straighter. Drake had said something like that, too. "College guys, you mean?"

"Yeah, I think so. And I remember your friend— the one working the microphone like a pole."

"Zuri," I supplied.

Genny went on. "She wanted one of those Cokes sweetened with stevia. We don't typically serve those, but I found some samples in the back. When I came back with it, there was this girl hanging around that wasn't there before. And, I don't know, she looked like she didn't quite fit."

I sat up straighter. "What do you mean, she didn't fit?"

"Well, you can just tell, you know? Which sort of people fit together. She was dressed different, had a different way about her. Like she was uncomfortable. The rest of you were all right at home, with the music and the guys and the dancing. But she looked like a fish out of water."

Was she talking about Sara?

"The girl was giving your friend something," Genny continued. "Looked like a pill—I assumed it was an Advil or something—but then she stuck around even though your friend stopped paying attention to her."

"What did she look like?" I asked.

"Brown hair, twisted up in a messy bun. Sort-of plain features."

Hmm, Sara was one of those platinum blondes, and her hair was too short to fit into a bun.

"And, get this," Genny added. "The girl was taking pictures. With one of those big, professional-looking cameras."

I didn't mean to, but my gaze slipped to Summer. Brown hair in a messy bun. Professional camera. Uncomfortable in a group of people.

Summer didn't notice my eyes on her. I looked away quickly, mentally kicking myself.

My voice came out a bit wobbly. "What was she taking pictures of?"

Genny shrugged. "Just everything. The club, the band, the crowd. A lot of people take pictures, but it was weird because she wasn't in any of them. And nobody posed for her. It seemed more like she was documenting something."

Another waitress breezed by our table and, when she saw Genny sitting with us, stopped dead in her tracks "Seriously? I've been covering your tables for you—I thought you were taking a serious dump."

"Oh, sorry, Mal," Genny said, jumping up. "Hey, good luck," she yelled at us as she hurried away.

Everyone at the table leaned in and started talking at once. I couldn't tell who was saying what.

"Pictures? That has to be R33S!"

"Aspen, do you know anyone who looks like that?"

"You know, she might not have anything to do with it. Maybe it's just a coincidence."

"Don't forget about those older guys—they were

probably drinking."

I said, "Well, now we have a new lead at least. Maybe Zuri will remember who gave her medicine that night and we can work from there."

We sat back and listened to the band. Despite the fact that Brogan's hand was still comfortably around mine, my mind was in knots. When we slid out of the bench later that night, I dropped Brogan's hand. I wasn't ready for anyone else to know about this. Not until I knew what it was myself.

On our way out, Brogan's brother called him over. Lia slumped an arm around my shoulder. "This is some crazy shiz, girl. Date rape drugs are no joke—are you sure you grabbed the right drink? Maybe that friend of yours—Chase, I think you called him—maybe he slipped something into Rhea's drink and you took hers on accident."

I recoiled. "Chase would never do that. He was drunk and acting stupid, but he's a good guy."

That's when it hit me. Chase was drunk that night. He'd used it as an excuse several times. But if the bartenders had been so sure not to serve us alcohol, how had Chase gotten some?

****

Dylan dropped me off first. I'd been hoping to have more time with Brogan before we all went home, but I lived closest to the club. And Lia ended up being squished between us in the backseat, due to some obvious poor planning on my part.

I climbed out of the car, but hesitated before shutting the door behind me.

Lia slid out of the middle seat and into the one I'd just vacated.

Brogan caught my eye and winked.

"Hey, thanks for coming with me. It meant a lot

that you were all there."

"We'll get to the bottom of this," Summer said. "I know we will. See you tomorrow."

Tomorrow.

What was tomorrow again?

"The photo shoot," Summer said, reminding me. "Mollie's sending a car."

Right. And then the demolition derby thing. It was a good thing we'd be wearing masks—nobody would be able to see the lack-of-sleep circles under my eyes. Because there was no way I'd be sleeping anytime soon.

Going to the club had filled in a couple missing pieces of my puzzle, but it had also made the puzzle bigger. How had Chase gotten drunk? Was he the one who'd spiked our drinks? Or was it the college guys? And who was the girl taking pictures?

It was well after midnight, and my house was dark. I let myself in through the garage, the inside door creaking slightly as I opened it. I eased it shut and crept toward the stairs.

A voice, thick with sleep, made me jump. "Aspen, is that you?"

I whirled around and saw a figure sitting on the couch—my dad. A dim table-lamp was on beside him. A book of Sudoku puzzles sat in his lap.

"Come sit." He patted the empty spot of couch beside him. His hair was mussed up and, even though it was short, I saw the echo of my own rebellious curls.

I did not have the mental capacity for this right now, but I went over and sat down, eyeing his hands. They were rough and scarred in places. It was a constant reminder that he'd worked his entire life in thankless, labor-intensive jobs—which he'd started right after high school when his mom died. All he'd ever wanted was for our lives to be better than his.

It wasn't fair. It really wasn't.

But he was still happy—it seemed like he always was, actually—despite the disappointments and pain life had dealt him.

He stifled a yawn. "So, want to tell me where you've been?"

I hesitated. This was my Dad—I couldn't lie to him. But the truth was such a tangled mess, it would take all night to catch him up. And I didn't want to worry him.

"I was just with some friends. Why are you still awake?"

"I'm doing nerd puzzles." He held up the Sudoku pad. "It's very important work, you know. And this particular one was just so riveting, I couldn't put it down."

I smiled, knowing the truth—he'd been waiting up for me. And struggling to stay awake.

My throat suddenly felt thick.

"We haven't talked much lately," he said.

I swallowed, but the thickness in my throat only got worse. "I know, I'm sorry. I've just been busy." I hesitated. Maybe I could tell him a little bit about what I'd been up to. I could just leave out all the crappy parts.

He raised an eyebrow.

"Okay, so I've been doing something crazy." I took a deep breath. "I found a pair of Jojo's old skates in the garage a while back and decided to start skating."

"Really?" He sounded just as skeptical as if I'd told him I was learning to fly.

Well, I *was* learning to fly. I just wore the wings on my feet.

"I'm not playing roller derby," I clarified. "I just wanted to skate. Like, outside, at the park. I've been doing tricks … picture a skateboarder on roller skates. There's this skate park nearby, and I've been going there with some new friends. Here, I'll show you."

I pulled up the first video Dylan had posted of us and played it for him.

When it finished, he said, "Wow. That looks dangerous."

"Well, not really. I always wear a helmet. And kneepads, and wrist guards and all that stuff, especially when I'm learning new tricks. Sure, I've gotten lots of scrapes and bruises, but it's not like I'm skydiving or anything. It's fun. When I skate, I feel like I'm flying, even more than I used to in gymnastics."

Dad studied me. "Well, you certainly look happy when you talk about it."

"Yeah. It makes me feel good."

"But when you came in just now, you didn't look happy."

Oh, man. How could I explain to him everything else that was going on?

The truth was that I couldn't. He'd feel the pain with me, because that's what a good dad did. But he had enough pain of his own—I couldn't add to his load, I just couldn't.

So I put on a smile. "I'm fine, Dad, I promise. Just stressed about school." I left it at that. There was no need to tell him that the reason school was stressful these days was not because of tests or grades.

"How's the puzzle coming?" I pulled his Sudoku out and studied the squares, eyeing the way the numbers fit together and waiting for them to make some sort of sense to me. Jojo always said they would if I just gave it enough time.

But they never did.

Chapter Twenty-Six: The Darkroom

We did the photo shoot.

We did the skating gig.

And we were amazing. The crowd loved us and Mollie loved us. It felt like the sky was at our fingertips and that if I simply reached up, I could grab a cloud. I was Skate-or-Dye, through and through. I didn't think about R33S or Rhea or Chase or anything else not related to skating.

But then, Monday morning, I had to be Aspen again.

I had to think about the gossip, because I still had some digging to do—a lot of digging, actually—and I wasn't looking forward to where I had to start. As I pulled open the door to the school, something caught my eye. A square stuck to the door frame that looked a lot like…

No way.

It was our new Flippin' Skaters logo—this must be one of the bumper stickers Skateopia had been handing out. Seeing it here made me smile. And it made me feel stronger.

Then, walking down the hallway, I saw one stuck to the back of someone's binder. A Flippin' Skaters keychain dangled from another person's backpack, and I even passed a guy wearing a Flippin' Skaters t-shirt. There were flyers on every bulletin board I passed announcing our events—the state fair we'd already done, a monster truck rally, a mall opening, and a string of similar events.

The smile died on my face when I reached my locker and saw a fresh set of vulgar drawings—the first in weeks—scrawled across the surface in black Sharpie. I didn't quite have it in me to appreciate the irony that crap like this kept happening even while support for my alter ego took off. Right now, I needed to bury all the hurt and focus on the task at hand—figuring out who had done this to me. I slammed my locker shut and headed for the cafeteria.

The permanent smell of cheap pizza and nacho cheese hit me before I'd even entered the room, even though it was hours before lunch. I stepped through the double doors and walked right up to the table where my former friends gathered every morning before school to discuss lipstick colors and run through all the latest gossip.

This morning they were talking about a girl on the volleyball team who, apparently, had not been born a girl. She'd transferred in from another school this year, as a senior. Everyone was wondering if the coach had known when he let her on the team. There was even an online poll.

People were sick.

Zuri noticed me first and looked down, suddenly hyper-focused on peeling her nail polish.

"Hey," I said.

The other girls looked up from their phones. Some of them mirrored Zuri's reaction, looking away carefully like they had something to be ashamed of. Sara was one of them. Rhea and some of the others just stared me down.

An apology sat on the tip of my tongue: *I'm sorry for using Taylor against you and I'm sorry for being a crappy friend...*

... even though you deserved it.

Yeah, I wasn't sure I wanted to apologize. She should apologize to me.

I ignored Rhea and everyone else and walked

right up to Zuri. "That night at the club, someone gave you some medicine. Who was it?"

Zuri's eyebrows arched up. "Umm."

"There was a girl there taking pictures, and she gave you some medicine—don't even try to deny it—I was at the bar last night and one of the waitresses saw it."

Zuri's eyes darted to the side. "Was that before...?" She trailed off, like she wasn't sure what to say next.

For the first time, it occurred to me that Zuri's memory might be as fuzzy as mine. I softened my tone. "Yes, before we got up onstage. How much do you remember about that night?"

Rhea stepped in between me and Zuri. "I don't need you messing with my girls' heads. You can go now."

I bristled. "Seriously? What is your problem? Zuri has a mind of her own—she doesn't need you controlling it for her."

Rhea seemed to grow in stature. "Well, right now, she's on *my* squad, and *we* are preparing for states. We can't have any distractions."

"Oh, you mean like reality? Because I know something very wrong went down that night. Zuri and I are victims, Rhea, and I would think that you, more than anyone else, would want to get to the bottom of it since the mental well-being of your squad is so important to you." I felt my face go red as heads at nearby tables swiveled to face us.

Rhea was getting heated as well. "The only thing that went down that night was that my squad stayed out too late and ignored the guidelines to keep themselves mentally and physically fit. Alcohol is not approved. I left early, and everyone else should have, too."

"Whatever. You left because you didn't want

Chase to see you with Drake."

Rhea was shaking. "Well, I've certainly never made a drunken fool out of myself in front of the whole school. I know you were the instigator of what happened that night, Aspen. Zuri just got caught up in it, and I won't let her take the fall for your bad behavior."

My hands were clenched so tightly that my fingers were going numb. How could Rhea possibly believe the garbage she was spouting? It was so completely ridiculous.

I stepped around Rhea and spoke to Zuri. "If you remember anything, you can talk to me. Maybe we can help each other remember. I want to get to the bottom of this just as much as you do."

I glanced at Sara. Her lower lip was trembling. She pulled out her phone and started tapping on it.

Rhea saw. "You'd better not be texting her," she said through clenched teeth.

Sara jumped and hastily turned off her phone.

Wait, *had* she been texting me?

Had Rhea somehow been monitoring the girls' phones? Was that why nobody was answering my texts anymore?

I didn't have it in me to be subtle. "Sara, where did you move here from again?"

She blinked, clearly thrown off by the question. "Uh, Kansas."

I faltered. "So, not Eastern Seattle, then?"

"No."

Hmm. I turned to Rhea. "You know, once they lose respect for you, it's only a matter of time before you have no control at all. Fear can only motivate for so long." I whirled around and stalked away, ignoring the sea of gazes that followed me. The one bonus of hitting rock bottom was that you had the luxury of not giving a crap.

Flippin' Skaters posters lined the hall like sentinels as I hurried away without a destination, trying to outrun all the things I didn't understand. I'd gone to Zuri for answers, not realizing that she wouldn't have any. And Sara didn't fit the description of the girl taking pictures, nor had she come from a squad we'd be competing against. Who was left?

A voice behind me said, "Aspen?"

I froze.

It was Chase. And he did not sound okay.

I turned around.

He was advancing toward me, his hands in his pockets and a guarded expression on his face. "What did you mean back there? When you said Rhea left because she didn't want me to see her with Drake?"

Oh no.

No.

I swallowed. "Chase, I…"

Something in his eyes made me stop. There was no way to save this. I had to tell him—no excuses, no lies.

The collar of Chase's t-shirt was worn and starting to fray, and I focused on that as I spoke. "Rhea was with Drake. That night at the club, when you couldn't find her—she was cheating on you. I told her to tell you—she should have told you—"

He cut me off. "*You* should have told me."

I looked up, finally meeting his gaze. "I'm sorry, Chase. I'm so, so sorry."

His expression was guarded. His jaw clenched and unclenched. "You should have told me," he repeated. Then he turned and walked away.

And in my mind's eye I saw a sandcastle crumbling.

****

I needed Summer. She would help me figure things out.

What was I going to do about Chase? What *could* I do about Chase? And now that I knew Zuri didn't remember anything, what was my next move?

Summer didn't answer my text asking if she could meet up for lunch, but she usually spent her breaks in the darkroom where we'd first met, so that's where I went.

I eased the door open and peeked in. "Summer?"

The room, as always, was silent and dark. I stepped in, closed the door behind me, and waited for my eyes to adjust. The first time we'd met, I'd thought the room was empty when it actually wasn't. "Summer?" I tried again. "Hello? Is anybody in here?"

It was silent, except for the gentle whir of a small fan circulating air in a corner. I stepped farther into the room, finding it empty. There was a row of recently developed pictures drying from a wire and I wandered over.

Wait ... was that...?

I peered closer at the nearest picture, taken in a locker room. It featured the latest victim of social media—the trans girl from the volleyball team. She was a senior, but I recognized her as one of the few friendly faces I'd encountered those first few days back at school. I thought her name was Ruth.

Beside the picture of Ruth was a picture of Ronald, and beside that was one of Saraya. Last was Keir, the baseball pitcher.

And then my throat went dry as I realized exactly what I was seeing ... these were physical copies of the pictures R33S had posted. Here, finally, was a lead.

I hadn't actually seen the post about Ruth—I'd only heard about it—but I could guess what picture of her was now online.

I continued down the row, my heart beating faster. The next picture was an artistic close-up of a single drink sitting on a table. The room and people in the background were fuzzy, but I could just make out two girls on a stage: me and Zuri.

My fingers found my bracelet. I tugged and twisted on the leather, pulling it tight around my wrist as I moved on.

And then my breath hitched in my throat.

Because the next few pictures had been taken at a skate park I knew like the back of my hand.

What was happening right now? Had R33S been spying on me at the skate park?

Or ... had R33S been *with* me at the skate park?

My world rocked. Like I was suddenly in one of those spinning tunnels at the fair, and it was spinning and spinning and I didn't know how to get off.

The logical conclusion was that Summer had been the girl taking pictures at the club that night, and that she was R33S. Because all the pictures were here, mashed up together—pictures from the club, pictures R33S had posted, and pictures of our skating sessions.

But that didn't make any sense. Summer was my friend. It couldn't have been her. And for all the times we'd talked about—or delicately avoided talking about—that night at the club, she'd never once hinted that she'd been there.

Then I remembered a few weeks ago when I'd asked to see some of her pictures. She'd freaked out, spouting something about the camera belonging to the school and how she didn't want me to break it and that her pictures weren't that good anyway. Maybe she'd actually been worried I'd see something that would give her away.

No. I shook my head, banishing the thoughts. There had to be another explanation. Summer wouldn't do something like that.

Unless she'd just been pretending to be my friend. Was it possible that the one real friend I'd thought I had had been faking it this whole time? Was this all some elaborate scheme to do something really clever and mean that I couldn't quite connect the dots to?

Again. No.

I refused to believe Summer could do anything that underhanded and mean. Summer was different.

But these photos belonged to somebody.

I pulled my phone out and started snapping pics so I could study them later. Because I felt sure I was missing something. And then someone pushed open the door and entered the room. I darted behind a table and crouched down, tucking my phone away.

The person's face was in shadow, but the outline of hair twisted into a pile on top of her head gave it away. The bun even had a pencil stuck through the middle, just like the first time I'd met her.

It was Summer.

She closed the door.

I waited for my eyes to readjust to the darkness, and then stood up. I tried to make my voice light. "Hey, Summer."

She jumped. "Aspen! What are you doing in here?"

"I was looking for you." I darted a glance at the row of pictures.

"Have you seen all the Flippin' Skaters stuff? Mollie said they had an event at the store over the weekend and gave out a bunch of free merch. I texted Dylan—it's the same at his school."

If those pictures were hers, she was acting totally

oblivious to the fact that I might have seen them.

She headed for the row of pictures, all the way to the end where the skating ones were. "Wanna see my latest shots? They've been drying all weekend—I didn't have time to get them until now."

"Well, um." I faltered.

She stopped, studying me. "What's wrong?"

"Nothing." I fiddled with my bracelet. "I just, already saw the pictures. They're really good."

"Oh." She eyed me, then turned back to the pictures. "Thanks." She started unclipping them, working down the line toward the pictures of the social media victims.

Okay, the other pictures clearly weren't hers—if they were she would have freaked as soon as I told her I'd seen them. But, then, whose were they?

I was just about to ask her who else had access to this room when she sucked in a breath. "Aspen, did you see this? I think that's you." She continued down the line of pictures. "And all the other R33S victims..." She trailed off.

Then she whirled around. "Wait, did you think these shots were mine? They aren't, obviously, the angles are all wrong and I would have used different lighting."

"I know," I said, even though I hadn't known about the lighting and angles.

She narrowed her eyes as she studied me.

I fidgeted.

When she spoke, her voice was soft. "That's why you were acting weird when I came in, wasn't it? Because you thought these shots were mine." Her voice broke on the last word.

"No!" I spluttered. "I mean, maybe at first, but seriously only for like a sec—"

She cut me off, hurt flashing in her eyes. "Aspen,

how could you think I would do something like that to you, even for one second? I have been nothing but your friend, even agreeing to those stupid face masks just to keep you happy."

"I know, I'm sorry."

"A lot of people use this room, you know—anyone taking a photography class, plus yearbook people and school newspaper people and some students who just like to take pictures and have gotten permission to use the room." She was breathing hard.

"I promise, I knew it wasn't you. I was just confused for the tiniest little second. This morning I confronted Rhea again, but didn't really get any answers, but then Chase heard the whole thing and now he's mad at me…" I trailed off. "I was hoping you could help me sort things out."

She shook her head—one slow shake. "You are just like all the other popular kids. I thought you were different." She turned and gathered up her pictures, then headed for the door. She paused with one hand on the knob. "Just so you know, I was with my great-grandma for her ninetieth birthday the weekend your social life crumbled. My mom posted pictures and tagged me in them so you can check up on me if you really want, even though a real friend wouldn't have to. Have a nice life, Aspen."

"Summer, wait!"

The sound of the door slamming was her only reply.

Wait … *have a nice life?* We had practice this afternoon, and an event this weekend. She couldn't be mad enough to want to throw all that away because of a silly misunderstanding.

Had she really not been at the club that night?

I scrambled to open my social feed and typed in

Summer's name. I scrolled back through her pics and found them—several of her with an old lady wearing a birthday crown and blowing out a cake full of candles the same night I'd been at the club.

My face burned in shame. I shouldered my bag and walked to the door, trying to figure out how I'd believed, even for one second, that Summer was capable of betraying me.

Then a voice said, "The pictures are mine, actually."

Chapter Twenty-Seven: Farther to Fall

My heart skipped into my throat as I whirled to see who had spoken.

A figure stood from a stool beside a tall cabinet at the back of the room. "So, do you like them?"

"Huh?"

"My pictures—do you like them?" The voice sounded female.

"Not really."

The figure walked over and started clipping them down. "They should be dry—I slipped in last night during the PTO meeting to work on them and came back to check on them just before you showed up."

I yanked out my phone and turned on the flashlight, shining it in the speaker's face.

It was Marissa. And she had long, dark hair, similar to Summer's.

She snatched the phone out of my hand. "This is a darkroom—you can't just go shining light everywhere." She turned the flashlight off and plunked my phone down on a table.

My body shook, simmering with an emotion too big to name. "Why do you have these pictures?"

"For my story."

Right. Marissa wrote for the school newspaper.

The simmering turned to a boil. "What story?" My voice sounded strained. It was the lid on a teakettle ready to wail.

"The story that's going to earn me a scholarship to Northwestern." Marissa hadn't looked at me since she'd snatched my phone away, and was now taking her photos down and laying them carefully on a table.

"You're writing a story about us?" I waved an

arm to indicate everyone in the pictures. "How is that right?"

"Oh, it's not. Or, maybe it is. Maybe you all deserved it and I'm just giving Karma a helping hand. I don't really care either way. It's a great story idea."

I narrowed my eyes at her. "It was you, wasn't it? You're the one who spiked my drink and drugged Zuri. You orchestrated everything."

Was this why she was always hanging around being fake-nice and offering a shoulder to cry on? Because she was looking for dirt?

For the first time, Marissa deigned to look at me. "Oh, grow up. Nobody orchestrated anything. And I definitely didn't drug Zuri's drink—I just gave her a Midol."

"But you were at the club that night."

"Of course. How else would I have gotten all those great shots?"

"Shots which you then posted?"

"Naturally." Marissa blew on one of the photographs, then clipped it back up. "But that was one photo shoot I did not orchestrate. You girls did that all on your own."

My hands clenched and unclenched by my side. "I definitely didn't get myself drunk, if that's what you're saying."

Marissa raised an eyebrow. "Whatever you say."

A rattling was building up inside me, filling me with pressure I didn't know how to relieve. "What about the others? You've been systematically targeting people from different groups and taking them down."

Marissa scoffed. "You are so clueless. I haven't been targeting anyone. I'm a silent observer—a gatherer, if you will—scooping up news wherever it is. I'm turning the stuff people do to each other every day into a social experiment. How much pressure can each nut take? What has to happen to get them to crack? Stuff like that. It's going to earn me a scholarship—you'll see."

"You can't just write an article messing up everyone's lives."

"Oh, really? Who's going to stop me?"

I put my hands on my hips.

She laughed. "You? You can't even keep one single friend. How are you going to get anyone to listen to you? I'm not breaking any rules, and I'm not hurting anyone. I'm just reporting the facts."

Hissing, screaming rage filled me from top to bottom. I shook with the sheer force of it. "You're not *hurting* anyone? What about the string of people whose lives have gone down the toilet since you started your little experiment?"

Marissa stopped what she was doing and looked at me, hard. Then she said, "Oh, wow. *Wow.* You really think this is a new thing? That you were the first in a stream of masterminded social media take-downs? Grow up, Aspen. This stuff happens all. The. Time. You were just too self-centered to notice until it actually happened to you. And, by the way, you're welcome—you needed a good hard look at your friendships."

"My friendships were fine until you started messing with them."

"Were they, though? Those pictures were actually a litmus test, revealing the true colors of your friends. So, again, you're welcome. Now you don't have to live a lie." She did a little curtsy.

"You are unbeliev—"

She cut me off. "That Chase, though, he's the real deal—you should hang on to him."

I actually snorted. "Friends don't post pictures like that."

Her eyes widened in surprise. "Oh, I thought for sure he would have told you … but, yeah, maybe he was too drunk to remember. He didn't make that post about you, I did. From his phone."

Hold up.

What?

"How'd you get his phone unlocked?"

She shrugged. "I told him mine died and asked if I could borrow his to call my mom."

The teakettle inside me shattered, sending razor-sharp shards flying through the air. "You're wrong. This stuff does *not* happen all the time, and you are a truly terrible person." I was shaking. Marissa was to blame for my social downfall, and that of the others. "You're R33S, aren't you?"

She blew on one of her photos and examined it. "I am."

"So, what, you posted once from Chase's phone and then again as R33S?"

"Yep."

She was so smug and cavalier it made me want to puke and then wipe her face in it. "How'd you know all that stuff, anyway, about the others? Did you break into the front office or something?"

Again, she laughed. "I told you, I haven't done anything wrong. You can learn a lot if you just pay attention. I notice things—details other people miss—and then I stay close and observe."

"What does that stupid code name even mean?"

"It's my nickname, and the name I write under— Rees. If you write it in all caps and turn the Es backward it becomes R33S. A good writer never passes up an opportunity to include her byline." She smirked.

I felt sick. And drained. Marissa had definitely orchestrated everything. I didn't buy it for one single second that she hadn't. She probably did break into the office—maybe she'd left some fingerprints or something.

But … wait…

She'd tagged her work along the way with her byline, R33S. That might actually help me put together a case against her. I just had to figure out how she'd initiated it—she had to have messed with my drink somehow. Maybe she'd used some sort of date rape drug. She could probably go to jail for that.

Why hadn't I been recording this conversation? Then I could go straight to the administration and take her down. But I hadn't been that smart. I searched for the perfect words instead—a fiery retort that would cut to her core. But I had nothing.

So I headed for the exit. "You're a horrible person."

"Says the girl who took her friend down with her," she fired back. "You might want to research Zannies, by the way."

I slammed the door behind me and put some distance between myself and the darkroom, trying to ignore what she'd said.

But I couldn't.

Why would she say I'd taken my friend down with me? Which friend was she referring to? And what the heck were Zannies?

Chapter Twenty-Eight: Digging for Truth

A folded-up piece of paper slid out of my locker at the end of the day. I unfolded it, angling myself so the note was inside my locker as I read.

Aspen—

I'm sorry I couldn't help you today in the cafeteria. Rhea has been crazy, demanding that we not talk to you. She even checks our phones before each practice and she made us all delete your contact info. Something's up with her, but nobody wants to say anything after what she did to you. I think we're all just waiting for states to be over before rocking the boat too much.

So, yeah, I'm going old-school here. Zuri doesn't remember going onstage, and I guess you don't either. There was a girl hanging around our table talking to Zuri, but I didn't pay much attention to her once all the cute guys came over. And Chase was wasted. He showed up at the table halfway through your, um, performance.

Also… and you might want to sit down for this … I overheard Rhea talking about how she tagged your locker a few times—I think she did the baby coupons, too. I'm still not sure why she's so pissed. Actually, I'm not sure why she does anything anymore. It's like she's Jekyll and Hyde these days and we're all just trying not to get eaten.

For what it's worth, everyone misses you and we all hate what happened. It's super messed up.

—Sara

I slammed my locker shut, then pounded a fist against the Sharpied artwork.

Why, Rhea?

Okay. I didn't care what Marissa said or how

many times she denied it—she'd been at the club, and she *must* have started it all.

The grass outside was damp and the sky overcast, but it wasn't raining. Chase was all geared up for practice, heading out to the football field. He probably didn't want to see me, but this couldn't wait.

I yelled his name.

He didn't react, so I tried again, louder. "Chase!"

He turned around. The shadow from his football helmet hid his expression, but his movements were stiff as he jogged toward me, helmet strap flapping beneath his chin.

"Aspen, practice is about to start. Why are you here?"

"Chase, I'm really, *really* sorry for not telling you about Rhea. I just knew it would hurt you, and I didn't want to do that to you."

He sniffed. "Okay. Is that all?"

"Um … no." I fidgeted, took a deep breath, and dove in. "How did you get drunk the night Appellooza played? The bartenders weren't serving alcohol to minors."

He frowned. "Huh?"

"Last night I went to the music club to try and figure out what really happened—why I would have gotten on stage in my underwear—and they claimed they wouldn't have given me alcohol because I'm a minor. But I was obviously under the influence of something or I wouldn't have done what I did. Since the club didn't serve it to me, I'm trying to figure out who did." I caught his gaze and held it. "*You* had booze that night. Did Marissa give it to you? Did she tell you to spike our drinks?"

Chase's expression froze into one of careful composure. "I wasn't dr—"

"Don't even try to deny it," I said, cutting him off. "I knew you were drunk when you asked me to find Rhea. And you've said yourself—more than once—that you were wasted that night. Is that how Marissa got you to unlock your phone for her?"

Chase fidgeted. "Who's Marissa?"

"You know, that girl on the school newspaper who acts like everyone's best friend? She's the one who posted the first picture of me, and she did it from your phone, as you."

His expression went blank.

"Come on, Chase. You owe me the truth." I held his gaze.

He ran a hand down his face, squeezing his eyes shut. When he opened them, he said, "Aspen, if I tell you what happened, you have to promise not to blab. To anyone."

All the blood drained from my face and pooled at my feet, anchoring me in place. So there *was* something to tell. My head bobbed up and down in a nod.

Chase closed the distance between us and said quietly, "There was this waitress. I met her the weekend before at a party, and when she saw me that night, she invited me outside during her break."

I raised an eyebrow. Why would a hot, twenty-something waitress waste time on a high school guy?

He shrugged, hearing my unasked question. "She thought I was older."

"Was this before or after you asked me to find Rhea?"

Chase looked at me like I was an idiot. "Before."

It took me a beat to figure out what he was saying. And then I realized. "Did Rhea know?"

Chase nodded. "She found me out there. I'd already had three beers by then. Tam—" Chase stopped and amended. "The waitress had a stash of booze outside. She and a couple of the others keep it out there for their breaks. If they just take a little, then the customers and bosses don't notice, and it takes the drag out of being at work while everyone else is partying. That's what she told me, anyway."

My head spun, everything suddenly going off kilter. Rhea wasn't the bad guy after all. Chase was. He'd cheated on her first, and then she'd cheated to get back at him.

But, wait, she'd said Drake wasn't the first. So maybe she had actually been the first to cheat and then Chase had cheated to get back at her and it had turned into this cycle. Did Chase know about the others, though? He'd seemed totally thrown by learning Rhea had been making out with Drake. Maybe he hadn't known about any of them.

Oh, this was so messed up. Both of my former best friends were liars and cheats.

Chase sighed. "Look, Aspen, I messed up. I get it. And I deserve whatever Rhea throws at me. But I had nothing to do with getting you drunk, I *swear*. I would never do anything to hurt you. And I don't remember loaning my phone to anyone, but I guess I could have. That makes more sense to me than the idea that I would have ever posted that stuff about you, even if I was drunk. You're my best friend."

I sniffed. *Best friend.* What did those words even mean anymore?

"Hey, don't snitch on the waitresses at the club. They shouldn't go down for this."

I frowned, studying him. "But someone should. Tell me how Marissa comes into play. What did she do to get me to act like that?"

"Nothing. At least, not that I know of."

His words hit me like a physical blow. Marissa so obviously had something to do with it. She had all those pictures. She'd admitted outright that she was using us to get a scholarship. She had to have set the whole thing up.

The coach blew a whistle, and Chase's teammates ran out to the field. Chase fastened his helmet strap under his chin, then hesitated, eyeing me. "Are you okay?"

"I haven't been okay in months." I swiped a hand across my face, feeling totally and completely drained. "But I am sorry I didn't tell you about Rhea. Really and truly. I should have been a better friend."

"Okay." It was all he said. He gave me one final look and then joined his teammates on the field.

****

As I stalked away from the football field, I pulled out my phone and saw I'd missed some texts—one from Dylan and one from Jojo. The first had come in right at the end of school, probably as I was reading that note from Sara.

Dylan: **summer says no practice today. Everything ok?**

That was a loaded question. The text had come over an hour ago and Summer had probably filled him in by now anyway, so I just left it.

I started typing out an apology to Summer, but something made me stop. She was the most real friend I'd ever had, and I'd basically accused her of stabbing me in the back. For all she knew, I actually believed she had. I could not fix this over text.

Not that I knew how to fix it at all—this was bigger than I knew how to handle. But, one way or another, I was going to figure it out. Summer's friendship was worth fighting for. So I simply wrote:

Aspen: **can I come over?**

Send.

I waited.

Summer didn't respond.

Maybe she just needed some time.

I moved on to my next missed message—a text from Jojo that had come in just after Dylan's.

Jojo: **are you coming to my bout tonight? We can go out for ice cream after, just us. Its been a while since we talked and I neeeeed to hear how the skating is going**

Then fifteen minutes after that.

Jojo: **so are we on for ice cream?**

She'd probably be in practice by now, but I texted her back.

Aspen: **sorry, busy afternoon. sure lets hang tonight**

Normally I would have included a smiley face or a heart or something, but I just didn't have it in me today.

I also didn't have it in me to go home. I needed to think, and, although my bedroom was the ideal place to do that, I couldn't bear facing my family. The conversation I'd had with my dad the other night had been hard enough. And now I'd lost every single friend I had. I was afraid that, at a single glance from my mom, I'd start crying and never stop.

I'd tell her everything, and then she'd tell me it would be okay, but that it would get worse before it got better and that I'd just have to tough things out a bit longer. And then I'd tough it out and, hopefully, it would get better. So what point was there in breaking down about it now?

The answer was that there was no point. I was better off avoiding my mom and all of her motherly perceptiveness until things got better. Until I made them better by figuring out how Marissa had caused my social downfall, finding solid proof—beyond some anonymous profiles and a few incriminating pictures—and bringing her to justice. For me and for everyone else she'd victimized.

Then I could honestly look my mom in the face and say 'fine' when she asked how my day was. But today I couldn't say fine, and I didn't feel like explaining why.

So I went to the local library, found a quiet spot, and pulled out a piece of paper. I wrote down all the names of Marissa's victims and listed everything I knew about them.

The list included two cheerleaders, a brainiac, a nerd, a jock, and an all-around nice girl. The classic eclectic eighties movie gathering. But real life was never that neat. Marissa had to be choosing her targets strategically. What had she called it ... a social experiment?

I rested my head on my arms and closed my eyes.

When my eyes fluttered open, the shadows filtering through the library windows had shifted. A lot.

Oh, no, what time was it?

I glanced at my phone—I'd spent so long at the library that my family had probably already left to watch the pre-show and see Jojo warm up. I could take the bus and meet them there, but I really didn't want to see my family, and I really didn't want to sit and watch other people skate. Right now, *I* needed to skate.

So I went home to get my gear, then headed to the park. I'd just need to leave with enough time to catch the end of Jojo's bout so we could meet up for ice cream. She'd never even know I missed the main event.

Chapter Twenty-Nine: Climbing Trees

Brogan and Lia were teaching some younger skaters how to slide the rail when I got to the skate park. I debated going over to say hi, but I really just needed to think. Plus, I hadn't seen Brogan since we'd held hands a few nights ago and things might be awkward.

So I put on my mask like I always did when I skated and took a lap around the park to warm up. Then I started in on the course Summer, Dylan, and I usually did at the beginning of each practice. I ended in the bowl where, most recently, we'd been crafting a twist on the classic skateboarding ollie 360, but for roller skaters.

My legs were on fire, but I skated on, loving the feel of my wheels gliding over the smooth pavement and hearing the scrape of skateboards in the background. I didn't love the feeling inside my heart, though—I'd broken something valuable and I had no idea how to fix it.

The streetlights creeped on as I skated, the artificial light growing so subtly that I almost didn't notice. When I stopped for a break, Lia was packing up. I scanned the area for Brogan, but he was nowhere in sight. The younger boys were scattering, heading home.

"Hey, Aspen," Lia called. "Where's your gang?"

I skated over. "Just me today."

Lia pulled the ponytail holder out of her hair and let her half-head of braids fall loose.

"Where's Brogan?" The words slipped out before I could stop them. I bit my lip, wishing I could take them back.

Lia grinned. "He left. But I saw him looking your way more than once."

My face warmed.

"Are you done for the day?" Lia said.

"Nope, just taking a break."

"Cool. Well, you have the park to yourself. Have fun." Lia pulled out her car keys and headed for the parking lot.

There was nothing quite as magical as being alone in an empty skate park. I skated to my bag for some water and then checked my phone—I still had an hour to kill.

I also had a text from Dylan, in all caps. It was probably a scathing lecture on what I'd done to Summer. I definitely deserved a scathing lecture. But when I opened the full message, it was something else entirely.

Dylan: **DID YOU SEE MOLLIE'S EMAIL???? KINDA FREAKING OUT RN**

It took me a moment to process the fact that his message wasn't about Summer. Had she not told him what I'd done?

I scrambled to check my email and found one from Mollie.

Hi Flippin' Skaters—great news! This hasn't been publicly announced yet, but I wanted you to be the first to know—we got you in at Flipfezt! The organizers saw you at the demolition derby and loved what you did. You won't be competing, since there's no roller skating element, but you'll kick the competition off with a showcase performance. This is a fantastic opportunity to introduce your style to the world and present the possibility of opening up Flipfezt to roller skaters in the future. The official announcement will be made tomorrow morning—please keep it a secret until then. Since Flipfezt is coming up so soon, I'm pushing back some other things in your schedule to make room. Congrats!

—Mollie

I reread the message. And then read it again for good measure, a smile growing on my face. We were skating at Flipfezt! This was huge!

But … Summer wasn't speaking to me. I didn't know if she'd ever forgive me for what I'd done, even with Flipfezt on the line.

I wanted her friendship back even more than I wanted to go to Flipfezt.

I texted Dylan.

Aspen: **thats AMAZING news. does summer know?**

Dylan: **I texted her but she hasn't responded**

Dylan: **headed to her house now**

Dylan: **want to meet me there?**

I did. I really did. But it probably wasn't a good idea. Dylan would find out why soon enough.

Aspen: **I can't**

I almost added something else—*Let me know how it goes*, or *Tell Summer I'm sorry*, but thought better of it. Summer deserved to tell him her side of the story from scratch.

The empty skate park, which had seemed magical only moments ago, now just felt lonely.

What I really wanted was a giant half-pipe. Something bigger than I'd ever been on before. I could stand at the top and let my toe stops hang over the edge while I savored that feeling of being moments away from plunging to the ground. That would fill the emptiness inside me.

But this park didn't have a half-pipe. So I stashed my water bottle back in my bag and, after a moment of hesitation, pulled off my mask. There was nobody here but me—I didn't need to hide. Then I went to the top of the bowl.

It wasn't as high as I would have liked, but it was high enough to get that feeling—that electric ball of nerves in your gut—as you stand just a hair away from letting gravity have you. I let the nerves work up inside me, staring down into the bowl while I balanced on the edge.

And then, I let myself fall.

I careened down the slope, keeping my knees bent and my arms tucked in as my stomach did that thing where it gets left behind and then catches up all in a whoosh. It was terrifying and delicious all at the same time.

When I got to the bottom, I pumped, propelling myself around the bowl and back up. At the top, I did a handstand and came out of it in a backward skate. My backward skate was so much better now than it had been all those weeks ago when I'd wiped out at the skate-off. At the bottom of the bowl, I spun so I was skating forward, then repeated the move on the other side.

I was breathing hard, but I kept going, pushing myself harder, faster, higher—focusing only on my body, my skates, and the pavement beneath my feet.

Then I heard an extra set of wheels.

And I didn't have my mask on.

I started panicking, but then I saw the gray beanie. Brogan's body flew past mine, his torso arching as he grabbed the lip of his skateboard and did a trick at the top of the bowl.

I breathed a sigh of relief—he already knew who I was underneath the mask, so I was safe. I had too much momentum to just stop, so I did a quick skate-grab at the top and let my skates carry me back down, skidding to a halt in the center.

Brogan kept skating.

I put a hand on my hip. "You crashed my solo session."

"No, I didn't." He slid to a stop beside me. "I made it a duet."

"You are so weird."

He grinned. "Guilty. And you work too hard. You've been here for hours."

"I'm not working, I'm thinking. But I'm done now." I definitely couldn't think while he was smiling at me like that. Why was he smiling at me like that?

I headed for the bench where my stuff was.

Brogan followed, and silence fell between us.

I sat down and stretched my feet out, letting my skates roll on their back wheels. The toes had some scuff marks that hadn't been there a few weeks ago, but the purple taffy color was still just as beautiful as ever.

The silence became too much. "Okay, fine. I'll tell you what I was thinking about."

"I didn't ask," Brogan said.

"I know, but you wanted to."

He sat down beside me, his lips quirking up into a grin. "I did."

"First of all, I've been a crap friend. Summer and I had a misunderstanding today. It was completely my fault and I don't know how to fix it."

"That's easy. Apologize."

"I know, I'm just not sure she'll accept it. This is bigger than a simple 'I'm sorry'. But we have an event coming up, and we need to be good before then. I'm not sure what Mollie would do if we backed out."

"Yikes," Brogan said.

"Oh, there's more. I think I know who spiked my drink at the club, but I have no proof. And, even if I did, what then? Should I get revenge or just let it go? Part of me wants the girl to pay, but I also can't see how that will make anything better. I've given up trying to be anyone other than Skate-or-Dye. But bringing her to justice might stop what happened to me from happening to more people, you know?"

Brogan exhaled loudly.

"Oh, and to top it all off, I just found out my two best friends are liars and cheats."

"Summer and Dylan?"

"Oh. No. My two *former* best friends—Rhea and Chase. See, I caught Rhea cheating on Chase, and I told her to tell him but she didn't. Then he found out I knew and didn't tell him, so he got all mad at me. But it turns out he was cheating on her, too."

"Okay, maybe you do need to skate some more."

I gave him a playful punch in the arm.

Brogan's feet were still on his skateboard, even though he was sitting beside me, and he rolled the board from side to side as we talked. "I have a story for you. It might help."

"Okay, shoot."

"I'm afraid of heights."

I raised an eyebrow, not buying it. "But you never have a problem dropping in on your skateboard."

He shook his head. "It only *looks* like I don't have a problem. There's the tiniest moment, every time just before I do it, that I'm terrified."

"Okay, even if I believed you, how is that relevant?"

"I'm working up to that part." He straightened his torso and made his voice all official—like the narrator on some stuffy documentary—and said, "My height-o-phobia stems from a tree climbing incident when I was five years old. The hours-long ordeal began with a dare and ended with firemen and a ladder."

I giggled, still thinking he was joking. But then I looked at him—really looked at him—and saw something deeper. He was straddling the line between melodrama and real drama, and I couldn't tell which side he meant to end up on. So I said, "Wow, okay. Was it a very tall ladder?"

He made a show of sniffling, playing up the melodrama. "It had to be, because it was a very tall tree."

I laughed. I couldn't help it. "Okay, so why'd you choose skateboarding, then? There are plenty of things you can do for fun where both feet stay on the ground."

Brogan kicked the lip of his board down, popping the other end up. "Because it scares me. That's why I do it. But I'm not done with my story yet."

"Oh, I thought the firetruck-slash-getting-stuck-in-a-tree thing was the story."

"That was the pre-story," Brogan said. "The real story involves my brother—you met him, remember?"

"Oh, yeah, at the bar. What was his name?"

"Slate."

"Right." I rolled my skate-encased feet back and forth on the ground beneath me, letting the bumps in the pavement jostle my legs. "Okay, tell me about Slate."

"Well, Slate was never afraid of anything. He's a couple years older than me, but after the tree incident he started taking me to the skate park. He taught me how to skateboard. He told me not to be scared—that fear was for sissies and it would only hurt you. I tried to believe him—I really did. But there was a part of me that didn't understand. I'd been afraid when I started climbing that tree, but my friends had been watching so I ignored the fear and kept going up. And that's how I got stuck. So it seemed to me that, sometimes, fear can keep you safe. It can keep you from doing something stupid and getting hurt because of it."

The streetlight hit his face just so, highlighting his strong jawline. I couldn't take my eyes off him as he spoke.

"But he was my big brother and he knew best, right? So I tried to be just like him. Fearless. Carefree.

All of that."

Brogan kept fidgeting with his board, his hands alternating between grabbing the lip of the board and resting on his thighs, which were jolting up and down as his feet moved. The edge of his beanie taunted me, practically begging me to take it off so I could finally see his hair.

Instead, I took a chance and grabbed one of his hands.

His body went still. Then he smiled and wound his hand around mine. The same feelings I'd felt at the club, when we'd held hands under the table, came rushing back.

But then he said, "Slate got busted for possession of drugs. It started as a routine traffic stop, but he mouthed off to the cop, the cop made him get out of the car, and they found him with weed." Brogan's grip tightened around mine.

"I thought weed was legal now."

"Not if you're under twenty-one. Slate ended up with three months of jail time right in the middle of his senior year. He was supposed to finish school once he got out, but now he doesn't want to."

Brogan's thumb traced a pattern on my hand as I processed what he'd just told me. We were now solidly on the real-drama side of the line, and I wasn't sure what that meant. But I understood I was seeing a side of Brogan that he didn't let many people see.

He continued. "So it turns out I was right about fear. Slate wasn't afraid of anything, and that's what got him in trouble. If he had been more afraid, he wouldn't have had pot. He wouldn't have mouthed off to the cop who pulled him over. And he would have gone back to school once he got out of jail because he'd be too afraid of what his life would look like as a high school dropout.

But he's still not afraid of anything." He paused, looking me in the eyes. "You asked why I was on roller skates the day we met, even though I knew I was bad at it."

"I remember," I said.

"Okay, so I do things that scare me—things that push me out of my comfort zone—as a reminder that it's normal to feel that way. Because if you're never afraid of anything, well, then there's something wrong with you. But you also can't let the fear keep you from doing things you love. So I do them anyway, even though I'm afraid, to prove to myself that my fear doesn't control me, I control it."

Wow. Just … *wow*.

Wait.

The point of this story had been to help me with my problem. I dropped his hand. "You think I'm afraid?"

"Well, yeah. Aren't you?"

I bristled. "No. I'm trying to figure out what happened and stop it from happening to anyone else. Which is, like, the complete opposite of fear."

"But the one thing you've been doing ever since that night is hiding. I did the same thing after Slate got put away. You're holding up a version of yourself that's not really you, but I promise—you don't need to. I've seen the real you. And the real Aspen has nothing to be ashamed of. Just let go of the image you're trying to keep up and you'll be free."

Nope. Nuh uh. He was flat-out wrong.

Brogan continued, apparently oblivious to the fact that he'd basically just called me a poser and a coward. "See, there are two kinds of fear—one that keeps you alive and one that prevents you from living. You're letting fear prevent you from living. The girl I saw just now—in the bowl when you didn't think anyone was watching. That girl was fierce. Unafraid. And the girl I saw in the skating rink that day you threw your phone at me—she was also fierce. But when you're being Skate-or-Dye, you withdraw into a shell. You put on a mask and hide the most beautiful part of yourself. You're afraid of being seen, Aspen Heathrow. But I've seen you. And, trust me, you don't need to be afraid."

Part of me wanted to punch him.

And the other part of me wanted to melt right into him. He'd called me beautiful. And fierce. And unafraid.

Was he right?

His expression was too intense, but I couldn't look away. It was like he was seeing me as no one had ever seen me before. The real me—the good, the bad, the beautiful, and the ugly all rolled into one.

And still, he looked at me like I was the best thing he'd ever seen.

Electricity zinged between us, just like it had that night after the rigged competition when we'd stood face to face. Only, this time, it didn't scare me. Plenty of other things did. But he didn't. Not anymore.

I'd tried to kiss him once before, and it hadn't gone so well. But maybe … maybe I could give it another try.

He beat me to it.

His lips came to mine and, oh, they felt good. Warm and soft and perfect. And the electricity I'd felt before was nothing compared to the fireworks that went off now. Our lips moved together. His hand found my face, cupping my cheek gently as he laced his fingers through my hair.

I tried to scoot closer to him, but I was already as close as I could get without taking off my skates. Why had I left them on?

But then he pulled me into his lap, ignoring my weighed-down feet, and I wound my arms around his neck, breathing him in.

We kissed and kissed and kissed under the haze of the streetlamps and a dusting of stars.

****

When we came up for air, I felt like a different person, and when I looked at him, I knew he was telling the truth about being able to see the real me, and that he liked what he saw.

But that didn't mean anybody else would like the real me. I couldn't let my two worlds collide, I just couldn't. The people at school couldn't know I was Skate-or-Dye, and I couldn't be Aspen when I skated. For one thing, there was the contract. Even worse, if people knew I was Skate-or-Dye, it would take away the power she gave me. At school, I was just a washed-up cheerleader who used to be cool. When I put on my mask, though, I was somebody else. Somebody strong, with real power to make a difference. I had to leverage that.

I still wasn't sure whether Brogan was right about the fact that I was afraid of being seen and that's why I liked my mask, or that it was the wrong kind of fear driving me. But it didn't really matter why I was wearing my mask. It only mattered that I had one, and that it gave me power. I couldn't risk losing that.

I traced a finger along Brogan's jawline. My gaze caught on a curl of brown hair sticking out from beneath his beanie. I fingered the edge of the hat, tugging on it slightly. "Can I see your hair?"

He grimaced. "It'll be a mess. I've had this hat on all day."

"You've had that hat on for months," I said, laughing.

"Umm, I take it off at night, crazy."

I clasped my hands together in front of me.

"Please?"

"Ugh, fine." He tugged the beanie off and ran a hand through his mussed-up hair.

I pulled back so I could see him better.

And then, there he was. Brogan, with no gray beanie, and floppy, sort-of curly brown hair. I couldn't tell if his hair was wavy because it had been under a hat all day or if it was naturally like that, but he looked even more like his brother now.

I fingered one of his loose curls. "You're not bald. I'm so glad."

He laughed. "You thought I was bald?"

"I don't know! Or that you had horrible dandruff of something. Why else would you wear the same hat every single day? It's like that story of a man who married a woman who always wore a ribbon around her neck. And he kept asking her to take it off and she wouldn't. And then one night he untied it while she was sleeping and her head fell off and rolled to the ground."

Brogan's jaw dropped. "What the heck kind of a story is that?"

"Just a story my sister, Jojo, used to tell to scare me at night."

I sucked in a breath.

Jojo.

We had an ice cream date.

"That's the worst story I've ever heard," Brogan said. "I just like wearing hats, and this one is really comfortable.'"

I leaned in and kissed him. "That's super weird. And kind of adorable."

He kissed me back. "*You're* adorable."

My body flooded with heat.

Okay, I really just wanted to sit on this park bench with him all night, but for the first time in a really long time, Jojo had reached out to me. I couldn't blow her off.

I stood up. "So, I just remembered that I'm supposed to meet my sister for ice cream tonight."

Brogan made an overly dramatic wounded face. "Oh, see? I told you my hat-hair would scare you off."

I tugged him up from the park bench and leaned into him. "I'm not that easy to scare off," I said, tangling my fingers into his hair and kissing him long and hard.

When we parted for air, he said, "Glad you don't scare easily. That means you can tell your sister you have a secret identity."

"She basically already knows, though we haven't talked about it or anything—she recognized my voice at the skate-off."

"Good. Take the next step and tell your family."

My mouth went dry. "Nuh uh. No way. They would never understand."

"So? They're your family—they don't have to understand. They'll love you anyway."

His words rang true. They probably would love me anyway. But the whole story was so complicated, I couldn't imagine coming clean at this point. Not to mention the fact that I'd forged my mom's signature on an official document—who knew what she'd do to me if she ever found out about that.

Brogan was eyeing me.

"I'll think about it."

"Secrets have a way of coming out," Brogan said. "Better to just get it over with and tell them."

I frowned. "I really have to go. See you tomorrow?"

He plopped the beanie back on his head. "Of course."

We skated in opposite directions, and leaving him was almost physically painful.

I pulled out my phone to check the time and saw a text from Jojo that had been sent eight minutes ago.

Jojo: **exciting bout, huh? meet me outside the locker room in ten?**

Chapter Thirty: Sisters

Oh, crap. I was at least a fifteen minute bus ride from the rink. The nearest stop was five minutes away, and who knew how long it would take for the right bus to show up?

There was no way out of this one. I had to tell my sister I'd missed her bout.

I typed out a response.

Aspen: **don't be mad … can u pick me up?? im at the skate park by our house**

I pressed send and cringed. She was going to be so mad. But there was no other option—I couldn't get to the rink in less than two minutes, even if I had turbo boosters on my skates.

Jojo: **wait, you missed it?! it was our best one of the season**

Aspen: **im rly sorry, ok? i got tied up**

My cheeks flushed at the thought of my legs tangled up with Brogan's and my fingers twisted in his hair.

Jojo: **umm, tied up how?**

I typed the one thing I knew would get me out of hot water.

Aspen: **i was with a guy, ok?**

Jojo sent back an almost immediate string of happy/excited/gasp-y emojis, then added:

Jojo: **im leaving the rink now!!**
****

"So, a guy, huh?" Jojo said once we were settled in a booth at The Tin Roof. She dug into her banana split. "Who is he?"

I took a sip of my chocolate malt to hide the grin I felt creeping onto my face. "His name is Brogan." Still, I couldn't keep the smile out of my voice. Just saying his name made me go all weak at the knees.

Jojo's face went blank, her brow furrowing.

"He doesn't go to our school," I added, "so you wouldn't know him."

"Oh, really?" Jojo's mouth twisted into a playful grin. "Where'd you meet him?"

I thought back to that first day at the rink and the look on his face when I'd almost hit him with my phone. Then I thought about our kiss-fail. The memory didn't fill me with mortification anymore, which was new.

"Technically, the roller rink." I pictured myself back there. I pictured *him* there, in his band t-shirt and beanie. "But he's also one of the boarders we skated against at the skate-off."

"Ooh. Enemy turned lover. Hot." Jojo eased a spoonful of vanilla, dripping with chocolate sauce, into her mouth. "Tell me about him."

Where to even start? I tapped a finger against my lips, thinking, and then felt a blush crawl up my cheeks when I remembered what my lips had been doing twenty minutes ago. My skin tingled with the memory of his lips on mine.

I circled my straw slowly around my malt, letting my words come out in lazy waves. "Okay, so he's adorable, with these deep, dark eyes and mussed-up brown hair, which he usually hides beneath a beanie so that just the bottom ends curl up at the edge." I watched my ice cream swirl inside my glass, matching the way my insides felt. "He's loyal and kind and talented. He loves his family. And he pushes himself to try new things, even if they scare him."

Jojo cut me off. "He admitted that things scare him? If that's true, he's way ahead of the guy curve."

I'd been reduced to a sweet, sugary puddle, just

like my dessert. "I know, right?"

"Well, he sounds perfect." She took a sip of her water. "Why were you at the roller rink, anyway? I thought you only practiced outside."

I chewed on my straw while I tried to come up with a response better than: *I got kicked off the cheer squad and everyone was hazing me online, so I decided to hide out on roller skates.* Because now, sitting here with Jojo in the fluorescent lights of the ice cream shop, that explanation sounded completely ridiculous. Why had I thought that changing who I was would fix anything? Sure, my life as Skate-or-Dye was pretty awesome, but my life as Aspen still sucked. Becoming a skater girl hadn't changed that.

I didn't know how to change that.

"Aspen?" Jojo was eyeing me carefully. "What's really going on?"

I pushed my malt away. "I just went skating there, okay? Just for fun, before I started the Flippin' Skaters. I'm allowed to do that, right? And then I met Brogan, so it turned out to be a good idea."

"Okay, chill." Jojo set her spoon down, leaving the rest of her banana split uneaten. "But can we talk about this? For real?"

I eyed her. "Talk about what?"

"The skating thing. You are wicked talented, but I just don't understand what made you go there. I always thought you didn't like skating."

"I never said that."

She cocked her head to one side. "You know, you were just as good as I was when we were kids. Why didn't you do roller derby with me?"

I gaped at her. "Seriously?"

"Yeah, we should have done it together. Why didn't we?"

"Um, because you told me I sucked and that skating was *your* thing and that if I even *thought* about joining roller derby, you would hang me from the treehouse by my toenails."

Jojo's mouth popped open.

"I believe that's a direct quote."

"No way. I never said that."

"You did. It was the day after Christmas, the year we both got new skates. Dad took us to the rink while Mom stayed home because she was pregnant and puking everywhere. That song by Vanessa Carlton was playing on the loudspeaker—a thousand miles or whatever—while you told me I was a copycat wannabe faker and to leave the skating to you or you'd pound me. On or off the rink—you said it didn't matter."

Jojo's face drained of color. She was shaking her head.

I pressed on, avoiding my sister's gaze and looking only at the straw wrapper I was slowly shredding to bits. "I buried my skates in the closet the next day. Later when Mom asked why I hadn't been using them I told her they gave me blisters. They're still there—I saw them the other day—but I never used them again."

My sister's hand was pressed over her mouth. "Aspen," she breathed. "I'm so sorry. I really don't remember saying that, but … I mean, I was eleven … eleven-year-olds are stupid and they say stupid things." She reached out and grabbed my hand. "I'm so sorry."

I finally looked into my sister's eyes. She was seeing me. Really seeing me. Not as a fan at her next bout, or one of the Flippin' Skaters, or even the sister who once lived down the hall. She was seeing me as a real person.

Tears pricked behind my eyes and I hastily wiped them away. "It's not a big deal, really. I mean, I do like skating. But the aggression that goes with derby—that's your thing, not mine. And I'm okay with that."

"Are you sure?" Jojo said. "Because I could start training you—I bet I could get you derby-ready by next season if you wanted to try it."

"I'm okay, really."

Was I okay, though? Sure, I was okay with Jojo being the roller derby girl. But, in general, I was not okay.

Jojo must have seen something change on my face, because she said, "Okay, I wasn't going to bring this up, but ... I saw what Chase posted online. So, I'm asking you again, Aspen—for real this time—*what* is going on?"

My lower lip trembled.

"I emailed customer service," Jojo added. "They took all the pictures of you down."

That got my attention. I scrambled for my phone, opening my social feed and scrolling back through all my notifications until I found one connected with the pictures. When I clicked on it, a page popped up that said:

Content Removed—if you feel you've reached this page in error, please check the address and try again.

I clicked on another notification—for one of the other pictures—and got the same message. A third time brought me to the same page.

I looked up at Jojo, unable to form words.

"They're all gone. Inappropriate content gets taken down if someone reports it—why didn't you report it?"

"I didn't know you could do that," I stammered. "And I didn't think whining about it would make any difference. You told me yourself to suck it up—during the pie fight in the locker room."

She huffed. "I was a little distracted. And I didn't realize how serious it was. Reporting something like this is not whining—it's standing up for yourself. Look, Aspen, people do all sorts of stupid, mean things. Especially in high school. But that doesn't mean you have to sit back and take it."

"I know, I know ... punch them all in the throat. I tried to do that, but I'm not you. I can't just go around fighting the world."

Jojo looked at me. "No, you can't. But you don't have to fight the same way I would. Be you. Fight back in your own way. It'll be just as powerful as punching them in the throat—maybe even more so."

Fight back in my own way. How could I fight Marissa in my own way? What could I do that would offset everything she'd done?

"Hey, what if I help you figure it out?" Jojo pulled her shoulder bag into her lap and dug through it until she found her phone. Something hanging from her bag caught my eye, just before she dumped it back on the chair beside her.

"What was that? On your bag?"

She pulled it back into her lap, her brow furrowing as she examined it.

I reached out and fingered the cord of leather that had caught my eye. It exactly matched the one I wore on my wrist—the twin bracelets our parents had brought back for us from Mexico. "You still have this?"

She snatched the bag away, going quiet.

"What?" I said, unable to account for the flash of pain that had just crossed her face.

"Okay, fine. Yes, I still have it—it reminds me of a simpler time. When we shared everything."

She refused to meet my gaze, and the vulnerability in her expression left me at a loss for words.

My big, tough sister had a sentimental attachment to the same thing I did—a thing that connected us.

Did she actually miss me as much as I missed her?

I waited until she met my gaze, and then I took a chance. "I miss us, too." I showed her my wrist, where my own bracelet sat. I'd been trying to stop fiddling with it, and the skin was mostly healed up.

Jojo's chin quivered. "Being a grown-up is hard. Watching your relationships change and not being able to do a single thing about it is awful."

"Our relationship doesn't have to change, you know. We'll always be sisters."

She laughed, her eyes glistening. "I know. It's just hard being so disconnected from you. I can't just run down the hall when I need to talk anymore. And texting isn't the same."

Warmth filled me from the inside out. My sister actually needed me.

I squeezed some chocolate sauce into my malt, then stirred it with my straw and watched the colors swirl together. "No, texting isn't the same. But it's better than nothing."

"That's true. Let's do better, okay? Like, I'll actually listen when a picture of you goes viral if you promise not to tell me in the middle of a food fight."

I laughed. "Hopefully no more pictures of me go viral."

"Amen to that!" Jojo grabbed the chocolate sauce I'd just put down and drizzled some into her bowl of mostly-melted sundae. "Now, do you want me to help you figure out how to fight back or what?"

"Um, how is that even a question? Of course I want your help."

"Good. Cause I have an idea."

Chapter Thirty-One: Lie Detector

Jojo's idea revolved around a news story she'd seen of this celebrity who'd posted the QR code for a $100 coffee shop gift card. He'd included the hashtag #payitforwardchallenge and told his fans to enjoy a drink on him and then add more money to the gift card, if they could, so that someone else could get one, too. His fans responded in droves, posting pictures of their coffees with receipts showing that they'd reloaded the gift card.

"I don't get it—you think I should buy coffees for everyone?" I said when she'd finished explaining.

"No, of course not. I think you should start a pay it forward challenge at your school. Only it won't involve money. The currency will be pictures. Good pictures—spreading love, not hate."

I frowned. So instead of posting stuff like Marissa had, I'd post the opposite type of stuff? I guessed that could be a way of fighting back—fighting her—without actually stooping to her level. Was it big enough, though? Would that actually make a difference?

Jojo's eyes were bright, full of excitement. "Do you get it?"

"Yeah, I think so. It's a good idea."

Jojo took me home, then decided to stay the night rather than driving back to school so late. We snuck in the backdoor together. Jojo tripped over the threshold and started giggling.

"Shh," I hissed. "Are you *trying* to wake everyone up?"

From the darkness of the kitchen, our mom's voice said, "I'm already awake."

I jumped.

Jojo flipped a light on.

Our mom was sitting at the kitchen table, running a finger around the rim of a coffee mug.

"Why were you sitting in the dark?" I asked.

"Oh, no, young lady. *I* will be the one asking questions tonight."

Jojo and I exchanged a look.

"I got an interesting letter today." She pulled a piece of paper out of an envelope sitting on the table, and read out loud:

"Dear Ms. Heathrow,

I know you're busy, so I appreciate you being so on top of this, but since Aspen is no longer on the squad, you will obviously no longer be responsible for the lodging and transportation fees for states. I'm returning your payment. Additionally, this reminded me to look into getting you a refund for the fall fees you paid at the beginning of the year. I was able to authorize a partial refund, which you should see come through shortly on your credit card statement. Aspen was a joy to have on the squad and we miss her terribly.

Best,

Coach Irina"

Jojo's eyes went wide. "You're not on the squad anymore? I knew things were bad at school, but—"

My mom cut her off. "Joelle, please."

Mom raised an eyebrow, waiting for me to say something. The lines in her face were deeper, it seemed, than they had been yesterday. Her hair was pulled back into a messy ponytail with a few loose strands hanging limply around her face.

I stood by the fridge, scared to get any closer. My old cheer bag—now full of skating stuff—hung over my shoulder. It was an elephant in the room trying to pass as a puppy.

Jojo's gaze darted between me and our mother.

"Am I missing something?"

"Go to bed, Joelle."

Jojo didn't move.

My mom sighed. "This is about Aspen." Her tone was the one she reserved for the worst kinds of offenses. She looked at me. "Sit."

I scrambled to a chair and sat, my butt slamming into the seat harder than I'd intended. My skate-slash-cheer bag clunked to the ground.

Jojo sat, too.

My mom pinned her gaze on me and said, "Why have you been lying to me about going to cheer practice for the past three months?"

I twisted my fingers together in my lap. Looked at my mom. Took a deep breath. "Okay, um … so you remember the friend drama I told you about on the park swings?"

She nodded.

"The drama included this rumor about me…" I trailed off. I couldn't tell my mom I'd originally gotten kicked off squad because everyone thought I was pregnant. It was just so humiliating.

I glanced at Jojo.

Mom raised an eyebrow.

"It's not true," Jojo said. "What everyone said about her."

"*What's* not true?" Mom said, visibly losing patience.

I swallowed, fisting my hands so tight that my fingernails pressed into the fleshy part of my palms. "Rhea told Coach I got pregnant."

My mom blanched.

"It's not true," I said, even though I'd already said it.

Mom's tone was steely. "Then why would she say

it?"

"I don't know, because she was afraid?"

"Afraid of what? Aspen, I don't understand!"

"Okay, okay." I held my hands up in surrender. "I'll start at the beginning. Remember the night I went with some friends to see Appellooza play?"

"Apple-what?" my mom said.

"Appellooza," Jojo said. "It's a band."

She didn't give any hint of recognition. "You were working an overnight shift and Dad fell asleep on the couch, so no one was awake when I got home. It was a tournament weekend—we met you at the rink the next morning for Jojo's bout with..." I trailed off, looking to my sister for help.

"Umm, I think we faced the Skull Smashers that morning," she said. "And I got the Bloodsucker award."

My mom nodded. "Okay, yes. I remember that."

I continued. "Well, that's the night I caught Rhea cheating on Chase with this guy named Drake. And I told her she should tell Chase, but of course she didn't want to. So she started this rumor about me, I guess so no one would believe me if I decided to tell the truth."

"Was she trying to get you kicked off the squad?" Mom said.

"I think so. Or, I don't know if she actually wanted me off the squad or if she just wanted to humiliate and discredit me. Honestly, I don't understand anything she does anymore."

"But once your coaches learned the truth, why didn't you re-join?"

My cheeks burned. So much had happened that night—things that had changed me and made it impossible to ever re-join my old life. I took a deep breath. "Mom—can you just listen for a minute? Let me get the rest of the story out?"

Worry lines appeared in the crease between my mom's eyebrows, but she nodded.

I told her the whole story. Starting with the matching bra and underwear set I'd bought with the squad and ending with the avalanche of pictures and comments about me online. Somewhere in the middle of it, my fingers found my bracelet and I started slowly spinning. By the end of the story, the skin underneath the leather cord was stinging.

My mom sucked in a breath when she saw my wrist. She grabbed my hands and made me stop. Then she looked straight in my eyes. "Aspen, you really don't remember anything after sharing Zuri's drink?"

I shook my head.

"You could have been drugged. Sexually abused out back behind the club." My mom's voice was shrill. "How do you even know who brought you home? When was your last period?"

"Mom, relax. I'm not pregnant, I'm sure. And Sara brought me home."

"Does she remember what happened?" My mom got up and rifled through the nearest junk drawer.

"I've talked to a few people, actually. All of them just say they remember me and Zuri getting onstage and dancing." I gulped. "And me taking my clothes off. But after that, Sara took me home. Nothing else happened. But because of the pictures, people started saying horrible things about me, and then my friends turned against me, and it just snowballed from there." I was close to tears now, shaking from the effort of telling my humiliating story.

Mom plucked something from the drawer and came back to the table.

My fingers were back on my bracelet, spinning, spinning, spinning. The action was comforting. Safe.

Something I could rely on.

Mom produced a pair of scissors—the ones we kept in the junk drawer—and reached for my bracelet. "You're hurting yourself."

"No!" I shrieked, snatching my arm away.

"Look at your arm, Sweetie. It's swollen and red."

Jojo said, "Whoa, are you allergic to the leather or something?"

"Of course not. And I like this bracelet—I don't want you to cut it."

My mom's voice was gentle. "But it's hurting you."

"No, it's not. It's my fault—I'll stop messing with it, I promise." I pulled my sleeve down over the bracelet.

"You know you could just tie it to your backpack or something, like I did with mine," Jojo said.

I didn't respond.

My mom studied me, her lips pressing together. Then she set the scissors down on the table and opened her arms. "Come here."

I hesitated for the smallest moment. Then I went to her and let her fold me into a hug. Jojo came over and rubbed my back. Then I cried until my eyes were puffy and my throat felt raw.

"Go to bed," Mom said, stroking my hair. "We'll talk more in the morning."

I wasn't looking forward to that. But I felt a lightness I hadn't since this whole thing had started. My mom was on my side. Jojo was on my side. And I knew they would fight for me just as fiercely as Skate-or-Dye skated.

****

My mom was already at the breakfast table in her scrubs when I got down the next morning. It was early—too early—but I'd had a restless night, and once the sun started peeking through my window, it had seemed silly to keep trying to sleep.

Mom set a cup of hot cocoa in front of me. A mound of marshmallows floated on top and I grinned in spite of everything. "You never let me have that many marshmallows."

Mom shrugged. "It's a different sort of day."

The junk-drawer scissors were still sitting on the table from last night. I shifted away from them.

Mom took a seat across from me at the table, sipping her own mug of cocoa. "You've really been off the squad for three whole months without telling me?"

I nodded.

"So, the question is, where have you been spending all your time?"

"Just … around." I avoided her gaze, watching the edge of one of the marshmallows slowly melt into the cocoa. I couldn't exactly tell her what I'd been doing. I'd signed a contract—with *her* signature, no less—not to tell anyone.

"Okay, let me be more direct. What is this?"

My head jerked up. One of my face masks dangled from her fingers. I snatched it away from her, panicking. "You went through my stuff?"

"Well, yeah. This bag could have been full of drugs."

"You had no right to do that."

"Actually, as your mother, I do have that right. It's my job to keep you safe. Now, please explain."

Crap, how could I explain without breaking my contract and letting on that I'd forged her signature to get it? Of course, Jojo knew my secret identity. But she's guessed—I hadn't actually told her.

I started slowly, considering every word before it left my mouth. I just couldn't tell her I was a Flippin'

Skater. She couldn't know I was Skate-or-Dye, but I could tell her I'd been skating, right?

"Okay, one day shortly after … the incident … I found a pair of Jojo's old skates in the garage and went to the roller rink. It was really fun, so I started doing it more. And then it kind of turned into … well … I'll just show you." I pulled up the very first video Dylan had posted of Summer and me—the same one I'd shown my dad—and pressed play.

When the video finished playing, Mom said. "I don't understand. What does this have to do with you?"

I laughed. "Mom, that *is* me."

It took a moment for that to sink in, and when it did, her eyes went all buggy. She grabbed my phone and started the video again. "No, that's not you!"

"It is. My hair's in braids, and I spray colored it. And with my helmet on and the long camera angle, well … I promise, it's me. It's just hard to tell."

"Wow. You're nearly unrecognizable." She peered closer at the screen. "Your father told me you were making skating videos, but I thought you were just filming skaters at Joelle's bouts—getting into derby like the rest of us. I had no idea you were actually *in* the videos." She held up the eye mask. "But why do you have this?"

"Oh," I hedged. "Sometimes we like to dress up. It makes it more fun."

"We?"

"Yeah, me and my friend, Summer. We skate together." I held my breath. Now would really be a good time to fess up about forging her signature.

"I can't believe this is you," my mom breathed, watching the video a third time with a new light in her eyes.

"Well, it is. So, that's where I've been spending

my time—at the skate park."

She tore her eyes away from the phone screen and looked at me. "Why didn't you just tell me? You know how much I love skating."

I twisted my hands together. "I don't know. I guess I thought that if I did, I'd have to explain why I wasn't doing cheer anymore, and that would mean telling you what happened at the club."

My mom turned my phone off and handed it back to me. "This video is impressive. You have a real talent, and I'm glad you've found something you love to do." She paused. "But we can't ignore what's been happening to you online."

And with that shift, the moment to confess passed.

She continued. "People spreading rumors that you're pregnant, posting pictures of you half-naked on a stage? It's not okay, Aspen. This world you're growing up in is crazy—with cameras everywhere and social feeds running like heroine through everyone's veins. People need to learn it's not okay to hide behind an anonymous profile and destroy someone, even if it's easy to do."

"Mom, this is the way things are. It's not going to change."

"How do you know? We'll start by contacting your school administration."

"They already know. I really don't think they can do anything."

"Of course they can. Suspension is a real threat. Each of those online accounts—the people who posted lies about you—each one is linked to a person, right?"

"Technically, but a lot of them are anonymous—connected to fake identities or whatever."

Mom pursed her lips. "Still. I think it's worth a visit to the school, don't you?"

"No, Mom. *Please* don't go to the school. You'll

only make things worse."

Mom drained the rest of the cocoa from her cup. "Hmm."

"Please tell me that non-committal *hmm* means you're not going to my school."

She ignored my plea and took her mug to the sink to rinse it out. "Okay, on to the next item of business. I need you to walk me through everything that happened at the club that night—everything you remember and everything you've learned from talking to other people. The fact that you still can't remember the details is—quite frankly—alarming. Also, you are coming in to work with me today for a couple of tests."

I opened my mouth to protest, but she cut me off. "This is not up for debate, Aspen. I know you don't think you did anything after leaving the club that night, but we have to make sure."

"Will the tests involve needles?"

"There will be a blood test, yes. Now start talking."

I sighed. "Okay."

We combed through everything I could think of about that night. Every. Little. Thing. I pulled from my memory, from the pictures I'd seen, and from stuff Drake, Genny, Marissa, and Sara had told me. My mom stopped me often to ask questions. She even jotted some things down. When I'd finished, she was tapping the end of her pen on the table and muttering to herself.

"Alcohol alone probably wouldn't account for this long of a memory lapse. Mixed with something else, though... Benadryl would have made her sleepy, but the forgetfulness wouldn't have lasted this long. Ketamine or GHB would have done the trick."

She cast a worried glance my way, then shook her head. "But there would have been other side effects." She clicked her tongue a few times. "Maybe Ativan or Xanax? Do kids carry their Zannies around these days? Or a Valium, perhaps?"

"Wait." I snapped my fingers. "Marissa said something about Zannies."

What had she said about Zannies? I couldn't remember, exactly, only that she'd said the word.

My mom's head jerked up. "It's slang for Xanax, an anti-anxiety drug. If you took some, especially on top of alcohol, that could definitely cause a degree of memory loss. It's one of the most common side effects of the drug, actually. It can also impair judgement and inhibit self-control. Do you think you took a Xanax?"

"I honestly don't know. But one of the girls I talked to who was there that night said something about Zannies. I'll ask her."

I pulled out my phone. I didn't have Marissa's number, but she was easy enough to find in my social app. I messaged her.

Aspen: **ok, time for some straight talk. what do you know about zannies and what do they have to do with the night i went onstage?**

I waited for any indication that she'd seen my message or was typing a response but got nothing.

"She's not responding."

"Well, a Xanax would explain some things for sure. Let's see if anything comes up at the hospital and go from there. Let me know when you hear back from her."

****

I was sitting on the exam table waiting for my mom to come in and draw my blood when Marissa finally responded. The paper on the table crinkled beneath me as I opened my phone.

Marissa: **ok aspen, ill throw you a bone. the guys u were hanging out with gave u a zannie. thats**

what they called it anyway. Zuri took one too. i even caught it on film

I waited for her to attach a picture, but nothing else came.

Aspen: **marissa, please will you send me that pic? u owe me**

Marissa: **um, i owe you nothing. but just to prove I'm not the bad guy …**

A picture appeared on my phone.

In it, Zuri and I sat with two guys, our heads bent together like we were all looking at something. The guy I sat beside was wearing a U-dub zip-up hoodie—the same one I'd woken up in. I zoomed in, but couldn't tell what we were looking at.

Then Marissa sent another picture. This one was a close-up of the group. One of the guys held a prescription bottle in his hand and was tipping some pills out into his palm.

And then, staring at that pill bottle, a memory finally surfaced.

I'd just left Rhea and Drake and was headed back to our table, trying to figure out how Rhea could have cheated on Chase like that. Didn't she care for him at all? How had I not noticed something was off? And what was I going to say to Chase when I saw him?

The questions circled, tangling up my thoughts, and I realized I couldn't face Chase on my own, just like that. So I went up to a group of older guys and snatched a drink out of one of their hands.

It was out of character for me. So out of character. But this was an out-of-character moment— finding your best friend cheating was not something that happened every day.

I took a swig.

The clear liquid burned my throat on the way

down. I spluttered.

The guys at the table hooted. I handed the drink back. "Sorry, I needed that."

The guy I'd taken it from eyed me. "Yeah, more than me, apparently. You want the rest?" He held the glass out.

I'd always been a rule follower. Both my parents and my cheer coaches lectured often on the evils of underage drinking. So I'd never had alcohol before.

But I only hesitated a moment before grabbing the glass and draining it. I needed all the help I could get if I was going to face Chase.

One of the other guys slid his glass toward me. Have another.

I gulped it down without a second thought. "Okay, I think I'm good now. Thanks." As I walked away from them, my head drifted into the clouds and my worry about what I'd say to Chase faded. But when I got back to our table, Chase wasn't there.

And then the guys appeared behind me, bringing their drinks along with them, and started talking to my friends.

I accepted a sip of Zuri's Coke, then grabbed her arm, stopping her from going onstage to meet the drummer.

"You think that Coke is good, try this," I said, handing her one of the guys' drinks.

"What is it?" Zuri shouted over the noise of the band.

"I don't know, but it makes me feel lighter."

Zuri accepted the drink.

One of the guys stopped the waitress to ask for another round.

"You seem jumpy," another guy said to me. He was wearing a U-dub zip-up hoodie.

Words I normally wouldn't have said out loud came tumbling from my mouth. The drink was already knocking down my filters. "I just caught my best friend cheating on my other best friend and she told me not to tell him, but I think I have to, you know? And I thought he'd be here now, but he's not. But he might come back and then what will I say? So, yeah, I'm a bit jumpy." I took another swig of his drink. "But this is definitely helping."

I was already feeling more relaxed, the alcohol buzzing through my head.

"That's messed up," the guy said.

"I know." My hair flew around as I bobbed my head in time with the music.

The guy punched one of his friends to get his attention. "Dude, give her one of your Zannies."

The friend produced one of those little prescription bottles.

I shook my head. "Nuh uh, I don't do drugs." My words were beginning to slur together. I laughed because it sounded funny.

"They're just anti-anxiety meds. One won't hurt you—it'll just help you relax."

"Yeah, they're harmless." The guy who'd produced the pills swallowed one. "See? I use them to loosen up before tests—my dad's a doctor."

People danced and laughed and partied around me. They were having fun.

My head felt foggy, but I still didn't know what I'd say to Chase when he got back. Maybe I did need help loosening up. "Yeah, okay, I'll have one." I held my hand out and the guy tipped a pill into my palm.

The band finished their song and the lead singer said, "We're going to take a twenty-minute break. Give it up for deejay Dwayne."

Thumping bass came on over the loudspeakers just as the waitress returned with more drinks for our college friends.

Zuri sidled up to the guy with the meds. "You're kinda hot," she said, purring into his ear. He offered her one of the pills, which she accepted.

The guy with the U-dub sweatshirt put an arm around my shoulder and I giggled, leaning into him. We partied. We had a good time.

I forgot all about Chase and Rhea and let loose.

This time, when someone suggested we go on stage, it had sounded like the best idea ever.

Chapter Thirty-Two: Truth

My mind reeled. All this time I'd been so sure that someone had done this *to* me. Someone had Photoshopped the pics. Someone had spiked my drink. Someone had masterminded a school-wide social media takedown.

But no, it was all on me. I'd approached the college guys. I'd accepted those pills. And the guys had come back to our table because of me. That's what Marissa must have meant when she'd said I'd taken my friend down with me. Not only had I set myself on fire, I'd lit Zuri up, too.

The door opened and I jumped. My mom came in, armed with her torture devices.

"Uh, Mom?"

"Yeah, Baby?" she said without looking up.

"I heard back from Marissa. She sent me a picture and then I remembered something."

My mom stopped what she was doing and looked up. "And?"

"I did take a Xanax. And had a few drinks beforehand." There was a tremor in my voice. "I'm really sorry."

My mom collected herself. "Okay. Thank you for telling me. But now I'm even more concerned about what happened after. Kids in our area have started to use Xanax and other anti-anxiety meds in place of date-rape drugs. The effects are comparable, but anti-anxiety meds are easier to get."

"Mom nobody like, took advantage of me or anything."

"How do you know?" My mom shouted, stamping her foot.

I flinched. My mom never lost her cool.

But now she grabbed my hands and held them in hers, her grip vicelike. Her voice shook. "How do you know, Aspen? You didn't remember even taking the pills until just now. How do you know you're not forgetting something else?"

I opened my mouth but had no answer.

I'd know if somebody *did* something to me. Like, something big. I'd know.

Wouldn't I?

Then I remembered the hoodie, and a cold pit settled in my stomach. I wrapped my arms around myself. Why would I have some random guy's hoodie if I hadn't…?

"Okay, these tests are way past due." Mom turned her attention gruffly back to the supplies she'd brought in, hooking everything up, cleaning my arm, and stabbing the needle in before I could even protest.

I tried hard to keep my body from shaking, but the room suddenly felt very cold.

"Oh, I can call Sara!" I blurted out, remembering. "She brought me home. She'd know if anything else happened."

My mom concentrated on the vial currently filling up with my blood. When it was full, she switched it out for another one.

"Geez, how much do you need?"

"We have a lot of tests to run."

I watched in silence as my blood flowed into the vial. "So should I call Sara when we're done? You can talk to her if you want."

"Sure," my mom said. She capped off the last vial, pressed a cotton ball into the crook of my elbow, and slid the needle out. "Put pressure on that and hold your arm up."

I obeyed while she organized the vials and cleaned up the supplies. I shivered some more. She came over and checked my arm, then put a Band-Aid on over the cotton roll. "I'll go get these started. If you want to get Sara on the phone, I'll be right back in to talk to her."

I pulled out my phone and dialed Sara's number. She answered on the third ring.

"Aspen? Is everything okay?"

"Yeah, hi, Sara."

"Did you get my note?"

Her ... note?

"I slipped it in your locker."

"Oh, right. Yeah, I got it. Thanks." I shifted on the table. "Hey, I'm with my mom and she's got a lot of questions about that night at the club. Would you be willing to talk to her for a sec?"

"Um, okay."

"You brought me home, right?"

"Yeah."

"Did you know those college guys gave me and Zuri some meds?"

Sara sucked in a breath. "I had no idea."

"So they didn't give you any? Or did you see them offering some to anyone else?"

"No. But honestly, I wasn't paying much attention to you until you got on stage. When I saw you get up there, I was like, 'Okay, something's off'. I haven't known you that long, obviously, but it really seemed out of character for you. So when you came down, I convinced you it was time to go home. I got Jasmine to help me. She took Zuri home and I took you."

I released a breath and shifted my phone into my other hand. "So I never went anywhere with those guys?"

"No," Sara said. "I'm sure of it. They came over to our table and we were all hanging out there for a while.

And then you and Zuri went onstage, and after that we went home. They never took you anywhere, I promise."

But... "So how come I was wearing his hoodie?"

"You asked him if you could have it. You said something about missing your sister and that his sweatshirt reminded you of her. He seemed reluctant, but you were really insistent so he handed it over and then we left."

The knot in my stomach loosened. Yeah, I could see drunk me begging for something that reminded me of Jojo.

The door opened and my mom came in.

"Oh, hey, here's my mom."

"Okay."

I handed the phone over. My mom took it and proceeded to grill Sara a little harder than I had. I watched her expression, and it seemed to relax as she listened. Finally, she said, "Okay, thank you, Sara. And thank you for bringing Aspen home safely. You're a good friend."

She ended the call and handed my phone back. "The tests will take a while. Your father is going to come pick you up."

She held me at arm's length and fixed me with her most serious Mom look. "Aspen, if you want to be treated like an adult, you have to act like one. You can't let yourself lose control, not ever. Drinking a stranger's drink? Accepting prescription medication? I don't care how rattled you were—you don't ever do that. Not ever. Do you understand? You're extremely lucky you had friends there watching out for you."

Then she pulled me into a hug. "We'll see how the tests come out, but if everything Sara said is true, you should be in the clear. I love you so much." She released me. "I've got to go on shift. Dad will meet you at the main entrance."

"Okay. Thanks, Mom."

I made my way to the main hospital entrance as her words echoed in my head. *If you want to be treated like an adult you have to act like one.*

I definitely hadn't been acting like one—lying about cheer, being a bad friend and, of course, forging my mom's signature. Sigh. I had some cleaning up to do.

My dad's car pulled up and I climbed in. "Hey, Kiddo. Did Mom have you volunteering again?"

Wait, she hadn't told him why I'd been at the hospital with her?

Maybe this was some sort of test to see if I'd do the adult thing. Which would be telling the truth instead of dodging it. "No, she wanted me to take a blood test."

Dad raised an eyebrow. "Everything okay?"

"Yeah, I think so. It was just to be sure."

****

I rode my bike to Zuri's house. She deserved to know what had happened that night, too. Her mom answered the door. "Aspen, what a surprise. Zuri's still sleeping, I think."

I glanced at the time on my phone. It was nearly ten o'clock, but it was a Saturday and Zuri loved sleeping in. "I really need to talk to her. Can you wake her up, please? It's important."

Her mom stepped aside, waving me in. "Wake her up yourself. I don't want any part of that."

I laughed. Zuri was notoriously grumpy in the morning—a lesson I'd learned at the ripe old age of nine during our first sleepover.

I went upstairs and eased her door open.

She groaned and threw a stuffed animal at me. "Go away, Zane." Zane was her little brother.

I threw the stuffed animal back. "I'm not Zane."

Zuri leaned up onto one elbow, patting her silk sleeping cap down, and squinted at me. "Aspen? What are you doing here?"

"We need to talk."

She groaned and pulled the covers up over her head. "Come back in an hour."

I sat on the foot of her bed. "Nope. Now."

She kicked me, but since she was under the blankets, it wasn't very effective.

"Fine, I'll do the talking. You can just listen." She didn't respond, so I forged ahead. "I learned something about that night at the club..."

I told her everything, fessing up to giving her alcohol and watching her swallow a Xanax. I trailed off.

Zuri remained silent.

I jostled her legs. "Did you fall back asleep?"

She pulled the covers down and peeked out at me, all signs of sleepiness gone from her wide eyes. "People have been calling me Magic Mike. Someone started a channel called Magic Mike, Zuri edition, and they post stuff from that movie with Channing Tatum, only with my head spliced in. I never even saw the movie—my mom wouldn't let me." Her lower lip trembled.

My mouth dropped open. I'd seen some Magic Mike posts, but hadn't realized they were about her. "Oh, Zuri, I'm so sorry. I had no idea."

She sat up. "Yeah, it sucks. But, Aspen—it wasn't your fault. I made my own choices that night. We all did."

"But I gave you a drink and didn't tell you it was alcohol."

"I knew it was alcohol, dummy. I could have spit it out or not had any more or yanked you from the club insisting that we go home. But I didn't. That's on me. Not you."

I didn't know what to say. Why wasn't she searching for someone to blame? That's what I'd done.

Zuri was studying me with a look that held none of the anger I'd been expecting from her. "We both made bad decisions that night, and bad decisions have consequences—I get that. But we didn't deserve what happened to us online. Nobody deserves that."

My voice was small. "But what can we do about it?"

"I don't know," Zuri said. "None of us has a platform."

I looked at her blankly. "A platform?"

"An audience. Someone who will hear us if we tell our stories. Maybe telling them would make a difference."

"For who? The bullies or the bullied?"

"Can't it be both?"

We fell silent.

I'd clearly been going about this the wrong way. I'd been trying to save people by finding the person who'd taken me down—Marissa, I'd settled on—and stopping her from doing it to more people. But what about all the other Marissas out there? Who was going to stop them?

And what about owning the fact that everyone makes mistakes and that everyone has *stuff*? Stuff like Saraya and Ronald and Keir and Ruth. Since we all have it, why does it have to be such a big deal?

Zuri was right, we needed an audience.

Aspen didn't have one. But Skate-or-Dye did.

The question was, how could I use it without blowing my cover?

****

As I biked away from Zuri's house, I found myself slowing down as another house came into view.

So many hours of my life had been spent here, it almost felt like my own. Without even deciding to, I parked my bike and headed up the walkway to Rhea's front door.

I had no idea how to fix what was broken between us.

But it felt like time to try.

Her dad answered the door.

I eyed him. Did he have any idea what had been going on between me and Rhea? "Hi, Mr. Alessi."

"Hi, Aspen. Rhea's not home, I'm afraid."

"Oh."

Should I give him a message for her? Or wait until she got home? Honestly, I didn't even know what to say.

"She's out with her mother and they'll be gone all day. But I'll tell her you stopped by."

"Okay. Thanks." Not knowing what else to do, I turned to go.

"Aspen, wait."

I paused on the steps.

Mr. Alessi gripped the doorframe. "I'm sure you know Rhea has had a rough couple of months." He swallowed, visibly reining in some unnamed emotion. He made his tone lighter and continued. "I've heard enough of that Love Story album to last me a lifetime." He chuckled, but the humor didn't reach his eyes. "Anyway, thanks for being gentle with her. You're a good friend."

Oh, man.

Lightning, strike me now.

Love Story was not an album, it was a song on the Fearless album, one of Taylor's earliest. It was the album we always listened to when we were all up in our *feels*, because it was so nostalgic and hit all the deeply emotional levels that words couldn't quite touch.

"You should come around more often, Aspen,"

Mr. Alessi said.

I swallowed, my throat suddenly dry. "I'll try."

Yesterday, I'd believed that if anyone had had a rough couple of months, it was me, not Rhea. But today, after everything I'd learned, I knew that things weren't always what they seemed. Was it possible, maybe, that Rhea had *stuff* too?

Chapter Thirty-Three: Friendship

My emotions were all over the place as I rode to Summer's house, the lyrics from Fearless looping through my head. It was a song about first love, not friendship, but it still helped. Summer hadn't answered any of my texts, but I was going over anyway. Not that I knew what I'd say, exactly. Plain old words didn't seem like enough to make up for believing the worst about the one person who'd stood by me when things were darkest.

I needed to fix our friendship. Not because of our skating contract, or even because of Flipfezt. I needed to fix things because when you find something as rare as a true friend—someone who will really stand by you no matter what—you do whatever you can to hold onto them. I would give up our contract, our sponsorship—everything—to keep Summer as a friend.

That was all I knew.

But the sheer bigness of what I had to do, and what I stood to lose if I failed, was making it hard to breathe. My throat was tight, and my chest felt like it held a balloon that was slowly getting bigger and bigger, compressing everything else.

I'd never been to Summer's house before—she'd always insisted on meeting at the park or coming to my house, but I had her address because of the face masks I'd ordered and had sent to her when she was trying to find one that didn't drive her nuts.

Three cars were parked in her driveway. One of them was Dylan's.

Oh. That would complicate things.

I wove between the cars, studying the two that did not belong to Dylan. One was a beat-up Mitsubishi—I'd seen her mom drop her off in that one before.

The other was some foreign brand—boxy and small. Not nice, exactly, but definitely not a clunker. Summer was old enough to drive, but always said she didn't have a car. As far as I knew, it was just her, her mom, and a baby sister at home. So who did that third car belong to?

I parked my bike and walked up the front steps. My hand shook as I rang the doorbell. I still didn't know what I was going to say when she answered.

I waited one beat. Then two.

My legs wobbled. I almost turned around and walked away.

But no. This was worth any humiliation. Any horrible thing she had to say to me. I deserved to hear it, and Summer deserved the chance to say it.

I rang the bell again, then knocked.

Still no answer.

So I pulled out my phone and texted Dylan.

Aspen: **can u tell summer I'm here?**

He texted back almost immediately.

Dylan: **what for**

Aspen: **to apologize**

Dylan: **she doesn't want to talk to u**

Aspen: **tell her ill go pick up some raisinettes. raisinettes make everything better**

Dylan: **eew who eats those?**

Aspen: **just tell her ok?**

Dylan: **fine**

I held my breath, hoping Summer would remember that first day in the park when the mom was feeding Raisinettes to her toddler and calling them candies.

A moment later, I heard footsteps behind the door.

I straightened up, wiping my palms on the legs of my jeans. Not that it helped. My chest still felt like it was about to explode.

Dylan: **she's coming**

The text came right as the door opened.

Summer stood in the doorframe, grinning from ear to ear. "You are *so* not off the hook. But Dylan had no idea what you were talking about with the Raisinette thing, and I needed someone to laugh about that with."

I smiled, not daring to hope she was really as happy to see me as she looked. Summer was really good at hiding her emotions.

Behind Summer, the TV was on. A woman—Summer's mom, I guessed—sat on the couch, bouncing a baby on her knee. "Is that your sister? She's so cute!"

Summer's smile faded, and she moved to block my view.

The baby started crying. Her mom bounced harder, trying to soothe her.

Summer stepped out onto the front porch and closed the door behind her. She sat on the front steps, falling silent.

I hesitated, then sat beside her, keeping a cushion of space between us. Now was my chance to apologize. I struggled to find the right words, to form them into a sentence that didn't sound stupid or incoherent or offensive.

Instead of some brilliantly worded apology, what came out of my mouth was, "Why don't you drive one of those?" I pointed at the cars in the driveway.

"Umm." Summer's brow furrowed. "The Mitsubishi is my mom's. And the other one has been sitting there for, like, ten years—ever since my dad left. He bought it on the cheap from some guy who said all it needed was a new engine. He was going to fix it, but he never got around to it. At least, that's what my mom says. He knew nothing about cars. And then he left and took the keys with him. So it just sits there."

She dug her toes into the dirt, peeling up a few weeds at the edge of the walkway. From behind the closed door, the baby's cries got louder.

Summer talked over the crying like she didn't even hear it. "I don't think my mom even sees it anymore. After my dad left, she was busy trying to track him down and get him to pay child support, and then when she couldn't find him, trying to keep it all together herself. And then she got a boyfriend and another baby and, well, it's gone downhill from there."

I said another thing that wasn't an apology. "How do you stay so happy all the time?"

"I'm not happy all the time. I just pretend to be."

"That's not true. I've seen you genuinely happy, lots of times."

"Okay, well. I guess I pretend I'm happy until I actually am. Or, I don't know, I choose to focus on the good stuff instead of the bad stuff or whatever." Summer paused. In the background, the baby wailed. "Okay, seriously, Aspen. Why are you here? Because if you just came to talk about cars and poke at my happiness level, then I've had enough of this conversation."

"Okay, I know." I slid a hand down my legs. "Summer, you are an extraordinary person. You were my friend when no one else was. You saw something good in me that I still can't see in myself. You've consistently had my back. You deserved nothing but my absolute trust, and instead, I dumped my baggage on you. I shouldn't have thought, for even one second, that you might have posted those pictures, and I'm really sorry about that. I know you could never do something that backhanded and mean. Obviously, I know that. I've just been so focused on me that I didn't see you."

Summer opened her mouth to respond, but I said,

"Hang on, I'm not done. I shouldn't have pushed you into agreeing to the face masks and anonymity in our contract. I'm so, so sorry. Our friendship means more to me than any contract, and I'm willing to give up everything in order to keep you as my friend."

The baby was no longer crying.

"If you'll forgive me," I continued, "I promise to stop letting my own stuff keep me from being the friend you deserve."

She folded her arms across her chest. "What about Flipfezt? It's this weekend."

If we didn't skate the event, we'd be breaking our contract. Who knew what Mollie would do? But Summer was more important. "We'll back out."

She raised an eyebrow. "Aren't we contract-bound to skate whatever events Mollie sets up for us?"

"Maybe," I hedged.

Summer sighed. "Look, Aspen, I love skating, and I love being part of the Flippin' Skaters. I love how far we've come together. The only thing I don't like are the masks—one, because they get in my way while I'm skating, and two, because this is the first amazing thing I've ever done and I want to share it. But I don't want to lose what we have. I don't want to back out of Flipfezt, and I don't want to break our contracts. I just hate knowing that you don't trust me."

"But I do trust you, I swear. I had a momentary, paranoid freak-out, and I'm so, so sorry. I would have suspected my own mother if she'd been there." I bit my lip, realizing I was borderline groveling. "Oh, and there's one more thing. I found out who R33S is."

Summer's eyes went wide. "Shut up."

"It's Marissa. She was in the darkroom with us that day. After you left, she totally confessed—said she's working on some social experiment for a college scholarship essay. *She* posted the stuff about me, *from Chase's phone*, and the stuff about the other people, too."

"What are you going to do?"

"I don't know. My sister had this idea—a pay-it-forward thing where the currency is pictures, not money. Like, feel-good pictures. I'm just not sure it would change anything."

Summer's lips twitched and she pressed them together. Then they twitched again. Like she really wanted to smile but was trying desperately not to.

I wished I'd thought to bring some Raisinettes.

"Okay, that could totally work," she finally said, a grin splitting her face. "It could be like, our own mini-revolution—a way to combat all the sucky stuff out there. I love it!"

"Really?" I said. "You think that could work?"

"Yeah. And, anyway, why not at least give it a try? Putting positive stuff out into the world never hurts."

"True." I studied her, then risked asking, "Does this mean you forgive me?"

"You're on trial," she said, without missing a beat. "How do we start?"

I risked a tiny smile. "Well, I hadn't really gotten that far—"

The front door swung open behind us, cutting me off. "It's about time," Dylan said. "Geez, girls take forever to make up."

I whirled around as Dylan came out with Summer's baby sister asleep on his shoulder.

"If you two were guys," he continued, "that conversation would have lasted ten seconds, tops."

"Shh," Summer said, jumping up and going over to him. "You'll wake her up."

"Nah, she's out," Dylan said.

I joined them. "Wow, Dylan. Are you, like, a

baby whisperer or something?"

"Not really," he said.

But Summer said, "He totally is—it's his superpower. He's the only one who can get Carly to stop crying when she's in one of her moods. Which means my mom loves him almost as much as I do."

They exchanged a syrup-y gaze.

Oh my gosh, so much cuteness.

Dylan said, "Okay, so, now that you two are friends again—"

"Trial friends," Summer interjected. But her smile said something different.

"Whatever," Dylan said. "I heard the word *revolution*. When can we start?"

Chapter Thirty-Four: Mini Revolution

I arrived at the park before the others, mask in place, and started warming up. Summer, Dylan, Brogan, and Lia were meeting me there. So was Jojo, since it had been her idea.

I'd also messaged Zuri, Saraya, Ronald, Keir, and Ruth, as Skate-or-Dye, and invited them to join. I had no idea if any of them would—Ruth was the only one who'd responded, and she'd just said *thanks for the invite*—but this fight belonged to all of us. Zuri had agreed to keep my secret after I confessed to her that I had a platform we could use, but none of Marissa's other victims knew my secret identity. As far as they knew, it was Aspen's family connection to Red Thunder that had gotten us an in with the Flippin' Skaters and if anyone actually asked, we'd make up some excuse for why Aspen wasn't here today.

In short, our mini-revolution would start small. Which was okay.

My hair was electric blue and in braids, as usual when I skated. The scrape of wheels on the pavement told me I had company as I made my way through the course. I looked over my shoulder to find Brogan skating up behind me. "A revolution, huh?"

I spun around just as he reached me and we ended up in each other's arms.

"A mini-one, yeah."

He kissed me, and my helmet nudged his beanie out of place.

He pulled away. "Why does it have to be mini?"

I frowned. "I guess because the thought of starting an actual revolution is too scary."

"How did ice cream with your sister go?"

"Really good, actually. But our mom caught us sneaking in after and it turned into this whole thing." I filled him in on confessing to her and then learning about the Xanax the next morning.

"Yikes." He'd been doing kickflips as I spoke—absently, almost like other people cleared their throat or picked at their nails. I wondered how many he could do in a row.

"Well, I'm really glad you got to the bottom of it," he said when I finished talking.

"Me, too."

The others joined us shortly. Zuri came, but there was no sign of any of Marissa's other victims. I introduced everyone while Dylan and Summer started setting up the camera.

"So, what's the plan?" Dylan said, holding the tripod steady while Summer adjusted it and tightened everything into place.

"Okay, most of this video is going to feature other people, not us. But we'll start with some skating, since that's why our viewers watch our videos. Dylan can string together some footage for an intro before we get real."

"Get real, how?" Lia said. "You never actually gave me any details. You just said you needed help with a project."

"Yep. That's because my sister's going to explain it." I nodded for her to take it away.

Jojo cleared her throat. "Okay, so, since leaving home, I've realized some things. The most influential parts of our lives actually happen in small moments that most people don't pay attention to. Like in helping a friend study for a test. Or trying to be the buffer that keeps two friends from fighting. Or, on the flip side, deliberately excluding someone or giving the new girl a fake phone number.

"People do all these things every day that make the world either a better or a worse place, and they add up quickly to shape our experiences and views. Usually no one notices the good things—they only notice the bad stuff. But life isn't just about bad hair days or bullies or lost championships. It's not even about corrupt politicians or natural disasters or online trolls. Focusing on all that stuff just spins a cycle of negativity. We want to do the opposite."

Hearing Jojo explain it, I knew we were doing the right thing. If anything could cut Marissa's legs out from under her, it was this—doing exactly the opposite of what she'd been doing.

Summer said, "I've noticed the same thing as I've searched for photography subjects. There are so many things that happen each day that go under the radar because no one sees them. We want to shine a light on those moments."

"We're taking a pay-it-forward approach," I added, "trying to encourage people to see the good, and do more good. We'll call it the Project, and we'll post pictures and statements on our social media."

"Our hope is that people will catch on and post their own stuff until the Project starts trending," Summer said.

"But it doesn't have to trend," I said. "We just want it to make a difference."

"That's really cool," Brogan said.

"Yeah, it is," Lia added. "I'm in."

"I'm in, too," said a voice I didn't recognize.

We all turned toward the speaker. It was Ruth, emerging from the shadows of a nearby tree. She was tall and serene, wearing a knee-length boho dress paired with white doc marten boots. Her blonde hair was straight, hanging to her shoulders, and she wore minimalist makeup done in an expert hand.

"I'm so glad you came!" I said.

Zuri introduced her. "Everyone, this is Ruth."

"Thanks for inviting me. This sounds like a really cool project." Her strength was apparent in the way she held herself and the way she spoke, and I was just so glad she'd decided to come.

"Well, the camera's ready," Dylan said. "Should we get started?"

****

By the end of the afternoon, the Project launch was looking like it would come together beautifully. We had footage of a kid at the skate park helping another kid with his rail trick. We had a mom pushing her toddler on a swing. We had a girl putting a plastic bottle in the recycling bin instead of the trash, a man buying a meal for a homeless woman, and a bus driver getting off the bus to help a person in a wheelchair on.

And those were just examples from the community. At school tomorrow, we'd all be on the lookout for those typically unnoticeable moments. Someone holding the door open for someone else. A janitor arriving at the butt-crack of dawn to get the school clean. Teachers using their lunch period to offer study sessions for an upcoming test. Someone making room for a new person at their lunch table.

It was all going to add up to something big, I could feel it in my bones.

As we were finishing up, a girl jumped down from a concrete ledge, where she'd been sitting, and walked over. With a jolt, I realized it was Saraya. How long had she been sitting there?

"I got your message," she said. Her hands were stuffed into the pockets of her jean jacket, but the rest of her body was constantly shifting, like there was just so much energy in her that it didn't have anywhere to go. "It's a nice idea and all, but I'm sorry, this is not gonna fly."

I tensed. "Why not?"

She laughed, a bitter sounding thing. "You actually think people are going to jump on some bandwagon of kindness? This isn't the land of Oz."

"No, but I still think we can make a difference," I said.

"It's not too late to join us," Summer said. "I can turn the camera back on and get some footage of you. Maybe picking up trash in the park?"

Saraya snorted. "Pass."

Ruth stepped forward. "You're right, this is not some fantasy land. It's real life. Where the ground is hard and words cuts like knives. But kindness still matters. And I'd rather be on the side that gives a crap than the side that has already given up."

"We're going to make a difference, you'll see," Summer said.

"I'm waiting with baited breath," Saraya said.

As she hunched her shoulders and walked away, I couldn't help thinking that Ruth was right. Saraya was the picture of a person so defeated she'd given up trying. Would that have been me if I hadn't found skating?

Chapter Thirty-Five: Final Victim

We skated at a mall opening and a city park dedication over the next two weeks, and our videos from both those events were doing awesome. But our first Project video only had a hundred or so views—way less than our other videos—and the second one, which we'd uploaded recently, wasn't doing much better.

"Be patient," Summer said as we entered school together one day. "It takes time to change the world."

"I was just hoping for a little more … I don't know, enthusiasm? There are hardly any comments on our two Project videos, and the ones we did get are mostly negative."

The comments rattled around in my head.

Gotta be honest, not liking the change in content
Get back to the flippin' skating, flippin' skaters
This is the stupidest idea I've ever heard

And on. People clearly weren't *getting* it.

"I finally caught up with Ronald yesterday," I said, lowering my voice as a group of our peers walked past. "I waited for him outside the band room."

Summer fiddled with her backpack straps. "What did he say?"

"Well, first he thought I had him confused with someone else, and then he tried to sell me a candy bar for some band fundraiser, which I bought, obviously—it had caramel. But then, when he figured out what I was really asking, he kind of turned in on himself and just kept saying no, he wasn't interested. So, basically the same reaction as Saraya, only with less … passion, I guess? Like he's already super jaded against the world and resigned that things will never get better."

Summer looked up. "But what we're doing will

reverse that—show people like Ronald that not everyone is awful."

"Will it, though?" I said, biting on my lower lip. "Maybe we were wrong. Maybe it was a stupid idea."

"Stop it," Summer said sternly. "We're not wrong about this. The Project will catch on, you'll see."

And with that, she went down one hallway while I turned down another, and we knew we wouldn't cross paths for the rest of the day. Tomorrow was Flipfezt and we had the perfect evening all planned out—some low-key time on the ramps after school and a movie night with our guys. But I was already feeling the tiniest bit nervous about tomorrow.

On my way to class, I passed Keir's locker and, for once, he was actually there. I'd been keeping an eye out for him since the message he hadn't responded to about joining us on the Project. I took a chance and went over.

"Hey, Keir."

He glanced at me but didn't say anything. We'd never really spoken before.

"Hey, um, I think one of the Flippin' Skaters messaged you a while back about a project they're working on. They messaged me, too, and I was wondering if you're going to join us?"

He shifted some stuff around in his locker. "Yeah, I saw. What are you, like, their little ambassador?"

I kept my response vague. "Something like that."

"Well, it doesn't really sound like my thing."

"So you don't know how to be nice?"

His brow furrowed. "Umm..."

"Or maybe you just don't believe in it. Niceness, that is." My tone was snappy and I knew it was because of the comments I'd read this morning. Those weren't his fault. I needed to tone it down.

"Look, of course I know how to be nice. But what you all are doing…" He ran a hand through his hair. "…it's a little juvenile, don't you think?"

I blinked. "Being nice is juvenile?"

"Well, no, I guess … that's not what I meant, exactly."

"Okay. What did you mean?"

He huffed. "You're just … you're like Sunshine Dora off to save the world in three easy steps. The plan is a little simplistic. That's all."

My hands fisted. "At least we're doing *something* to fight back." I whirled around.

"Aspen, wait," he said, and I heard the slam of his locker.

He caught up to me. "Look, it really is a nice idea. If I'm being honest, I don't think it's going to work, but … I guess that's no reason not to try. Count me in."

I stopped. "Really?"

"Yeah."

"Why the sudden change?" I asked.

"We have to stick together."

"We, as in, the bullied?"

He shrugged. "If the label fits… Anyway, I volunteer with my brother's little league as an assistant coach. I'll take some pictures this weekend and post them. I've seen the hashtag."

"Keir, that would be so great! Thank you."

"Sure. And Aspen?"

"Yeah?"

"You're okay." His smile said he meant it as a compliment.

I smiled back. "So are you."

****

A voice stopped me on my way into second period. "Hey, Aspen."

I whirled around to find Marissa standing there, smirking. "Welcome to the last day of my social experiment. After today, I'll have everything I need to write a killer story and cinch my scholarship. Thanks for your help!" She walked into the classroom ahead of me.

Wait, no, it was too soon. The Project needed time to grow into something big enough to fight her.

Then I realized what her words meant: someone else was going down today.

As my teacher plowed through a lecture on Ohms and Watts and I shot imaginary laser beams into the back of Marissa's head, my mind spun. Was there a way to figure out who her final target would be? My fingers drummed on the desktop as I mentally circled back to that day in the darkroom and combed over everything she'd said. There'd been no clues about any upcoming victims.

But...

I straightened, remembering the pics I'd snapped of Marissa's photos hanging to dry. I'd never looked back through them—maybe I'd missed something.

I held my phone under the desk and started scrolling through my pictures until I found the ones from that day in the darkroom. They weren't very good—I'd had only seconds to snap them before Summer had walked in—but I'd have to work with it.

I zoomed in on the first one—a blurry shot of me and Zuri at the club.

The second was mostly in-focus and included the shots of both Saraya and Keir.

Yet another shot showed Ronald, and half of Ruth.

My final shot showed just the bottom half of the picture of Ruth. But ... it actually looked like there had been another picture hanging to dry behind the one of Ruth, like maybe on a separate wire. Only one side of it was visible, since Ruth's picture was in the forefront. And since my shot had cut off the top half of this view, only the bottom corner of this new picture was visible. In it were some legs, with a row of lockers in the background, and someone's backpack was sitting on the ground, with a gold cat keychain dangling from one of the zippers.

Wait ... that backpack. That keychain.

It was Rhea's.

Could *Rhea* be the next victim?

But why would Marissa go after another cheerleader? Did she have a vendetta against us or something? Or maybe this picture didn't mean what I thought it did—I was missing almost three-fourths of it, after all—there could be another person in the shot.

Still, I should probably try to warn Rhea. Just in case. I think I would have appreciated some warning before my world imploded. Maybe if I'd been prepared it wouldn't have flattened me like it did.

I started a text to Rhea, but couldn't think of anything that didn't sound all doomsday or conspiracy theory. I'd go find her after class—I still had her schedule memorized.

The very moment class ended, I bolted from my seat and made my way to room 207, where Rhea would be headed for AP Calc. The hallways filled quickly, muffling the sound of my shoes slapping against the floor. When I got to the right room, I peeked inside. Rhea was already there, seated in the front row, staring at something on her phone.

"Rhea," I hissed, standing in the doorway.

Her expression went slack when she saw me. "Aspen?"

I beckoned her over. "I need to talk to you."

She took one last look at her phone, then sighed

and stood up from her desk. She pulled me out of the doorway and into the hall. "What?"

"I just wanted to warn you—I think you might be the next online victim. I don't know if knowing will make any difference, or if I'm even right, but I just wanted to give you a heads up because I would have wanted one. It turns out that Marissa is—"

Rhea cut me off. "You're too late."

"What? No."

Rhea huffed and held her phone out. On the screen was a picture of her—the rest of the picture I'd seen hanging in the darkroom. It showed her at her locker, looking frazzled and sloppy, with a look on her face that bordered on psychotic.

"How long has this been up?"

"Like, a minute."

The post itself was long. Some bombshells needed more explaining than others, apparently.

R33S: **It's time for a closer look at Rhea Hammond, our school's beloved student body president, cheer captain, national honor scholar, and all-around teacher's pet. Rhea has secretly been on anti-depressants and anti-anxiety meds for years, but over the past several months, they've no longer been doing the trick. Doctors are recommending institutionalization, and suspect she may be bi-polar, but Rhea's parents can't face the facts and have chosen to ignore the problem instead. The school administration is doing the same. In the meantime, South High, beware—your student body president is doctor-certified unstable. Let's see how much pep your favorite Bulldog actually has, now that she's the one in the pressure cooker. Who's ready for some sparks?**

I handed the phone back. "I'm so sorr—"

"It's bull," she said, cutting me off again.

"So it's not true, then?"

"Of course not."

I searched her expression. If it *was* true, it could explain her erratic behavior over the past few months.

She sighed. "I mean, yeah, I've been to the doctor a few times this year. And they've given me a few different meds to try. But they're not labeling it as any specific thing yet." She flicked her hair over one shoulder. "And my parents aren't ignoring it—they've been the ones pushing me to try different options. But none of it helps, really. I still feel like I'm either sitting at the bottom of a black hole or about to jump out of an airplane all the time. There's no middle."

My voice was soft. "Rhea, I had no idea. Why didn't you tell me?"

"It's not a big deal." She sniffed. "Everyone gets anxious and depressed. I just have to pull out of it."

"Sometimes you can't pull out of it on your own," I said gently. "Sometimes you need help. There's nothing wrong with that."

Her expression softened. "Why do you care, anyway?"

"Rhea, we've been friends forever. That doesn't just stop."

"But I wasn't a good friend."

"I wasn't either. And maybe I can forgive you if you can forgive me for not noticing that you needed help."

Rhea's eyes flashed, the hardness coming back into her features. "I don't need your help."

I stepped back. "Okay. But maybe you'd like to get out of here before this gets around the school? I'll ditch with you if you want."

She gawked at me. "Aspen, you can't just ditch

whenever you don't feel like going to class. There are consequences, you know."

"I know. And I've accepted those consequences."

"Well, I haven't. I've worked hard to get where I am. I need the AP study session in the class I'm about to have. Plus, I have a history paper due and a presentation in AP Bio." She turned away. "I'm going back to class."

I opened my mouth, hesitated, then said, "Bye, meanie."

She paused, then half-turned toward me. I thought I caught an eye roll. But she said, "Bye, meanie." Then she ducked into her class.

That was as much of an apology as I was going to get—I could tell. But maybe it was all she was capable of right now.

I pulled out my own phone, found the post, and read it again. The comment frenzy was already starting.

Beckers_the_great: **i always knew she was nuts**

yoitsjess: **runs in the family, i hear**

Thenextjamesbond: **would be kind of fun to watch her crack, actually #keeperoffmeds**

I started adding my own comment as Aspen, and then realized it would have a bigger impact if I did it as Skate-or-Dye. I switched accounts, then typed:

Skate_or_Dye: **this girl probably works really hard, and she seems good at what she does. she needs compassion right now, not hate**

Marissa's whole social experiment thing had seemed so stupid at first—the idea that a person would let a negative spotlight completely destroy their life. That they'd let it break them.

And yet … that's exactly what I'd let it do to mine.

Sure, I had the Flippin' Skaters. Being Skate-or-Dye was amazing—better than any dream I could have imagined—and, up until now, I'd believed that was enough to compensate for the total annihilation of Aspen Heathrow.

But … was it, really? Should I have fought harder to hang onto myself, like it appeared Rhea was going to, rather than skipping class and creating fake online personas to hide behind?

The bell rang seconds after I walked inside my next class, saving me from getting yet another tardy. But there wasn't any bell that could save me from myself. In less than twenty-four hours, I would be on a nationally televised stage, skating my heart out for a world full of strangers.

So now would be a really good time to untangle my heart.

I spun my bracelet around my wrist as I sat in class, and I hated myself for it. The spinning hurt my skin, and I was so sick of the endless loops. It was like a single song lyric on constant repeat in my mind, and I couldn't, for the life of me, remember what came next. I'd seen Summer exchanging looks with Dylan lately whenever she caught me spinning the bracelet.

But I didn't know how to stop.

Chapter Thirty-Six: What Movie Night?

Summer and I were on the floor in my living room trying to pick a movie to watch with Dylan and Brogan when my mom walked in the door. My dad had been trying to get Nate to take a bath for, like, an hour, and somehow that had turned into the two of them playing Uno at the kitchen table—something about Nate taking a bath as soon as he lost a round, but he kept winning, and I could tell my dad was reaching the end of his rope.

Mom set her purse on the kitchen counter and said, "Aspen, could you come here please?"

Something about the way she said it put me on edge.

"I'll be right back," I said to Summer, and then got up and went to the kitchen.

Mom didn't wait for me to say anything. "Aspen, would you care to explain why I got a phone call from your manager while I was at work today?"

My heart stopped. It literally stopped beating right then and there, and I'm not even sure how I stayed on my feet.

"What?" my dad said, his attention jerking away from the game even as Nate put down another card and yelled "Uno!"

Mom acted like she hadn't heard any of it. She continued, "At first, I thought maybe you'd gotten a job without telling me, but then she started talking about skating events and photo shoots, and then she said she had a direct deposit form she needed filled out right away in order to avoid delaying your first check. I asked this woman—Mollie, she said her name was—how you were getting paid for skating informally at the park. And that's when I learned about your contract. Which you apparently signed—*as me*—without my consent."

All the air left my lungs in a single breath, like I'd been punched in the gut.

"Aspen, really?" my dad said. "Why would you do something like that?"

My thoughts crashed into each other, cornered, searching for a way out.

Both my parents' gazes were locked on me. Nate was staring open-mouthed at the three of us like he was trying to figure out what was going on.

My mom's piercing gaze cut to my core. She waited for me to say something, but I'd apparently lost the ability to speak. And the longer I went without speaking, the stonier her expression got.

Finally, I opened my mouth. "Jojo helped me."

It was the wrong thing to say.

My mom's anger seemed to grow in stature, like a living, breathing thing. Her eyes went steely. "This is *not* about Joelle, this is about you. You have been sneaking around and lying to our faces for three months now. We have given you countless do-overs because we know you've been dealing with a lot. And I've tried to be patient—believe it or not, I remember what it's like to be a teenage girl. But, Aspen, there are some things that are just so far over the line. Forging my signature on a legally binding document is one of those things. I can't just let that go."

I'd messed up. Big time.

My gaze shifted from my mom to my dad and back to my mom. I swallowed. "I'm sorry." The words were quiet because of the lump in my throat.

I'd never been a liar. And I hadn't flat-out lied—not really—but I'd left out some very big details that kind-of made it the same thing. Tears pressed behind my eyelids.

My mom steeled herself—like she was gearing up for something. "So … your punishment."

I drew in a breath and held it. Flipfezt was tomorrow. What was she going to dole out?

"I'm going to need your phone."

I exhaled and fished it from my pocket.

"You'll need to disable the passcode."

I took off the passcode and handed it over.

"Okay." She tucked it into her purse. "You'll get this back in two weeks. I need your laptop as well."

"Mom, I'm really sorry." My words sounded watery and timid, but I meant them. "I'm going to figure my stuff out and start making better decisions, I promise."

She smiled, but it didn't touch her eyes. "That's good, Aspen. But I'm not finished."

I snapped my mouth shut. There was more?

"You're also grounded. For the next two weeks, no skating, no hanging out with friends, no fun of any sort. You'll need to send your friend home now and hand over your skates."

The collective intake of breaths was audible—from me, my dad, and Summer from the next room.

My mouth hung open. "But, Mom, Flipfezt is tomorrow!"

"That doesn't change anything."

Words started tumbling out of me. "No, you don't understand. Flipfezt is like this huge, major deal, and the fact that we got in at all is just … it's unbelievable. It's going to be nationally televised and everything. I promise, if you let me skate tomorrow, I'll hand my skates over as soon as it's done. In fact, you can have them for three weeks. Or a whole month if you want!"

"Aspen, this isn't a negotiation."

"Maybe we should talk about this," my dad said, getting up and putting a hand on my mom's arm.

She shrugged him off. "No. We should have acted sooner—punished her that very first time she skipped school. Then maybe she wouldn't be taking other people's prescription meds and forging legal documents! This is a big deal—we can't just let it slide."

My dad angled himself so his back was to me, but I still heard every word he said. "I'm not suggesting we let it slide. But to take away something that brings her genuine happiness when she's so lost is not the right answer."

When she's so lost.

The words stung. But the fact that they were true, and that he'd noticed, was not lost on me.

"A punishment isn't a punishment unless it stings a little," my mom said.

"Mom, this is going to sting a *lot*. I'll do extra chores around the house. I'll take Nate to the park every day. I'll volunteer at the hospital. Just please, *please,* don't make me miss Flipfezt."

"Aspen, you are no longer a part of this conversation," Dad said. "Go send your friend home."

"And tell her you won't be skating tomorrow," Mom added.

"No, tomorrow is still up in the air," Dad said, giving her a hard look.

My mom gaped at him. "Seriously? You're really going to undermine me right here in front of the kids?"

I hovered in the doorway, watching them. Poor Nate was glued to the scene, his eyes wider than when he watched roller derby. Our parents never fought about anything more substantial than which flavor of ice cream to buy.

The two of them looked at each other, gazes

locked, bodies tensed. No more words were exchanged. When you'd been married as long as they had, apparently, you didn't always need words.

My dad finally broke the silence. "Aspen, go tell your friend you won't be skating tomorrow." Then he took Nate by the hand and left the kitchen. "Come on, it's time for bed. You can skip your bath tonight."

I was still standing in the doorway.

"Aspen, move!" my mom thundered.

I scrambled around the corner to the living room and ran right into Summer. She folded me into a hug, and I started sobbing.

"We won't do it," Summer said. "We're not skating in Flipfezt without you."

"You have ... to do it," I said between sobs. "I won't let ... you miss this."

Summer started to protest again, but I cut her off. "If you all don't skate ... I will never, ever forgive myself. Please." I pulled away and looked at her. "Please skate. Promise me."

She pressed her lips together and nodded once. "Okay, we'll skate."

"Will you tell the guys for me? My mom has my phone."

"Yeah, I'll tell them." Her eyes were shimmery. She blinked a few times, like she was trying not to cry.

"I'll watch it on TV," I said. "You're going to kill it."

Summer nodded again, then let herself out the front door.

My feet were heavy as I made my way to my room. In one single moment, Skate-or-Dye had been reduced to ash, and I was the one who'd lit the match. I collapsed onto my bed, my body quaking with big, heaving sobs. I cried and cried until my head throbbed and my eyeballs burned and my pillow was soaked through.

****

It was the longest night of my life.

I dreamed my dog got hit by a car. I'd never in my life had a dog, but I was heartbroken and sobbing uncontrollably, kneeling beside him in the street as the car sped away. And then these horrible black birds came and started picking at his flesh. I swatted them away, but then they started picking at my flesh, too. I woke up screaming and crying into the blackness, only to remember what had actually happened and burst into tears all over again.

The cycle repeated too many times to count. Each time, I jolted out of some strange and awful dream only to remember all over again how badly I'd screwed things up.

****

Jojo's knee slammed into my back, and I became aware of light filtering in through the blinds. "Get up, sleepyhead."

My eyes felt puffy and raw. My head throbbed.

Why was Jojo here?

I blinked a few times, trying to remember what day it was and why Jojo was waking me up. Then everything came flooding back with crushing clarity. Again.

Jojo was here to drive me to Flipfezt. Only, I wasn't skating in Flipfezt. I'd flushed the one good thing I had down the toilet.

I tugged the covers over my head. "I can't go so I don't need a ride."

"I know. Last night when I texted to see what time you wanted to leave, Mom answered and told me what happened. So I came over—I was here all night."

She pulled the covers down, making me look at her. "You need to come talk to Mom."

A weight pressed down on my chest. In just a few hours, my team would be skating without me. I wanted to stay in bed all day with my eyes squeezed shut so I could pretend it wasn't happening.

"Come on, Aspen, it's important." She pulled the comforter off the bed, leaving me shivering in my tank top and shorts.

"Fine." I tugged on a sweatshirt and followed her down the hallway to our parents' bedroom.

Mom was sitting up in her bed, reading a magazine—a sight I almost never saw. Why wasn't she in her scrubs ready to run out the door? She put the magazine down and patted the spot beside her.

I sat, hesitantly, and Jojo settled down at the foot of the bed.

Then Mom said, "Aspen, do you really believe I don't love you?"

"Umm, what?" My gaze darted between my mom and my sister.

"I had a talk with Joelle last night, and she said you feel like your father and I don't love you as much as we love her. She said we always celebrate her successes while you're left watching from the sidelines, and she thinks it's time that we focus on you for a change."

I felt my mouth hanging open. "Dang, Jojo."

Jojo jumped in. "I mean, it's true, right? You feel like you always come in second—with grades and skating and stuff, and that Mom and Dad don't really see you."

I mean, yeah, that was basically how I felt, but I had no idea Jojo knew that. I stared at my sister. "How long have you known?"

"I'm not blind, Aspen—I've known you for a long time. I know I've been really focused on myself lately, but I also knew you weren't okay. I'm really sorry I got so caught up in my own life that I left you behind."

Suddenly my eyes were stinging with unshed tears. She'd pinned my feelings down exactly.

I blinked the tears back. "It *has* always felt like the Jojo show around here. And then, even after you left, somehow things were still always about you. And I hated that. But also I really missed you."

My mom put an arm around my shoulder and pulled me in for a side hug. "Aspen, I'm so sorry. I never meant for you to feel that way. You are kind and hardworking, and amazingly talented, in so many ways. I admit I've been really caught up in roller derby, for a really long time. It was just so far outside my own experience and that made it exciting, but I'm incredibly sorry it pulled my attention away from you. Your gifts may be different from Joelle's, but that doesn't make them any less beautiful."

She squeezed me tighter, and I blinked some more. "Thanks."

She continued. "But it seems like you've found one thing you both excel at, and that's skating. So. About today…"

I tensed.

"Your sister thinks we should let you go. She said this is your moment to shine and that we would be the worst parents on the planet if we took that away from you. She even offered to complete your sentence for you, missing her next bout so you could skate today. But I decided on something else."

I waited, not daring to breathe, as my mom paused dramatically.

Then she said, "You are still grounded for two weeks, and you still can't have your phone or laptop during that time. But I will let you skate today. In place of today's indoor sentence, I'd like you to research the penalties of forging someone's signature and write a ten page paper on the legal ramifications of contract forgery."

Jojo started laughing. "Mom, really? A paper?"

But all I heard was *I will let you skate today.*

"What's wrong with a paper?" Mom said. "I want her to understand the seriousness of what she did."

"It's not like she's going to become some sort of contract criminal—she just wanted to skate without telling you," Jojo said.

"I'll do the paper," I said, cutting them off. I slid off the bed and stood there, the biggest grin stretching across my face. "But, today, I'm skating in Flipfezt. *Oh, my gosh, I'm skating in Flipfezt!* We have to go. I have to get ready."

I gave my mom a tight hug. "Thank you, Mom. Thank you *so* much."

"Thank your sister," my mom said.

Jojo jumped off the bed. "I'll help you get ready. I already texted everyone to let them know. We're picking Brogan up in a half hour."

"Your father, Nate, and I will meet you all there," my mom added.

Holy half-pipe. I was skating in Flipfezt! And my family was coming to watch.

Chapter Thirty-Seven: Flipfezt XVI

I never got nervous anymore before we skated. The last few events we'd done had been huge successes, and my skates now felt like natural extensions of me. Even with the Project video flops, things were still going really well for the Flippin' Skaters—Mollie said we had some money coming our way from merch sales, and that the exposure at Flipfezt would help us lock in some ad revenue. We were masked superheroes, doing something no one had done before, and we were on fire.

So I shouldn't have been nervous.

But my hand wouldn't stop shaking as I colored my hair and tried to put it in braids. I was shaking so hard Jojo had to help me. Dozens of professional skateboarders and thousands of fans would be there, along with big-name sponsors like Monster and Zumiez.

Also, news crews. Lots of news crews.

I focused on deep breathing as I got ready, but it didn't seem to help.

Then I was in Jojo's car, and she was driving Brogan and me to the event, where Summer, Dylan, and Lia were going to meet us.

After our first Project video, we'd asked about making Jojo, Brogan, and Lia official members of our skating team, but Mollie wanted to keep the Flippin' Skaters capped at three. Which was a major bummer. I'd always envisioned us growing. What good was starting a movement if the membership was capped?

My hands clammed up as Jojo drove. The closer we got to the venue, the more my stomach felt like it was full of bad seafood.

Two hours, seven minutes, twenty-something seconds until showtime.

The venue came into view way too soon. Jojo flashed the participant parking pass Mollie had given me, and the attendant directed us to a back lot.

"Ready, sis?" Jojo said.

I blew into my cupped hands, shivering even though I wasn't cold. "Do you get nervous before bouts?"

"Sometimes. But you have nothing to be nervous about. I've seen you skate and you are a force to be reckoned with. Seriously, Aspen, those skateboarders aren't going to know what to think. Their minds will be blown."

"It's true," Brogan said, climbing out of the backseat.

Jojo opened her door and jumped out, reaching her hands high above her head in a stretch.

I stayed put and focused on my breathing.

One deep breath in—all the way—let it fill up your lungs.

Hold.

Now let it out, along with everything else.

And breathe in again—focus on skating—only on skating.

Hold.

Picture yourself flying into the bowl, completely free, with nobody watching and nothing on the line. Picture Aspen Heathrow, with nothing to hide.

Let it out.

Jojo's voice broke through my reverie. "Umm … Aspen? You need to get checked in."

"Ugh. Fine." I opened my door and stepped out.

"Hey, don't forget this." Brogan was holding my favorite mask—the purple one with silver accents that screamed *Steampunk Pirates at a Venetian Masquerade.*

I took it from him. It must have fallen out of my bag. I put the mask on and felt the familiar comfort of wearing it, the confidence of becoming someone else.

My attachment to the mask was probably reaching addiction-level. But, was being addicted to my secret identity really such a bad thing? And if it *was* a bad thing, how bad was it, exactly? Was it like being addicted to M&Ms or fizzy caffeinated beverages? Or was it more like being addicted to painkillers or alcohol or … worse?

As we walked toward the participant check-in, we had to pass the main entrance, and a chorus of shrill screams erupted.

"Look, it's Skate-or-Dye!" a girl yelled.

Another said, "She's here! She's here!"

A gaggle of girls—age ten or eleven—stood in a group just outside the entrance with a few adults. The girls held poster boards glitter-glued with phrases like *I Flip for the Flippin' Skaters* and *Flip Out Today* and *Roller Skates are the Flippin' Best!*

Jojo grabbed my arm. "Aspen, you have a fan club! That is so cute!"

I gawked at the girls, who were screaming and waving. "Should I go say hi?"

"Definitely yes." Brogan nudged me toward them.

"Hey, everyone," I said when I got close enough. "Are you excited to see some skating today?"

They screamed in response.

"Do you like to roller skate?" I asked.

Several of the girls nodded. One of them said, "We started our own skate team, and we practice at the park every weekend."

Another girl said, "We're not as good as you yet. But we've gotten really good at doing cartwheels on the grass."

"*Without* skates on," said one of the adults nearby.

"Right," said the same girl. "But I can skate backward."

"Wow, that is so great!" I said. "Skating backward is really hard—it took me a long time to get it right."

"Will you sign my poster?" A girl held up a poster that read, *Roller Skates 4 Evah.*

"Sure!"

One of the parents produced a pen and I signed the poster. Then I signed another, and another. The girls without posters had me sign their tickets to the event. One of them had me sign a flyer for ten percent off lunch at a local pizza joint.

The girl holding the pizza flyer was smaller than the others—maybe eight. When I'd finished signing her flyer she said, "When I get bigger, I want to be as brave and strong as you."

"No, Annabelle," one of the other girls said. "We agreed she was fierce, remember? That's the word we're using. It's on our t-shirts, see?" The girl turned around so I could see the back of her t-shirt, where sparkly, purple letters read: *Fierce Girls Rule.*

"Oh, right," Annabelle said. "I forgot." She turned back to me. "I want to be brave and fierce, like you."

My arms dropped to my side. I gazed at the girls, so full of life and happiness, and felt a burn behind my eyes. I blinked, swallowed and said, "Wow. I bet you are all really brave and fierce already. I'm so happy I met you."

"Good luck today," one of them said.

"Thanks."

I turned around to find Jojo furiously tapping away at her phone, a mischievous smile on her face. I moved so I could see what she was doing. She'd posted a picture of me signing autographs, capturing the girls' awe-filled faces, and was tagging it #theProject.

"The mini-revolution is going to take off, Aspen,

you'll see. I really think it's the best way to fight back against all the haters."

I felt a little numb. "Did you hear what they said about me?"

"Something about being brave," Brogan said. "Which you are, by the way."

"They called me brave and fierce. They have it written on their t-shirts."

"See, that's really cool!" Jojo said. "You're already changing the world by inspiring young girls to be brave and dream big.

But I knew, deep down, that I wasn't brave or fierce. I was a coward hiding behind a freaking mask.

****

One hour, forty-two minutes and ten seconds until showtime.

We found Summer, Dylan, and Lia hanging out beneath a Skateopia awning. Mollie sat nearby, talking on her phone, but when she saw us she waved us in. A table filled with energy drinks, healthy snacks, and Flippin' Skaters merch was set up, with some folding chairs in a row behind it.

The Flipfezt course stretched out before us. There was a gaps section, a rails and stairs section, a ramps section, a bowl, and, apart from the rest, the mother of all half-pipes. A giant awning was stretched above the entire thing, providing shade and keeping the ramps dry in case of rain. So far, though, it was a beautiful day.

"Is this where the pre-game magic happens?" Brogan asked.

Dylan stood and gave him one of those guy greetings that was half fist-bump, half punch-in-the-shoulder. "Yeah, man. They told us to stay hydrated and fueled. I guess that's all there is to it." Dylan paused, then said, "Hey, I really wish you were going to be out there skating with us."

Brogan sniffed. "It's cool. My day will come."

Once again, I felt a pang that Mollie had shot down the idea of expanding the team.

Jojo put a hand on my wrist, and I realized I'd been spinning my bracelet as I studied the course. I hadn't even noticed. But now that it had stopped, I felt the burning pain. I looked at my sister—the Heathrow girl who really was brave and fierce—and my face suddenly felt hot.

I snapped the cap off a bottle of water and chugged.

Mollie stood from her chair, tapping away at her phone, and said, "The news crews are ready. They'd like to do some quick spotlights before your show. We'll save the longer interviews for after."

"Interviews?" I said, my voice catching. "I thought we were just skating today."

"Interviews are a part of going big," Mollie said, finishing up a text. She clicked her phone off and looked at me. "Don't worry, you'll do great. The fans just want to get to know you. Unfortunately, I don't have much control over the timing of these things, but you'll have plenty of time after to get ready to skate."

We followed Mollie as one big pack, but when she looked over her shoulder at us, she stopped. "I just need the Flippin' Skaters. Why don't the rest of you grab something to eat?"

I took Brogan's hand and pulled him to my side. "They've been skating with us—maybe they could add something to the interviews."

Mollie grinned as she glanced at Brogan's hand in mine. "I promise this won't take long—you'll be back together in no time. We don't want to crowd the press box."

Brogan, Lia, and Jojo were some of the best skaters I'd ever seen and they were being treated like nobodies. It sucked.

In the press box, there were lights. Reporters. Questions. I answered coherently, but my mind was a million miles away. Now that I had the new identity I'd so desperately wanted, everything felt sour.

****

Nineteen minutes to showtime.

The questions were over and my nerves had set in. Again. The crowd had swelled, along with the noise—people talking, skaters warming up, a local radio station broadcasting live.

Mollie was talking on her phone again, madly coordinating something. Brogan and Lia were watching the boarders on the ramps, with expressions matching the one Nate wore whenever we went to the dinosaur museum. Jojo was tapping away at her phone. Maybe she'd found more material for the Project.

Dylan was sitting in a folding chair with his earbuds in and his eyes closed.

"What's he doing?" I asked Summer.

"He downloaded a focus track this morning."

"What the heck is a focus track? Like, pump-up music?"

"I don't think its music. He called it *Auditory Stimuli.* The app store said it was designed to help you focus. There was a track for test-taking, one for auditions, one to prep for a big game—that's the one he's listening to, I think. There was even one for confronting your boss."

I giggled. "That's super weird."

"Yeah, well, he's kind-of geeking out. I mean, we're at Flipfezt! For Brogan, Dylan, and Lia this has been the moon for so long, and the fact that Dylan is here, *skating*, is crazy insane. Even though we're not official competitors, he's feeling the pressure, you know? If we do well, we could actually change Flipfezt."

"But he'll be okay, right? Dylan never cracks."

Summer gazed at him. He was all calm lines and focused concentration. "Yeah, he will."

That was good. Because I wasn't sure *I* would be okay.

"I have to pee," Summer said. "Help me find the restroom?"

I tore my eyes away from Dylan. "Sure."

Our skates were already on and the laces tied with just the right amount of pressure, so we left them on. When I emerged from the stall, Summer was staring into the mirror, fidgeting with her mask.

"It looks secure," I said, eyeing it as I skated to the sink to wash my hands.

"I know. It's just the same old stuff. I feel like I'm walking around with a pair of smudgy glasses on. I wish, for once, we could skate without masks."

The hand dryer clicked on after several unsuccessful waves. I scanned the bathroom graffiti as an unimpressive stream of warmish air blew onto my hands. The graffiti included the typical declarations of love, accusations of slut-ism, and hateful phrases with so many swear words I felt my eyes starting to bleed.

Then I noticed something else. Something different.

There, in the middle of the typical garbage people wrote on bathroom walls, was something atypical. Something so different that my wandering gaze stuttered to a halt and I moved closer to read it more carefully.

In purple Sharpie, someone had written: *Loving yourself is the greatest revolution.* There was a little heart drawn beneath it, and the words were boxed in with a series of artsy dots and lines.

The words rattled around in my mind, trying to find a place to sink in.

I had the odd sensation that there was the perfect spot for them—like when I was a kid, trying to fit a shaped peg into the correct hole.

Loving yourself is the greatest revolution.

The *greatest* revolution.

The greatest revolution was to *love yourself.*

Why was loving yourself the greatest revolution? Was loving yourself really such a hard thing to do? Everybody loved themselves—that's why the world was such a selfish place.

But then I thought about all the hours I'd spent at cheer practice. All the self-deprecating comments I'd both heard and uttered—I'm so fat, I'm so ugly, my hair is too frizzy, my chest is too flat.

And then there were the ones in my classes—I'm so dumb.

And in the hallways—I'm such a klutz.

And just in general—I'm a hot mess.

And I realized, loving yourself was hard. Maybe the hardest thing ever.

Which would make loving yourself the greatest way to revolt. Conventional wisdom said we shouldn't love ourselves. No one ever said it out loud, but that seemed to be the general rule—at least according to what was splashed on magazines and billboards.

Could loving myself be *my* greatest revolution? Even bigger than the Project? Even bigger than the Flippin' Skaters?

Did I love myself?

"Aspen!" A voice dragged me from my thoughts.

I looked at Summer, who was standing by the door.

"Your hands have got to be dry by now," she said.

"Oh. Right." I pulled them out from under the dryer.

"We're on in ten minutes," Summer continued. "Dylan will freak out if we're not there when his focus track ends."

My attention snapped back to the event, and a bolt of adrenaline shot through me. We were skating in the biggest event of our lives in *ten minutes*.

I joined Summer at the door.

"Are you okay?" she said, examining my face.

"Sure. Let's go skate."

****

Our role in Flipfezt was different than anybody else's. Rather than skating individually, like the competitors were going to do, today we were skating together. We were putting on a show. The purpose was to entertain and introduce the world to our skating style in the hopes that roller skaters would one day be invited to compete alongside boarders at Flipfezt.

We'd planned out what we were going to do based on the event map Mollie had given us weeks ago. Rather than ending in the bowl, we'd decided to start there, skating around each other in a choreographed type of almost-dance. Then we'd split up and go through the course, crisscrossing around and between each other, staying separate but still moving through the course as a single entity. Then we'd end up back at the bowl for some of our bigger tricks.

We'd had a chance to run through it on the course once that morning and everything had gone as planned. Still, standing there at the top of the bowl together, waiting for them to give us the go-ahead to start, my stomach was tighter than it'd ever been.

I couldn't stop thinking about the writing on the

bathroom wall.

Loving yourself is the greatest revolution.

We'd started a mini-revolution. And maybe Summer and Jojo were right—maybe the Project would pick up and change some things for the better. Maybe it would change a lot of things.

But it would not change the way I felt about the two halves of myself.

I was Skate-or-Dye and I was Aspen. And, up until ten minutes earlier, I hadn't understood how I could be both. I hadn't *wanted* to be both. Aspen was a mess, and Skate-or-Dye was not.

But Skate-or-Dye had no depth. Sure, she was brave and fierce, but when it came down to it, she had no reason to be. She had nothing to fight for. In the end, that would make her weak.

Aspen had something to fight for. She had friends. And a family. And a future.

All Skate-or-Dye had were fans who were strangers and a contract that told her how to act and think. If I wanted to do this—if I really wanted to start a revolution—it would have to start with me accepting me. *All* of me.

The realization hit me so hard, it gave me chills. There, on the top of a ramp in the heat of the day, surrounded by fans and news crews, and Flipfezt staff, I finally knew what I had to do.

"Two minutes," a guy with a headset said.

Then the deejay who'd been playing music all morning wrapped up and said, "Ladies and gentlemen, welcome to Flipfezt, the biggest, baddest skateboarding competition on the west coast. Today you will see the best of the best. Boarders who've been working their whole lives, who've sacrificed every day, skating in rain, sleet, and at least a dozen qualifying competitions in order to earn the right to be here."

Off to the side, I could see Mollie talking on her phone again. She gave me a quick thumbs up.

Summer was tugging at her face mask.

Dylan wiped the palms of his hands on his pants.

"Summer, Dylan," I hissed. They looked over and I motioned for them to circle up around me.

The announcer thanked the venue and started listing off the sponsors one by one. I heard Skateopia in the mix.

Looking at two of the closest friends I'd ever had, I knew I was doing the right thing. "Let's skate without our masks."

"Umm, I'd love to, but what about our contract?" Summer said.

"Back when we signed it, Dylan said we could back out whenever we wanted to. Let's be ourselves."

Summer and Dylan exchanged a glance. "There will still be consequences," Dylan said.

Summer added, "Anyway, are you really sure you're ready for that? You know everyone at school is probably watching this. All our channel subscribers will see it. You won't be Skate-or-Dye anymore. You'll be Aspen."

I took a deep breath. "I know. And I think I'm finally ready for that."

"You'd better be more certain than that. This is not something you can undo," Dylan said.

"But are you both okay with it?" I held my breath, trying to discern the expressions beneath their masks.

The announcer had finished listing off the sponsors. "And now, to kick off the first event, we have some special guests."

"Oh my gosh, we are up," Summer said. "Let's talk about this later. I'll be fine in the mask for one more day."

"No, I'm ready. I promise. If I don't own who I am now, I'm afraid I never will."

Dylan pressed his lips together. Then he grinned. "It *would* be nice to add more skaters to our team. And there are lots of other sponsors. Let's do it." He ripped off his face mask.

I glanced over at Mollie. She was focused on the giant screen overhead where the live feed now featured our logo, alongside Skateopia's.

I pulled off my own mask and released it, letting it fall to the ground beside me.

"Give it up for the Flippin' Skaters," the announcer said.

The crowd went wild.

"Guys, I can't get my mask off," Summer said, her voice high and frantic. "There are too many bobby pins."

"Crap," I said, reaching over to work on the ties while she pulled bobby pins out and handed them to Dylan.

I got it untied from the back and tugged on the front of the mask. It pulled loose, but not all the way off. Now Summer couldn't see at all.

"Crap, crap, crap." My fingers shook as I worked to untangle the ties from Summer's hair. We'd wound them in good and tight.

The guy in the headset who'd given us the two minute warning came running over. "What are you doing? You're on *now*!"

"Technical difficulties," Dylan said.

The guy's eyes bugged out and he ran over to the announcer. The announcer started listing off some of the recent events we'd done. When we still didn't come, he started saying stuff from off our website, which the tech guy must have pulled up for him.

"Just rip it," Summer said. "Rip the ties off— we're never going to get it out of my hair."

"Okay." I gripped the face mask in one hand and one of the ties in another and gave it a good tug. It didn't come free. Dylan tried the other side with the same result.

Another guy in a headset came over. "What's taking so long?" he hissed.

"We need a pair of scissors," I yelled.

"Seriously?" he screeched. But he darted away purposefully.

I continued tugging at Summer's mask, unsuccessfully.

When the guy returned with the scissors, I grabbed them and cut the straps of Summer's mask. The mask came off.

And, finally, there was Summer, grinning like a kid on Christmas. "Oh my gosh, I'm so ready. You all, let's do this."

But I still had the scissors in my hand. And there was one more thing I needed to cut.

I held the scissors around the leather band on my arm, wincing as the cord tugged on my raw skin. Then I snipped.

The bracelet fell to the ground, along with the hurt, the fear, the shame, the self-doubt, and every other crap thing I'd been carrying around with me since that night at the club.

I felt lighter than air.

Summer beamed at me and pulled me into a hug. "Aspen, I'm so proud of you."

"All right, ladies, it's now or never," Dylan said.

We took hands and skated to the bowl entrance. When the camera found us, there was a beat of silence while the crowd processed what they were seeing.

The announcer said, "Well, look at that, folks. It appears the Flippin' Skaters have chosen this moment to reveal their true identities."

My gaze darted toward Mollie. She stood gawking at us, her expression a mixture of hurt and disappointment. I felt a pang at letting her down—at breaking our contract this way with no warning, but this moment was bigger than any contract.

The announcer continued. "Doing what no one has ever done before, and doing it all on roller skates, give it up, folks, for the Flippin' Skaters!"

The crowd roared.

We dropped into the bowl.

And I had the greatest run of my life.

No. *Aspen* had the greatest run of her life.

Epilogue—Revolution for Real

I change my name one last time.

It needs to happen.

Skate-or-Dye has been good to me, but she was a mask, covering up who I really am.

Now my skater name is Veracity. Which means truth.

I still color my hair when I skate, but I'm a different person now than I was all those months ago when my life derailed. The change didn't happen overnight, of course. And it was the hardest freaking thing I've ever had to go through. But I wouldn't go back to who I was then, even if it meant erasing all the hurt.

The heat from the summer-warmed asphalt reaches the backs of my legs through my jeans as I sit scrolling through the comments from our latest video. There is a comment from Rhea. I accidentally read it.

CheerGirlRhea: **ugh why does everyone like this stuff???**

I keep scrolling.

Here's a truth for you: sometimes friends grow apart. That's just the way life is.

Rhea led our squad to a state victory without me. The doctors figured out her meds and she's been stable for months now. But we haven't hung out in ages. Maybe, to her, I represent a past she'd like to leave behind—a past where she felt unstable and scared and was just trying to keep her own head above the water. For us, growing up meant taking different paths. I still think about her every time I hear a Taylor song, and she will always be a part of my story. Just not this part. The good news is that I am stronger now than I've ever been, and I have real friends who I know I can count on. And that means everything.

Here's another truth: sometimes people surprise you. Like when Chase stepped up and started advocating for better treatment of women. He's been one of the strongest supporters of the Project, and we're back to being friends. And, ladies, he's single!

Finally, truth number three: harassing people until they crack is not something that good reporters do.

The journalism program Marissa got into actually rescinded her acceptance after she submitted her scholarship application, which included the article detailing her social experiment. According to the admissions department, her "reporting" actually fell under the category of bullying, and they would not be extending admission to a student who didn't understand the difference.

She also got suspended from school for a few days. It was supposed to be more, but her parents threatened to hire some fancy lawyer, so the school reduced her punishment. Of course, she had to take down the posts, and all her social accounts got suspended.

But then her article went viral, and even got picked up by a few online gossip sites. One of them called her piece "*edgy and provocative*". Another said it was "*a daring and innovative use of social media to shine a stark light on human nature.*" Then she was offered a job writing for one of them, with a focus on celebrity gossip. According to her latest blog post, they appreciate her "*special talent for hunting down the spiciest tea, by whatever means necessary.*"

So she's pretty happy with herself, even though she didn't actually get what she set out for. And it's whatever.

It turns out that the biggest truth of all is that life is a mixed bag. Sometimes rotten people get good things, and sometimes friends grow apart. Sometimes people surprise you and change. And sometimes you change in ways you never thought possible. It's about learning growing, and being big enough to admit when you've made a mistake.

The only regret I have is the way we let Mollie down. The absolute worst part of Flipfezt was the look on her face when we came off the ramps after our run. I still remember the exhilaration I felt after skating as myself. It was the first time I'd ever embraced my identity—really and truly loved everything about myself—and I was riding that high. Then I saw her face and it all came crashing down.

But she sent us a video a few days ago.

I pull it up on my phone so I can watch it again. And there is Mollie, wearing a camo-print jacket and silky black tank top, smiling at the camera. She says, "Hey, Flippin' Skaters. I heard you just reached a hundred-thousand followers, and I just wanted to say congratulations. Of course Skateopia regrets losing you, because you're all very talented, but I truly wish you the best, and I'm so glad you've been able to come into your own. Peace and love." She presses two fingers to her lips and then holds them out toward the camera like a peace sign.

I feel a sting behind my eyes, just like I did the first time I watched this. But the hole in my heart continues to heal.

The Flippin' Skaters is healing, too. There's an email that I need to tell the crew about. It's not a sponsorship offer—not exactly, anyway—but it could turn into one. For now, it's just a gig. But there are good things on the horizon for us, I can feel it. And if the past eight months have taught me anything, it's that even if storm clouds roll in and stay for a while, eventually, it will be okay. *I* will be okay.

"Aspen, come on!" Jojo says.

She's warming up in the bowl, along with a couple of her derby friends. Lia is with them—she hangs out with them a lot now, actually.

Zuri is sitting on the edge of the bowl taking pictures and videos—she started managing our social media accounts after we broke our contract with Skateopia.

Someone falls trying a basic jump-and-grab, and Zuri says, "That's a great one for the fail loop!"

Oh. And there's that. We post our fails now. If it takes us twenty tries to land a new trick, we post a mash-up of all the nineteen fails leading up to the success. We want people to know that we fall. A lot.

But those times when we fly—those times make all the falls worth it.

Summer and Dylan are kissing in the parking lot—I can see them from where I sit. But ever since I saw Dylan holding Summer's sleeping baby sister, I can forgive him for just about anything—including monopolizing time with my best friend.

I stand up and, almost immediately, arms wrap around me from behind. Brogan's warm lips kiss the back of my neck. "Good morning," he says.

"It's after lunch."

"But it's the first time I've seen you, so now my day can officially start."

I spin around and kiss him back.

He says, "You are looking awfully Voracious today."

"My name is Verrr-acity, not Voar-acity," I say, emphasizing the difference. "And, how can you look voracious anyway? You can have a voracious appetite, or be a voracious reader, but you can't look voracious. At least, I don't think you can. Maybe we should ask Jojo."

Brogan silences me with another kiss. "Later. For now, let's skate."

So we skate.

No. Scratch that.

We fly.

The End

Evernight Teen ®

www.evernightteen.com

Made in the USA
Monee, IL
24 August 2023